Community
on the
American Frontier

UNIVERSITY
OF OKLAHOMA
PRESS
NORMAN

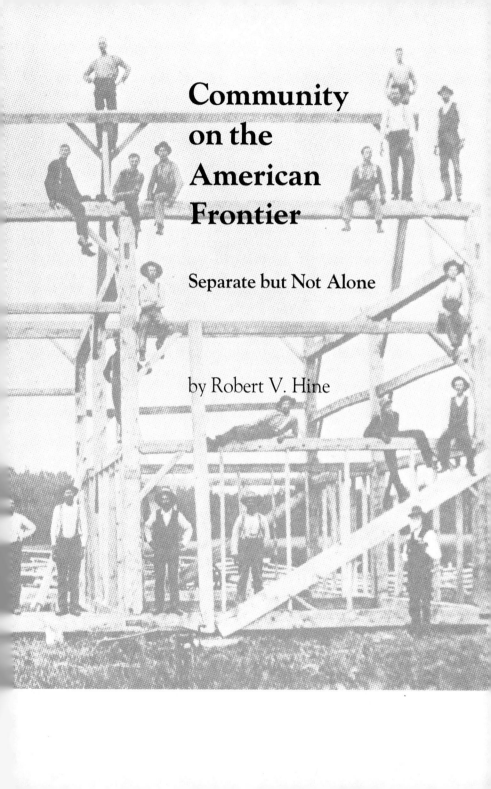

Community
on the
American
Frontier

Separate but Not Alone

by Robert V. Hine

By Robert V. Hine

California's Utopian Colonies (San Marino, Calif., 1953; New Haven, Conn., 1966; New York, 1973)

(editor) *William Andrew Spalding, Los Angeles Newspaperman: An Autobiographical Account* (San Marino, Calif., 1961)

Edward Kern and American Expansion (New Haven, Conn., 1962)

(editor) *The Irvine Ranch*, by Robert Glass Cleland (San Marino, Calif., 1962)

Bartlett's West: Drawing the Mexican Boundary (New Haven, Conn., 1968)

(editor) *Soldier in the West: Letters of Theodore Talbot During His Services in California, Mexico, and Oregon, 1845-53* (with Savoie Lottinville; Norman, 1972)

(editor) *The American Frontier: Readings and Documents* (with Edwin R. Bingham; Boston, 1972)

The American West: An Interpretive History (Boston, 1973)

Community on the American Frontier: Separate but Not Alone (Norman, 1980)

Library of Congress Cataloging in Publication Data

Hine, Robert V   1921–
  Community on the American frontier.

  Bibliography: p. 259
  Includes index.
  1. Frontier and pioneer life—United States. 2. City and town life—United States. 3. United States—Social conditions —To 1865. 4. United States—Social conditions—1865–1918. 5. Social structure. I. Title.
E179.5.H56   973   80–5238

To the students who have helped me —
especially John Calvin Spurlock, James T. Brown,
Robin Gass, Alan Curl, and Mary K. Scaff

Contents

Illustrations

Preface

I REMEMBER A YOUNG WOMAN who in 1970 ran away from home to join a commune. In her first night she was initiated into LSD, streaked naked through the woods, and lost her virginity. She claimed to have left family and school in search of community, but in her exhilaration she was forsaking one community, that of her past, and seeking another, one based on a personal quest for freedom. Because of this latter goal her story never touched on that essential ingredient, the daily sacrifices that the cooperative life demands. I think now that her experience, untypical as it might have been, said as much about our frontier tradition and its social thrust as it did about any other modern pursuit. I wondered if her ancestors on a frontier of hardship and endurance—the environment of covenanted Puritans, homesteading farmers, and homesick miners—had found the kind of community she sought. Was the frontiersmen's search based like hers on a personal quest for freedom, balanced by continuing commitments to the group? Or was their effort frustrated by unexpected losses and threats to the cooperative foundations? To venture answers to such questions involved leaps across time that are always hazardous, but my wonder was great enough to move me to try.

In the process I realized firsthand the meaning of cooperation through the many who helped me, most of whom gave as generously as the sunlight of an open prairie. Don Stoutenborough, for example, read the entire manuscript and guided its style. Colleagues at the University of California, Riverside, offered suggestions on portions:

Edwin S. Gaustad, Ernst Ekman, Ronald Tobey, Carlos Cortés, Kenneth Barkin, and Hal Bridges. Assistance came from Doyce Nunis, of the University of Southern California; Fred Erisman, of Texas Christian University; Robert A. Nisbet, then of Columbia University; Don Harrison Doyle, of Vanderbilt University; and Peter Decker, of Duke University. Sandra Turner kindly checked all references to the Western History Collection of the Denver Public Library. Ramon Sender Morningstar, Geoffrey Selth, Jim and Beth Nelson, and Stephen Gaskin added insights on the modern scene. In addition to those in the dedication, many other students helped, including Ronda Daniels, Carolyn Barnes, Marcella Waggoner, Raul Robles, Mario Mojarro, Edward Mierau, and Allison Hine.

The typing of the manuscript was done cheerfully and tirelessly by Virginia Stephens, Constance Young, and Susan Lasater.

Finances were supported by the National Endowment for the Humanities and the Research Committee of the University of California, Riverside.

And, most important, there is Shirley—to thank her is like expressing appreciation for my hands, my eyes, or the air I breathe.

ROBERT V. HINE

Riverside, California

Community
on the
American Frontier

Prologue

The Enigma of a
Pluralistic Community

The best in man can flourish only when he loses himself
in the community.

Albert Einstein, *Mein Weltbild* (1934)

AT THE AGE OF SEVENTY-ONE, a refugee from his northern
homeland and then a witness to a new community rising
from the Palestinian sands, Martin Buber wrote of utopia.
"The primary aspiration of all history," he said, "is a
genuine community of human beings." As Buber well
knew, the gestation of community is hard, full of tribula-
tion and heartache; yet the essence of community lies in
that heartache, as long as the trials are suffused with a
shared vision. "They are community only if they prepare
the way to the Promised Land through the thickets of this
pathless hour."[1]

A generation after Buber the eternal hope for community seems increasingly frustrated. A leading American
sociologist, Robert A. Nisbet, identifies the dominant
theme of our day as a pathetic quest of the uprooted individual "struggling for revelations of meaning [and] seeking
fellowship in some kind of moral community."[2] Nisbet's
argument builds upon the sociological prophet Emile
Durkheim, the social psychologist George Simmel, and

---

[1] Martin Buber, *Paths in Utopia*, pp. 133, 135.
[2] Robert A. Nisbet, *The Quest for Community*, p. 11.

3

psychologists like Karen Horney and Erich Fromm, who contend that the emphasis upon the individual at the expense of the community has led remorselessly to the fragmentation of personalities.

One of the sociologists upon whom Nisbet drew was Robert MacIver, who early in this century claimed that community was America's essential need. MacIver's concern may have reflected his schooling in the classics, inasmuch as the Greeks revered the close-knit *polis*. His ideas may also have been influenced by the contrasts between his native Scottish homogeneous village and New York City, where he long taught at Columbia University. In any case, he viewed history as a continuous widening of community. Primitive cultures unify themselves as "like calls to like across the barriers that have isolated them." But as time goes on, the wider community smothers the near community. Here is the tragedy, because the larger should be built upon the smaller. The personalization of the near could be balanced by the impersonalization of the wide; the petty tyrannies and dogmatism of the small could be corrected by the cool openness and independent spirit of the large. Our need, therefore, is "to fulfill and not to destroy the smaller. Our life is realized within not one but many communities, circling us round, grade beyond grade."[3]

The problem is not just the number of communities but the quality of those concentric circles around us. It may not be sufficient simply to restore the foundations; perhaps the quality of the foundations most needs our attention. Robert Heilbroner speaks in such a way. As an economist who has dealt with both past and future, he now predicts the decline of business and capitalist civilization, envisioning "the collective and communal destiny

---

[3] Robert MacIver, *Community* (London, 1917), pp. 252–53.

of man . . ., and the absolute subordination of private
interests to public requirements."[4]

Buber, Nisbet, MacIver, and Heilbroner concentrate
in different ways on the pluralistic plight of modern America, the pathless hour of our time. To shift our view, we
might ask how historians have seen the rise and fall of
community in America. Such will be a brief prelude to the
subsequent survey of community on the frontier.

For generations American historians and political theorists, rather than following collective communitarian
strains, stressed Lockean individualism, the importance
of the individual psyche, and the individualist labor theory
of value. We can assume without much discussion that
George Bancroft and Henry Adams and Francis Parkman
believed in the glory of the individual struggling against
nature and society. In this investigation, however, we will
give attention to and often imply more recent constructions
that emphasize the cooperative. In the early 1970s, for
example, two political theorists, Mason Drukman and
Wilson Carey McWilliams, interpreted the story in this
fashion, taking a much less sanguine view of American
individualism.

Drukman, examining American political thought, concluded that "the very national purpose that first united
America, liberty defined as economic individualism, may
have worked to prevent the country from achieving a
national sense of community."[5] Competition and a desire
for separate paths free from responsibility to others were
Drukman's chief culprits. The nation prospered, but without community; and the frontier kept internal friction to
a level that left the impression of harmony. The American
Adam needed no community, each Adam desiring to do
only as he saw fit. Fears of conformity expressed by de

[4]Robert Heilbroner, *Business Civilization in Decline* (New York,
1976), p. 120.
[5]Mason Drukman, *Community and Purpose in America,* p. 6.

Tocqueville, Emerson, and Thoreau strengthened the primary thrust of individualism. Contrary voices, like those of Orestes Brownson and Edward Bellamy, simply were not heard. When Drukman quoted Matthew Arnold: "Freedom is a good horse but you have to ride it somewhere," he obviously imagined America lost in its liberty and unable to locate the warmth of enduring community.

Wilson Carey McWilliams analyzed community through what he called fraternity. Although fraternity is more intensely personal than community, it is nevertheless based on shared values, mutual needs, and a sense of worth beyond the individual. Historically the promise of abundance combined with scarcity of available resources increased tension and suspicion between men. Laws and constitutions were biased against community. Liberalism discarded fraternity as a means of human perfection. Of course, some observers like Herman Melville hoped for an America in which fraternity would someday "open the gates to man's pilgrim quest."[6] But even Walt Whitman, who repaired so often to the rhetoric of fraternity, was speaking far more about individual selves, about himself, than about true community. As a result of our history, even modern movements of discontent are fractured by a sense of loneliness. The so-called youth culture of the late 1960s, for instance, was above all a romantic dream of self, never far from the anxieties of lonely fright. And so for McWilliams the cycle of American history closes against fraternity.

Such modern theorists are not unusual in their identification of individualism—only in ascribing to it negative connotations. Yet even on that score there have been earlier philosophers of American history who worried the point. Frederick Jackson Turner, for example, held fundamentally similar views. For him, of course, the frontier, "the outer edge of the wave," "the other side of the hedge,"

---

[6] Wilson C. McWilliams, *The Idea of Fraternity in America*, p. 371.

brought about in Shakespearean paraphrase "a forest-change." Thus a land with no history mirrored universal history, at least wherever society moved from the simple to the complex. In America the process diverted cooperative strains into individualism. When the frontier closed, the test would be to preserve some of that pioneer individualism in the face of rising cooperative and socialist tendencies. In these respects Turner was a nineteenth-century theorist in the tradition of de Tocqueville.

On the other hand, Turner appreciated the existence and value of community on the frontier. He described communal settlement, the convenanted community, pushing outward in New England and the Old Northwest. He saw common dangers producing united action. Hardship imbued the prairies particularly with a social destiny. In addition, the germs of community lay in such situations as garrison towns and the rough fellowship of the frontier. Above all, isolation encouraged associations like camp meetings, husking bees, and house-raisings—voluntary efforts for the common good, heavy with emotions of local attachment. And these associations were not mere window dressing but were for Turner highly significant: "In the spirit of the pioneer's 'house-raising' lies the salvation of the Republic."[7]

Nevertheless, the dominant thrust of Turner's frontier, and in turn for him the propellant of American history, was individualism, not community. In time Calvinist individualism overshadowed Calvinism's covenanted community. He noted with de Tocqueville that worker and master may have had more direct contact on the frontier but that they felt little real association, little sense of community based on shared values. For one thing, each was involved in a larger competition, struggling to engross natural resources. These competitive forces also led to a willingness to combine under the leadership of the strongest—the

[7]Frederick J. Turner, *The Frontier in American History,* p. 358.

Rockefellers and the Carnegies. Thus rising class conflict split what little there was of community.[8]

Frontier America built "the especial home of democracy." Frontier democracy, as Turner saw it, favored weak government based on a limited contract for the protection of the individual. In short, society became *atomic,* a word that Turner repeatedly used to mean "atomized," "broken apart." When he spoke of the frontier as a mecca for bands of reformers, his examples—Fourierists, Icarians, Dunkards, Mormons—were cooperative utopians or communitarians. For Turner, then, the atomized frontier had lost its sense of community, and its few reformers were engaged in a quest for a more collective or at least a more concordant way.

The most relentless observer of America's lost virginal communality was one of her leading philosophers, Josiah Royce. Philosophers are not often cited by historians, but Turner quoted Royce in both of his major works.[9] He emphasized Royce's belief that a vigorous provincialism, which Turner described in its western manifestations, might restore community in America. Royce and Turner actually held much in common: both made the educational hegira from West to East; both studied in graduate programs at Johns Hopkins; both considered their native

[8] Some historians have felt that Turner obscured conflict in American history: Jackson K. Putnam, "The Turner Thesis and the Westward Movement: A Reappraisal," *Western Historical Quarterly* 8 (October, 1976): 401–402; Howard R. Lamar, "Frederick Jackson Turner," in *Pastmasters,* ed. M. Cunliffe and R. Winks (New York, 1969), p. 87. For individualism see also articles by Mody Boatright and Allan Bogue in *Turner and the Sociology of the Frontier,* ed. Richard Hofstadter and Martin Lipset; for community see Michael Steiner, "The Significance of Turner's Sectional Thesis," *Western Historical Quarterly* 10 (October, 1979): 456–58.

[9] Turner, *The Frontier in American History,* pp. 157, 358; Frederick J. Turner, *The Significance of Sections in American History* (New York, 1932), p. 45.

West not a backwater but the central current in American history. Turner, however, saw the frontier as molding life and character, while Royce viewed it as a magnifier of strengths and weaknesses already there.[10]

Royce was the son of a strong-willed pioneer woman and was himself only five years younger than his birth state, California. Following graduation from the University of California and Johns Hopkins, he assumed the life of a philosopher on the young Berkeley campus. At this point an opportunity opened to teach at Harvard. On the one hand, he was happy to escape western antiintellectualism, if not provincialism, but on the other, he retained his allegiance to California and played the role of frontiersman, wearing boots and wool shirts in Cambridge. Thereafter he returned to the West only for brief visits, notably for research on his first book. That work appeared in 1885 as *California* and was significantly subtitled "A Study in American Character." His developing interpretation of American history was woven throughout subsequent philosophical writings, especially in *Race Questions, Provincialism, and Other American Problems, The Philosophy of Loyalty,* and *The Hope of the Great Community.*

Royce portrayed the national character, revealed to him in California, as fundamentally restless and irresponsible. America was a nation of strangers rather than "servants and lovers" of community.[11] People estranged from their communities are also estranged from themselves because only through loyal devotion to the community can the individual be fulfilled. Like Drukman and McWilliams, Royce complimented Americans for their political clever-

---

[10] For further comparisons see Earl Pomeroy, "Josiah Royce, Historian in Quest of Community," *Pacific Historical Review* 40 (February, 1971): 17–18; Earl Pomeroy, "Introduction," in Josiah Royce, *California.*

[11] Josiah Royce, *Race Questions, Provincialism, and Other American Problems,* p. 67.

ness with constitutions, while wondering if that knack had not led to a false confidence that laws and regulations produce community with the consequence that Americans failed to work at the hard day-to-day problems of living together. The first chapter of Royce's *California* described the tragedy of the Donner party, in which Sierra snows and impending death reduced men to isolated selves. What had begun as a cooperative wagon train became a bickering body of families unwilling to help one another. For Royce this degeneration was a portent of the demoralization to come.

Mining camps for him mirrored social dislocation, and vigilance committees were measures of social disintegration. Here he broke from contemporary interpreters like Hubert Howe Bancroft and Charles Shinn, who saw vigilantes as creative lawmakers and protectors of the society.

True, in frontier areas a communal spirit often flourished. But the eagerness of working together to forge new social forms out of the wilderness frequently drew "swift bankruptcy." "The young community flies too near the sun, and then lies prostrate and wingless in the despair of hard times."[12]

At the national level the causes of the breakdown lay in the competition for resources, the vastness of the country, imperial designs, class schism, and the general problems of industrial society, all tending to overcome local loyalties. These vast social forces excited loyalty "as little as do the trade-winds or the blizzard," and, Royce said, "the smoke of our civilization hides the very heavens that used to be so near, and the stars to which we were once loyal."[13]

Although Royce's model of community was religious—especially Christian communities in the time of Saint Paul—secular society could function in the same way.

[12] Ibid., p. 133.
[13] Josiah Royce, *Philosophy of Loyalty*, p. 242.

"We are all but dust save as the social order gives us life."[14] When secular, though, his community was not the modern nation-state; nationalism may not be evil, but to be a positive force it should grow from strong local attachments. Instead, a wandering, mobile population, bent on the preservation of intense individualism, had all but destroyed the prospect of community.

Daniel J. Boorstin, the contemporary historian, has also been engaged with the question of community in America. His picture of vigorous, burgeoning communities, however, is so divergent from Royce's that he seems to have stood the idea on its head. Of course, Boorstin writes three generations after Royce, and their backgrounds were very different, although they both were raised in the West — Royce in California, Boorstin in Oklahoma. Royce came to history through philosophy, Boorstin through the law. Where Royce embraced Hegel, Boorstin began with Blackstone. Royce distilled from history abstractions and intuitive longings; Boorstin, practical and technological trends. They were both Turnerians because the frontier became for each central to an understanding of American character.

As a Rhodes scholar at Oxford, fresh from Harvard, Boorstin also studied law at the Inner Temple. The following year he entered the Yale Law School and was later admitted to the Massachusetts bar. By the early 1940s, however, he had turned his attention to history and begun his historical writings with *The Lost World of Thomas Jefferson*. In his work there gradually emerged both a sense of American community and an awareness of the frontier. Less obvious in *Jefferson*, these themes were more evident in *The Genius of American Politics* and became increasingly prominent in his later work.

In exploring such themes, Boorstin assessed the ideas

[14] Peter Fuss, *The Moral Philosophy of Josiah Royce*, p. 237; Royce, *California*, p. 394.

of Royce as philosophical substitutes for the frontier.
Royce's loyalty to the community was an answer to a society
trying to cope with the absence of free land. Royce would
have agreed with Boorstin that the great American political
philosopher had been the Land. But Royce decried the
results, while Boorstin hailed them. In the end Boorstin felt
that Royce's efforts to find a new path had imprisoned
American values in "an absolutist strongbox" that when
opened was found to contain almost nothing.[15] The only
content of that box, deep loyalty to a cause, was worse
than nothing. Such loyalty implied the nineteenth-century
European state, presumably under Bismarck and Mazzini
and, if the shadows were lengthened, Adolph Hitler.
Royce was clearly not a man for Boorstin's seasons.

In his impressive trilogy, *The Americans,* Boorstin divides 350 years of Anglo-American experience into three
parts—colonial, national, and democratic. As the three
volumes progress, the theme of community swells. *The
Colonial Experience* pictures southerners as absorbed in
the past, reproducing older English society, too busy to
be concerned with new social patterns. The Puritans, however, were motivated by a quest accompanied by a common
way of life and cemented by a covenant as old as Abraham
and as new as John Winthrop. Consequently they were
community builders, and they believed their destiny to
be inseparable from that of their community.[16] Avoiding
the temptation of utopia, these practical nontheoretical
conformists devoted their efforts to making community
not so much ideal as effective. For them community existed even before government, as Boorstin points out in
his second volume. The Pilgrims in their Mayflower Compact pledged themselves to one another and to the community while still aboard ship. Their resolve initiated a

[15] Daniel Boorstin, *The Genius of American Politics* (Chicago, 1953),
pp. 164, 167.
[16] Daniel Boorstin, *The Americans: The Colonial Experience,* p. 15.

habit of group action to be repeated for generations.

Introducing *The National Experience,* Boorstin declared, "Americans were forming new communities and reforming old communities all over the wild expanse of the western world." Wanderers, they exported community wherever they went, and their creations, although "transient" and "upstart," were still communities. Indeed, this community-building process distinguished these nomads from other moving populations, like the Bedouins or the twelfth-century crusaders. In America people moved in groups, not alone as the myths have it. Their caravans and wagon trains were practical experiments in facing danger through group action. In thousands of situations—in trappers' rendezvous, in miners' camps, in claim clubs, and in cooperatively raising barns and threshing—the communal response got the job done.

In *The Democratic Experience,* Boorstin picked up the theme in the title of Book One: "Everywhere Community." Cowboys subjected themselves to the group spirit of trail or roundup, while their managers built community in the form of stockgrowers' associations. These men were variants of the "go-getter," and they too were forming community before government, as had the Puritans over two hundred years earlier. Even in twentieth-century urbanism the American propensity persisted in what Boorstin called communities of consumption. Here people were held together less by what they believed than by what they consumed—the brand of their cigarette or the make of their car. Mass production thus brought people together in shifting, evanescent communities. The Sears, Roebuck catalog became a bible, and advertising created the ingredient of loyalty that like "gossamer webs" weave the trivia of everyday lives.[17] Thus, the skeleton of American history

[17] Daniel Boorstin, *The Americans: The Democratic Experience,* p. 148. A trenchant criticism of Boorstin's mixing trivia with deeper meaning is in John P. Diggins, "Consciousness and Ideology in American

from the religious conformity of the Puritans to the gossamer trivia of modern advertising has been activated by
the muscle and sinew of community.

Where Royce described America in terms of disintegration and fragmentation, Boorstin saw creative experiments
in the building of community, unimpeded by obsessions
with values or theory. Where Royce worried over America's
direction, at least on the frontier, Boorstin was more positive, less value-oriented, perhaps more existential. The *is*
was the substance of the *ought*.[18] To Boorstin, then, community was no more than an immediate response to felt
needs and was a far cry from the enduring loyalties and
values championed by Royce.

In thinking as we have of Mason Drukman and Josiah
Royce and Daniel Boorstin, it would seem that community
in America is like a ship in a shifting fog—sometimes you
see it, sometimes you don't. The shape of community
ultimately depends on how we define the term. It is time
we turned to meanings and contexts. Without a compass,
what is the land? Without fixed stars, what is the sky?
Where is the compass and which are the stars to chart
the course of western community?

History: The Burden of Daniel J. Boorstin," *American Historical Review* 77 (February, 1971): 116. Arthur Bestor, *Backwoods Utopias,*
p. 17, as early as 1950 emphasized the same point of persistent group
formation.

[18] Referred to in J. R. Pole, "Daniel J. Boorstin," in *Pastmasters,* ed.
Cunliffe and Winks, p. 225.

Chapter One

What, Where, Why

What life have you if you have not life together? There
is no life that is not in community.

T. S. Eliot, "Choruses from 'The Rock'" (1934)

SAINT LOUIS IN 1904 was a surprisingly good place to theorize about community. There the Louisiana Purchase Exposition convened an international congress to explore man's intellectual progress in the previous one hundred years. The glitter of the fair, the lights along the Grand Lagoon, the cascades of music from the great organ in Festival Hall were matched in brilliance by the thinkers called together for one warm week in September. The world of scholarship would parade its disciplines in review like a jubilee to bury one century and launch another. Among them Ernest Rutherford talked on radioactivity; Julius Stieglitz, on organic chemistry; and Hugo De Vries, on natural selection in evolution. G. Stanley Hall and Pierre Jannet spoke on abnormal psychology and the mental sciences. James Bryce and Franz Boas discussed national politics and culture. Werner Sombart and Jane Addams reflected on factory and slum. President Woodrow Wilson of Princeton keynoted a session with Frederick Jackson Turner. American history, said Turner, was particularly rich for the study of developing community because it was a living exhibit of recently transplanted societies maturing in a wilderness.

Josiah Royce was at the congress too. He addressed a panel on the "normative sciences," philosophy and mathe-

15

Louisiana Purchase Exposition, Saint Louis, Missouri, 1904
Keystone-Mast Collection, University of California, Riverside

matics, the sciences of the ideal. These, like other and newer disciplines, he said, were united by a community of interest. His perceptive eyes, which once looked so unhappily on frontier individualism, seemed to observe among the hundreds of staid sessions the speeding specialization of knowledge. Here were the young shoots of professional associations destined to make this congress one of the last expressions of the unity of all scholars. Typically thereafter, historians, physicists, psychologists, and sociologists would meet separately.

Two Europeans in Saint Louis were profoundly important to community theory: the sociologists Max Weber and Ferdinand Toennies. Weber, "the most learned and imaginative of sociologists," had just completed the first part of his *Protestant Ethic and the Spirit of Capitalism,* and his trip to America would vitally influence the concluding parts of that seminal book.[1] He came with his wife, Marianne, who later wrote of their experiences. Weber stepped ashore, she said, "like a liberated eagle finally allowed to move its wings." He was awed by the capitalistic bustle, but the New York hotels were "loveless barracks" in which human beings, mere numbers, could fall ill with no one to care. Afterward he found Chicago "the crystallization of the American spirit," and "an endless human desert." He noted the prostitutes with their prices displayed and thought the city was like a man with his skin peeled off whose intestines were seen at work. Still, Weber sided with the New World. He saw much of good, much of love and spirituality, like Jane Addams, "the angel of Chicago," and the buoyant, hardworking students of the university.

He and Marianne traveled to Oklahoma and lived with a half-blood Indian. Like the genteel Parkman half a century earlier, he was interested in "the conquest of the

---

[1] Robert A. Nisbet, *The Social Bond,* p. 32; Reinhard Bendix, *Max Weber: An Intellectual Portrait,* p. 67.

wilderness by civilization." Actually, however, it was the
march of capitalism and industrialism that intrigued him,
the way factory-built houses supplanted log cabins, the
way oil derricks and railroad ties crept over the wild
prairie. Small-town officials in shirt sleeves received him,
and "together we put our legs on the window sills." He
loved the "marvelously free and easy atmosphere," a society of mutual respect, and felt more merry than at any
time since his first years in college. Nevertheless, he worried that capitalistic culture, like that of New York and
Chicago, would crush the delicious humor and warmth
of these rural communities.

Later, in Virginia, he observed a similar pattern. Fraternal orders with their health insurance, widow's benefits, obligatory credit, and pledges of mutual aid were
replacing the bonds of religion. It was the distinction he
would later make between intuitive, traditional communality with its feelings of belonging and rational association
based on expedient self-interest.

In his Saint Louis talk Weber laid the framework for
much of his theoretical study. He spoke of the condition
of the German rural community in the modern industrial
society. The older motivation from status had been supplanted by contract with the accompanying diminution of
communal ties. Such, he claimed, was also happening in
the American heartland. These wheat-producing areas had
little community because they were integrated into a wide
market and a fluid class structure, both of which were
parts of a contract system. In Saint Louis, then, Max Weber
wrestled with distinctions between the older communal
village and the modern associative society.[2]

Weber's German colleague in Saint Louis, Ferdinand
Toennies, appeared on a panel with an American, Lester

[2]Marianne Weber, *Max Weber*, pp. 281–99; International Congress
of Arts and Science, Universal Exposition, Saint Louis, 1904, *Congress
of Arts and Science*, ed. Howard Rogers (Boston, 1906), 7: 725–46.

Frank Ward. Tall, sunburned, reared in frontier Iowa, Ward is sometimes called the father of American sociology. But sociology then had no home for him; he worked as a member of the United States Geological Survey. He was combining ideas from both professions, however, since he was applying organic concepts from historical geology to the evolution of societies.

The Ward-Toennies session had a certain unity, because Toennies also reached for the biological metaphor. In "collective entities" like village communities he saw an organic wholeness — birth, growth, and death. But Toennies went beyond Ward in requiring for his definition of community psychological and sociological ingredients, including a sense of place and functioning interactions.

Although he made nothing like Weber's extensive tour, Toennies enjoyed his trip to America. He had stayed with a friend of his youth in upstate New York and spent two pleasant weeks in Cambridge, Massachusetts. Toennies was nearly ten years older than Weber, and America was not to have a comparable influence on him. His most enduring contribution to the theory of community had come in his first book, *Gemeinschaft und Gesellschaft* (Community and Society), which he wrote as a young man in the 1880s. Indeed, he was writing that work at the same time that his later colleague of the Saint Louis Fair, Josiah Royce, had been working on a first book, his history of California. Where Royce was historical and specific, Toennies was theoretical, devising abstractions not necessarily tied to history.

What Durkheim described as collective consciousness Toennies referred to as *Gemeinschaft*, a unity stemming from emotions, beliefs, and shared life experiences. It was often a religious commitment surrounding families and traditions and leading to brotherhood. *Gesellschaft*, on the other hand, was an ingredient of cities and states, public opinion, or industry. Individuals were more separate, and the links between them more pragmatic. Often associated with the marketplace, it was society in the sense of freely chosen associations, like fraternal orders, manufacturers' organizations, and professional societies.

Toennies disclaimed value judgments in his analysis, and yet it is difficult for us to avoid them. Fragmentation of lives in the modern world is surely attendant upon the *Gesellschaft* in our society, and all but those who cherish fragmentation would side with the *Gemeinschaft*. Toennies in his later life acted out political values, supporting consumers' cooperatives and working-class movements, finding in socialism the hope of the future. Ideal socialism must be based on the kind of ties that bind family or clan, and these, Toennies would seem to imply, were deeper and superior. So, although Toennies would agree with Weber that industrial society will triumph over the clan, Toennies would add that industrialism could lead in turn to a higher form of *Gemeinschaft*. He was not pointing to an inexorable determinism—an inevitable economic transition from capitalism to socialism—but rather, like Weber, identifying historic fluctuations between two, not necessarily equal, categories of community. The *Gemeinschaft* could exist within the *Gesellschaft*.

Thomas Bender, the modern sociologist, has recently emphasized this conclusion of Toennies. Bender cautions against a linear, sequential view in which simple agrarianism inexorably moves into complex industrialism and urbanism with the consequent collapse of close attachments. Bender describes a community of shared understandings and obligations, only incidentally tied to place or activity, and it becomes an unfolding network, a continuous ebbing and flowing between unity and separation. Even the tidal metaphor, he would say, is misleading, since conceivably both can rise or fall together. Mobility and nationalism, for example, may not destroy community but merely remold it.[3] In such a way the values of frontier

[3] Werner J. Cahnman, "Toennies in America," *History and Theory* 16 (May, 1977): 147–67; Thomas Bender, *Community and Social Change in America*, pp. x, 6, 30, 136.

communities could change in complexity, always carrying emotional and institutional elements of the old but on occasion breaking into new, revolutionary patterns and then reverting again.

Max Weber and Ferdinand Toennies will stand temporarily for the multitude of scholars who have dissected the subject. The ideas of others will later be applied directly to the American frontier. We must first, however, establish the features and values of the ideal community.

A sense of place is an ingredient common to almost all definitions of community. The group must exist in a definable space, and its geography and architecture feed its sense of belonging together. The shared knowledge that the sun in June will rise over that precise notch on the hill creates a climate of uniqueness: for no other group will the sun rise in quite that way. In our valley alone do white clouds back up against the mountain and bring rain on September afternoons. In this old building every nick is part of the shared experience. The known horizon and the familiar walls are the stuff of community. "Being together in one place," wrote Peter Laslett about village life, made possible "the bonds which are forged between human beings when they are permanently alongside each other; bonds of intermarriage and of kinship, of common ancestry and common experience and of friendship and cooperation in matters of common concern."[4]

Place is not the same as property, which implies ownership. Community may be enhanced if the group owns all its physical surroundings, but if only a few members possess "the place," the sense of fraternity may be diminished. The mystique of site, however, may be more seriously eroded by restlessness than by competitive ownership. Turner quoted Royce on just this point: on the frontier frequent change of dwelling hindered the growth of com-

---

[4]Peter Laslett, *The World We Have Lost* (London, 1965), pp. 78–79.

munity. "There is a fever in our blood," wrote George Pierson. "We have itching feet. Here today and gone tomorrow. Let's go. Scuse our dust."[5] Allan Bogue, in a study of frontier social theory, used a 1940 Farm Security Administration project to demonstrate how the "we" feeling slowly emerged from sacrifice and loyalty to common objectives. But almost as strong was the force of disintegration that came from mobility, the constant disruption caused by those who felt that they must move on. It became easy to predict who would first go: those who had the longest record of changes in address.[6]

Pitirim Sorokin, the Russian-American sociologist, once characterized mobile societies as more individualistic, more versatile, and more inventive but less socially intimate. Sorokin could have been describing, as Bogue suggested, frontier communities instead of mobile communities in general. In any case, mobility, because it generated strong individualism and weak social intimacy, nullified community.[7]

Places—the familiar surroundings of land, of buildings, of neighborhood—grow less important as the division of labor, interdependent skills, and the attachment to profession rise. Then place gradually translates into little more than physical identification. San Francisco and Wichita are distinguishable by the bay and the plains, but the water and the grass, the fog and the winds no longer infuse community because modern associations thrive irrespective of locale.

Size may be an even more critical key to genuine community. What is the optimum number of people for the good society? Too few would impoverish human resources

[5] George W. Pierson, *The Moving American*, pp. 7–8.

[6] Allan G. Bogue, "Social Theory and the Pioneer," in *Turner and the Sociology of the Frontier*, ed. Richard Hofstadter and S. Martin Lipset, p. 78.

[7] Pitirim Sorokin, *Social Mobility* (New York, 1927), p. 522; Bogue, "Social Theory," pp. 83–84.

and leave the group vulnerable to the idiosyncrasies of a minority. Too many would impersonalize, fragment, and alienate. The Greek city-state considered the ideally responsive community to be under 5,000. Charles Fourier's theories specified at least 1,600 in order to harmonize conflicting temperamental differences. The modern Israeli kibbutz chooses a size of 250 to 500. The Hutterite brotherhood, claiming 10,000 members living communally in America today, allows each farming community to grow to no larger than 200, when, like amoeba, it divides. Rosabeth Kanter, sociologist of the modern commune, defines the limits of community somewhere between a family of six and a village, presumably numbered in the hundreds. In fact, the modern commune is typically small, an understandable reaction to the behemoths of our industrial society.

As in a wolf pack or a beehive, size influences inner workings. A larger group makes possible specialized skills, discrepancies in wealth, and class structure. A smaller group generates participation in politics and transmutes technology into "sinews of confederation" rather than forces of dehumanization. Above all, smallness makes possible frequent, primary, face-to-face contacts, what Rebecca West meant when she described conversations as intersecting monologues, emanations from ourselves that form overlapping circles. At "The Farm" in Tennessee it has become common practice to look frequently and deeply into one another's eyes as a means to avoid misunderstanding. Baker Brownell, the Chicago journalist-philosopher-professor who retired to a commune in Alabama, asserted the humanistic significance of size: "Men are the measure of their communities, and groups which change in size or quality beyond the measure of a man or beyond his limits of experience, are not true communities."[8]

---

[8] Murray Bookchin, *Post-Scarcity Anarchism* (Berkeley, Calif., 1971), p. 135; Rebecca West, *The Harsh Voice* (London, 1935), p. 85; Baker

Thornton Wilder in *Our Town* caught the sentiments of the community, and he chose the old Baptist hymn "Blest Be the Tie that Binds [our hearts in Christian love]" as the theme. Over and over through the summer night the choir rehearses those words.[9] But not all scholars of community are willing to make "the tie that binds" so important. A Kentucky sociologist, Dennis Poplin, for example, is willing to accept geographical area and social contact in the definition but finds psychocultural common ties suspect. In the modern community, he feels, the demands of individual competition and unfettered mobility constrict the deeper attachments. Yet without these ties communities still exist, at least according to Poplin.[10]

Seeking a prescriptive definition, what community *ought* to be is not the same as the search for a description, what community actually *is*. The former tends to be the hu-

---

Brownell, *The Human Community*, p. 197. Robert Nisbet points out that such mutual awareness is possible through symbols; Nisbet, *Social Bond*, p. 81.

[9] The circumstances surrounding the hymn say a good deal about community. John Fawcett, an English Baptist, ministered to the farmers on the bleak Yorkshire moors. He had known poverty as an orphaned child, bound out at the age of twelve. His little meeting house at Wainsgate held only stools for pews, and he himself was trying to support a wife and four children. In 1782 came a dazzling call to a church in London. He momentarily accepted. After his farewell sermon, as his parishioners gathered for good-byes, he changed his mind. He remained for fifty-four years in his community. The week after his decision to stay he wrote "Blest Be the Tie That Binds," one of many hymns he later published. When George III once offered him a gift, he declined saying that he lived among his own people and did not need the gifts of kings. Albert Bailey, *The Gospel in Hymns* (New York, 1950), pp. 135–39.

[10] Dennis Poplin, *Communities: A Survey of Theories and Methods of Research*, p. 22. See also George Hillery, "Definitions of Community: Areas of Agreement," *Rural Sociology* 20 (June, 1955): 118.

manist's bailiwick, where some social scientists like Poplin prefer not to enter. But without shared perspectives there can be no community. Without binding ties, without commonly assumed values, whether they be religious, psychological, economic, or cultural, there can be no community. "The real beginning of a community," said Martin Buber, "is when its members have a common relation to the center overriding all other relations: the circle is described by the radii, not by the points along its circumference." Thomas Bender has described this dimension as the experience of community: "Community is where community happens."[11]

The primary value the community must assume is that the whole is greater than the sum of its parts. For the Greek the *polis* was prior to the citizen, and Socrates would accept death rather than be banished from his community even though it had condemned him. The ideal community believes in its own wholeness just as it hopes to touch its members as whole people rather than as fragments. Interest groups may be parts of the total body, but they cannot create communities in themselves. "There is nothing in the production of floor wax or burley tobacco," said Wilson Carey McWilliams, "to justify individual sacrifice."[12] Yet it is precisely the sacrifice of individual value that realizes community. The individual is not minimized, but his values are changed from competition to sharing. And although such a change is often associated with religion, it need not be strictly religious. When New Community Projects in San Francisco, a thoroughly secular group, defined its goals, it hoped to be "more growthful, sharing and ecological"; in other words, to make the individual more complete in his values, more cooperative in his small living unit, and more conscious of his environment. In the broadest sense these might be called religious

[11] Martin Buber, *Paths in Utopia*, p. 135; Bender, *Community and Social Change*, p. 6.

[12] Wilson C. McWilliams, *The Idea of Fraternity in America*, p. 70.

goals, and they fulfill the three primary elements of community: changed values, size, and place.

An engine is as definable by its sounds and the way it works as by a description of its parts. Another way, then, of identifying community is through the tensions that churn within it day by day. If we look, for example, at the points where the individuals intersect the group, a community might be seen as a plane where individual needs and desires are resolved in group action and, conversely, where group needs are furthered by individual behavior. Thus the community is an arena of individual-group tensions.

The nineteenth-century frontier was, of course, an heir of classical liberalism in which restraints on the individual were minimized. The community existed for the individual, not the other way around. A community was no more than a collection of its parts, with little if any right to suppress the human will. The psychic needs of man were attainable outside of the community. The individual good was thus separable from the public good. Boorstin called it "the blurred boundary between public and private," making it possible for the public sphere to be placed in the service of private interest.[13]

Of course, in the ideal community private and public interests would never conflict. What a member wants for himself is the same as what is required for the common good; indeed, Rosabeth Kanter defines community in that way.[14] In such a happy state the individual and the group coalesce. The actual workings of practically all communities would suggest, however, that such loss of identity on either side is a hopeless, unnecessary, and perhaps dangerous goal. Benjamin Nelson, a historical sociologist who has studied tribal brotherhood, warns that no society can survive if each member "calls himself 'I' and regards

[13] Daniel Boorstin, *The Americans: The National Experience*, p. 72; McWilliams, *Idea of Fraternity*, pp. 109–10.

[14] Rosabeth M. Kanter, *Commitment and Community*, pp. 2–3.

all others as a kind of inanimate 'They,'" or "if each 'I' is compelled to shout 'We' in utter unanimity."[15] Each position in its extreme, individualistic or communal, is destructive. Only in the right proportions will sodium and chlorine cease to be poisons and become salt. The group has its rights and needs, and so does the person; from the tension between the two emerges genuine community.

The family might be seen as the ideal expression of community: it is small, localized, and woven in the mesh of the one and the many. It is built upon the bonds to which community aspires—bonds often strong enough to compensate for any loss of personal identity. It maintains that level of loyalty so precious to Royce. In reality, however, it is the source of yet another tension, for the family is the offspring of blood or kinship and can, therefore, never be the same as community. Kinship is given; it is not voluntary; it is beyond the human will. Unlike those of community, family ties cannot be wholly severed. Community, on the other hand, should grow from at least the semblance of willing participation. Even if one is born into a community, there is a point at which free involvement in its affairs is essential to a sense of belonging. Royce and Nisbet hoped that community loyalty would enlarge upon family loyalty, but we know that family and community often become competitors. Either way, their joint existence will foster tensions.

Edward Shorter, contemporary social historian, describes the modern nuclear family not as merely parents and children living without other relatives but as a group isolated from the community. The traditional family was like a berthed ship tied securely to the dock of kin group and the community. The multiple connections were entwined in rituals like harvest festivals, baptisms, marriages, funerals—all confirming and enjoying the collective life. Restraints on the individuals, as, for example, in

---

[15] *Community (Nomos: II)*, ed. Carl Friedrich, p. 146.

sexual activity, tended to be as much communal as familial. The modern family sailed from the dock, distanced itself from the community, and signaled its own importance in the lives of its members. It proclaimed its solidarity no longer permeable to the outside world, with its members feeling far more in common with one another than with any outsider. In a different metaphor Shorter calls this modern family "a precious emotional fortress, . . . kindling a cosy fire in the household" while gutting the whole community.[16] Marriage became the offspring of romantic love, and communal supervision of the arrangement disappeared. When work was removed from the home to the factory, the man alone became a provider, and the family concentrated more and more on child rearing.

Until recently the nuclear family was seen as an offspring of the industrial revolution, and so the preindustrial frontier family should have been extended or traditional. But that conclusion is no longer certain if we accept the community-oriented approach. It appears that America has never experienced to any great extent the traditional extended family. Nuclear families have been found as far back as the seventeenth century in both England and America and even earlier in Europe. Where traditional families have existed, as perhaps in colonial New England, they were apparently deliberate efforts to recast much older forms, and their vitality in the circumstances of the New World was limited. If extended families survived on the frontier, they would not reflect the absence of industrialism but rather would expose the remnants of an older dream.[17]

[16] Edward Shorter, *The Making of the Modern Family*, pp. 205–206. Lawrence Stone, *The Family, Sex, and Marriage in England, 1500–1800*, pp. 4–8, 24–26, qualifies the distinctions more carefully.

[17] John Demos, *A Little Commonwealth*; Phillip Greven, Jr., *Four Generations*; Shorter, *Making of the Modern Family*, pp. 19, 205–206, 242.

Can a sense of community cross class lines? Can a community embrace workingmen and managers, proletariat and bourgeoisie? Some time ago Norman Ware, a Canadian historian (also, incidentally, a Turnerian) faced that question. He observed before the 1840s in America a community of interest between journeymen and masters, workers and employers. In a spirit of acceptance and good faith, intercourse between employer and employed extended beyond the job at hand into education, self-improvement, or temperance. Unlike later in the century, there was little thought of strike or political action. Thereafter wherever merchant-capitalist and absentee owners replaced simpler economic forms, the communal relationship weakened or died.[18] This dispersed control was analogous to the earlier transferral of work from the household to the factory. In any case, the hypothesis of class and community would begin with economic growth and the scarcity of certain resources creating economic subgroups. Increasing self-identification with these special interests ate away at the sense of total community and shifted the locus of that sense from the larger community to the special interest. The unified society fractured into the pluralistic society; the *Gemeinschaft* dissolved into the *Gesellschaft*. In the *Gemeinschaft* the tensions between the community and the class were resolvable. As the sense of community moved from the larger to the smaller interests, the tensions became conflicts, and the opportunities for resolution faded.[19]

[18]Norman Ware, *The Industrial Worker, 1840–1860* (Boston, 1924), pp. 18–19, 200–201. For a discussion of changing work habits see also Herbert Gutman, *Work, Culture, and Society in Industrializing America*, pp. 15, 33–36.

[19]In the context of another nation the intensification of class consciousness and its fracturing of the larger community has been explored in detail by E. P. Thompson in his *Making of the English Working Class* (Middlesex, England, 1968). Eighteenth-century village cohesiveness

As class consciousness emerged, the politics embodied increasing conflict. Where the individual or the family found the political system an ally, the developing special interests saw it as either a tool or a threat. Those in power confused their own good with the good of the community; in the same way capitalism's unseen hand transmuted self-interest into the good of all.[20]

The relationship between political structure, economic class, and community will obviously be different if members of the body politic do not feel themselves class-bound. Social and economic mobility can relieve community tensions. The frontiersmen believed their society to be the locus, the seedbed, and the acme of social mobility. It unified a decadent, class-ridden society. "Here was a magic fountain of youth," Turner once said, "in which America continually bathed and was rejuvenated."[21] Dwellers in both mansion and poorhouse once rode the same wagon train, and every president began in a log cabin. In fact, however, as Ray Billington has pointed out, western society

---

was undermined by the money economy and factory system. Ultimately workingmen's societies became the new forms of community. Through their "rituals of mutuality" (p. 456) collectivist values came to predominate in working-class communities, in contrast to the values of individualism in the middle class (pp. 462–63). The worker's subcommunity and its collective self-consciousness was, in Thompson's words, "the great spiritual gain of the Industrial Revolution, against which the disruption of an older and in many ways more humanly comprehensible way of life must be set" (p. 913).

[20] Utopians like Fourier and Owen believed that all class differences would be submerged in the true community. It was this point that caused Friedrich Engels to draw the line between utopian and scientific socialism. "Socialism: Utopian and Scientific," in Karl Marx and Friedrich Engels, *Basic Writings on Politics and Philosophy* (Garden City, N.Y., 1959), pp. 68–111.

[21] Frederick Jackson Turner as quoted in Henry N. Smith, *Virgin Land: The American West as Symbol and Myth,* p. 254.

remained "structured, despite a century and a half of fron-
tiering."[22] Nevertheless, the continuing faith in social mobility and its reflection in political aspiration, in spite of
all the violent and bloody contradictions, could mitigate
the corrosive effect of class tension.

Political structure—authority, laws, regulations—also
injects tension, if only because there is diversity in the way
human beings react to authority. How far the political
process orchestrates, heals, or tears apart may ultimately
depend on how wide the participation is in that process.
The essence of community may be in *doing* something,
not in *being* something; the community then should con-
ceive of itself as an active team, not a passive set of colleagues.[23] When people participate in a decision that cur-
tails their freedom, the process becomes less upsetting.
Furthermore, as communities live beyond their initial
members, the element of voluntary association becomes
more difficult to maintain. In the end it is the *doing*, the
participation, that perpetuates the free choice. Thus a high
level of political activity might be a test of the good community and might provide some relief from destructive
tensions.

Royce mused that historical memory is a prerequisite
for community. Just as "the self comes down to us from its
own past," just as the individual "needs and is a history,"
so when selves transcend the present flash of consciousness, when they link their common recollections, they constitute a community.[24] Memories encourage deep roots,
especially as the collective becomes suffused with new
group values. Time is essential for the crystallization and
internalization of these values, and until the continuities
are established, tension between the old and the new is

[22] Ray A. Billington, *America's Frontier Heritage,* p. 98.
[23] Robert J. Pranger, *Action, Symbolism, and Order* (Nashville, 1968),
pp. 17–18, 63.
[24] Josiah Royce, *The Problem of Christianity,* pp. 244, 248.

inevitable. Where new beliefs develop out of older ones, as, for example, communality in the midst of individualism, the process will be stormy. Psychological and social needs for conformity and stability are attacking equally compelling needs for freedom and wandering. In the reordering only time can bring historical memory.

Perhaps the ideal community would be culturally and ethnically homogeneous, politically egalitarian, socially and economically classless, and reasonably stable in time. A few groups, faced with conditions on the frontier, actually moved in those directions—New England villagers in the 1640s, Mormon settlers in the 1840s, Mormon communal experiments in the 1870s, and German farm colonists in the 1870s. These people nurtured, more or less, the basic elements of community: they felt a sense of place; their groups were small enough for face-to-face relationships; and they shared binding values which elevated their fellowship over individuality. Shading away from these combinations were thousands of others in which the ideal was less realized. In the social drama of dynamic, living communities, tensions almost inevitably arose. They swirled like dust devils around the individual and the family through the canyons of class, authority, and brevity. Careful examination of these tensions can reveal how strongly the community built upon the ingredients of place, size, and values; how far it departed from the definition of genuine community; or how new forms rose to replace the charms of the old.

Chapter Two

Puritan Communes
in the Wilderness

But hath not God left upon them the marks of his sore displeasure? whereby many such places are become ruinous heaps; upon which God hath in Righteousness stretched the line of confusion, and stones of emptiness.

Joseph Easterbrooks, "Abraham the Passenger"
(1705)

WHITE STEEPLES POKE through the elms of village greens; taciturn neighbors mend stone walls, sit on ladder-back chairs in simple rooms, or exude salt-box practicality at town meetings. These stereotypes only palely perpetuate the cohesive faith and participatory political life of the original New England covenanted town wherein people frequently submitted their private ends to the public good. The Puritan social sense was so strong that it generated community even before governmental forms were available. In fact, these colonists steadfastly practiced the highest levels of community that white Americans have ever achieved; Josiah Royce would heartily agree. He has been described as a spiritual brother to the leader of the Puritans, John Winthrop. Royce would have enthusiastically nodded as Winthrop held aloft the ideal: "We must be knit together in this work as one man. . . . We must delight in each other, make others' conditions our own, rejoice together, always having before our eyes our commission and community in the work, our community as members of the same body."[1]

Although he hoped to be a member of one body, each follower of John Winthrop was many things: an English farmer or artisan, an Anglican Calvinist dissenter, a loyal subject of King James, a local citizen, a father or brother, a lover or friend. The test of any community is always the extent to which the fragments of lives are somehow co-ordinated into one body. The remarkable success of the Puritans on that score stemmed from the way their sense of place and stability infused small village relationships with group values that in turn controlled the tensions within the community. But it was not easy, and in time the frontier, as much as anything else, would both undermine those values that once caused rejoicing together and at the same time introduce different forms of association.

What we call frontier the Puritan was more apt to call wilderness, and it was deep in his thoughts, an abiding presence. Men were being reborn and the new church was taking shape within a protected garden surrounded by what William Bradford at Plymouth found "a hideous and desolate wilderness, fall [sic] of wild beasts and wild men." It was a crucible, as Page Smith, historian of the New England town, referred to it, at whose brink the dangers were horrendous, not only for oneself but for the entire community.[2] In fact, in John Cotton's phrase, "All the world is a wildernesse," sinful, corrupt, with the Puritan community striving to redeem it. As Jonathan Edwards later said, such is "the land we have to travel through."

[1] John Winthrop, "A Model of Christian Charity," *Winthrop Papers* (Boston, 1931), 2:294; spelling modernized. For community before government see Daniel Boorstin, *The Americans: The National Experience,* p. 65.

[2] William Bradford, *Of Plymouth Plantation, 1620–1647,* ed. Samuel E. Morrison, p. 62; Page Smith, *As a City upon a Hill,* pp. 7–8.

This new pilgrim's progress echoed the Exodus, the wandering tribes of Israel, Christ's forty days, John the Baptist, and, above all, the images of garden and wilderness in the Song of Songs and the book of Revelation. In the last was the woman with child "clothed with the sun," threatened by the red dragon of seven heads, and forced to flee into the wilderness, "where she hath a place prepared of God."[3] Similarly the Puritans saw themselves. "God's people are sometimes called by Him," said a seventeenth-century preacher, "to remove from the places of their nativity, into a country afar off, . . . when they cannot live comfortably where they are, and have a plain prospect of mending themselves in another land."[4] The Puritans would thus repair to a land with no history to give that land meaning for all men and all time.

Against the wilderness the settled garden can be a joyful place. There was harsh winter, but there was also New England spring. Even Bradford described lovingly the little running brooks on a sunny day inland from Plymouth harbor, and we sense that his garden had become less metaphoric and much more concretely a simple love of place.

The wilderness was not only metaphor but immediate fact. During the frontier phase of most Puritan towns, say the first ten years, the wilderness stretched, like the sea for the sailor, brooding and fearful. Yet it was also a challenge and a force in itself. It imposed isolation both from Europe and from town to town, initiating a phenomenon that demarked the American frontier, particularly later on the Great Plains. It demanded a concentration on survival, turning the community's eyes inward toward its own re-

---

[3] Cotton and Edwards quoted in George H. Williams, *Wilderness and Paradise in Christian Thought*, pp. 106, 98–111; Revelation 12:1–6.

[4] Joseph Easterbrooks, *Abraham the Passenger* (Boston, 1705), p. 2.

sources. In 1636 the founders of Dedham were granted two hundred square miles of rolling hills southwest of Boston, and if we can believe Kenneth Lockridge, the historian of Dedham, the "catalyst" in the growth of its institutions was the wilderness, the fear of which inclined the settlers toward "the old ways engrained in them and their forebears."[5] The frontier thus predisposed the Puritans to live in compact communal peasant villages where people met daily face to face.

As for the European village, it was the land that bound these people together. They were farmers and animal husbandmen, sons of both Cain and Abel. When the seaboard centers became crowded and commercial, groups of them naturally looked inland. Thus within five or six years of the founding of Massachusetts Bay the dynamic reproduction of Puritan towns began. Between 1636 and the early 1640s a dozen new settlements ushered in a period in which a town was planted in New England practically every year for two generations. It was truly a golden age of community building.

The motives for new settlement were, of course, varied. Sometimes they were religious, the result of theological disagreement, as when John Wheelwright and a small group joined twenty-nine others to found Exeter after violent disagreements in Boston over the relation between good works and salvation. But the mainspring was more often, as William Haller put it, "no more than a simple, straightforward and familiar attack on the problem of getting a livelihood." Thus a little cluster in Watertown, Massachusetts, broke off to form Sudbury because in their situation there had developed a "straightness of accommodation, and a want of meadow." No matter the motive, the process involved not individuals but groups. Hence

[5] Kenneth A. Lockridge, *A New England Town: The First Hundred Years*, p. 21.

came their term the "hiving off" of a new community. The new companies, usually the relatively young of a congregation, would select a minister and then petition the legislature for land. Sometimes these groups knew the precise area they wanted; sometimes they accepted land already officially surveyed. The colonial legislature would allot about six square miles, occasionally more, and give the settlement a name. In the 1630s this communitarian fission was often wrapped in deep emotion—ceremonies in the church, hymns, tears of parting, and solemn signings of the fresh covenant. Psalm 50 was often repeated: "they that have made a covenant with me by sacrifice."[6] Each male head of a household pledged before his God and his fellows with sincere heart to work for the common good. In Salem the agreement was to "bynd ourselves in the presence of God, to walke together in all his waies"; in Hampton Falls, "in Brotherly Love faithfully to watch over one Another's Souls"; in Windsor, "to erect a particular ecclesiastical body, and kingdom, and visible family and household of God." These were church covenants, the social or brotherly side of the commandments, in contrast with the covenant of grace, the personal bond between the believer and his God. The church covenant created a body of visible saints with full power to govern themselves. "Those inside the church fellowship," wrote one historian of the covenant, "had something very special; those outside were very far away indeed."[7]

Plans for new settlement were carefully drawn and

[6] Psalm 50:5.

[7] William Haller, *The Puritan Frontier*, pp. 77–79, 104, 108–109; John W. Reps, *Town Planning in Frontier America*, pp. 151, 152; John Demos, "Families in Colonial Bristol, Rhode Island," *William and Mary Quarterly* 25 (January, 1968): 46; Williston Walker, *The Creeds and Platforms of Congregationalism*, pp. 116, 155; Smith, *City upon a Hill*, pp. 9–10; Ola E. Winslow, *Meetinghouse Hill*, pp. 23–28.

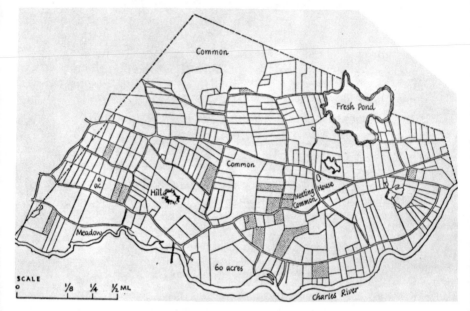

Watertown Center, about 1638
Copyright © 1963 by Wesleyan University. Reprinted from
Puritan Village: The Formation of a New England Town, by
Sumner C. Powell, by permission of Wesleyan University Press.

highly traditional. At the center was communal land. The
village commons or green belonged to all and functioned
as churchyard, pasture, drill ground, and later as school
ground. Its land focused the communal sense of place.
Its buildings spoke of mutuality: the church, the town hall,
the schoolhouse. Indeed, the first structure erected by the
Pilgrims in 1620 was for common use, a symbol of all those
later structures on town greens. The nineteenth-century
town in America would build on that tradition, so that
similar schoolhouses and meeting halls and churches in
public squares would strengthen community through fairs,

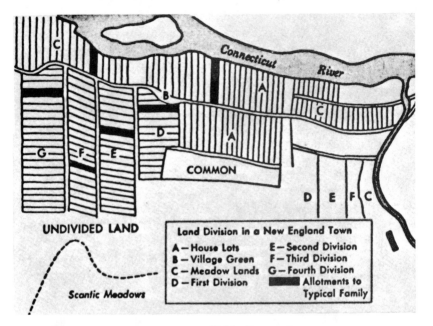

Typical New England town, Enfield, Connecticut
From *Westward Expansion*, 4/E by Ray Allen Billington.
Copyright © 1974 by Macmillan Publishing Co., Inc.

debating societies, baseball games, and Fourth of July cele-
brations.

   In the Puritan town each family received a home lot of
about one or two acres around or near the commons, within sight of the house of God and the houses of neighbors —
all of them. Plans tended to be compact — either geometric,
like the perfect square in New Haven, or nongeometric,
like the ship-deck shape of Woodstock. Otherwise they
were linear, especially if demanded by the terrain. Thus
Springfield, overlooking the Connecticut River, designed
its houses on one side of the main street with a shaded

brook on the other. Providence followed the contours of
the bay but kept its home lots very narrow to maintain
neighborliness.[8]

Each settler also received outlying farmland, to which
he walked in the morning to work, returning at night to
the home village. The farms were planned in strips, and
one family often held several, part of the best and part of
the worst, to ensure equality. The farmland was fenced
as a whole, however, not individually, and everyone helped
maintain that common protection. Robert Frost's fence
that made good neighbors because it kept them apart came
later. Decisions about what crop to plant, what sections
to leave fallow, and when to harvest were by necessity
mutual. Yet in the end each farmer owned only the produce from his allotted strip. Outside the farmland lay other
holdings of the community: pasturage for animals and less
valuable land from which stones could be gathered and
firewood cut.

Most of these land-use patterns were very old, largely
medieval; but faced with the American frontier they underwent subtle changes. For one thing, the land holdings were
much larger. The size, from 75 to 150 acres, made tedious
the walk from home to field and so encouraged the moving
first of barn and then of dwelling to the farmland. In
Dedham by 1686 a number of these farms had risen
around outlying holdings, and, as Lockridge wrote, "the
forces pulling their owners away from the village had
grown quite intense." By the eighteenth century such a
process was well under way, with a consequent erosion
of contacts within the village and of the sense of place.
Thus frontier conditions that in the beginning supported
village compactness produced an almost opposite effect
when land opportunities were fully realized.

[8]Reps, *Town Planning*, pp. 153, 162; Michael H. Frisch, *Town into City: Springfield, Massachusetts and the Meaning of Community, 1840–1880*, p. 12.

Growth and expansion relate ultimately to what William Haller called "the economics of optimum size." Institutions rooted in face-to-face contacts cannot thrive in too large a population. Helping one another means knowing one another. Democracy demands widespread participation in the affairs of the body politic, and that happens more readily in small groups. The Puritans were not democratic in the sense that they believed all men equal in talent and virtue. Yet their trust in one another made certain formalities of democracy unnecessary. And that trust in turn was based on an intimate knowledge of the neighbor's needs and sensibilities. In society, politics, and religion the small worked best, or, as Page Smith said of later years, "The smaller the town the closer it was to its heroic age."[9]

Dedham was planned for sixty families, but only thirty signed its original covenant. When the town had grown to forty-six families, there were moves to limit growth, and the distribution of the land was stopped when the population reached seventy-nine families. In New England as a whole a critical zone of town size lay in the area of two hundred households, when tendencies toward division became evident.

The ideal size of a community relates to its geography, its occupations, and its system of communication. These will limit or expand the number and quality of human contacts. A hurried "good-morning" is not the same as a long conversation. The optimum size of the colonial New England town was governed by the nature of the town itself. Not all towns were of the planned, covenanted type. Page Smith described at least one other kind as cumulative, growing by accretion, usually bent primarily on commercial success. These towns courted large size. In con-

[9] Rowland Berthoff, *An Unsettled People*, p. 50; Lockridge, *New England Town*, p. 94; Haller, *The Puritan Frontier*, p. 52; Smith, *City upon a Hill*, p. 234.

trast, the covenanted or colonized communities remained relatively small.

Ultimately, however, more than its geography or dimensions, its cohesive social values set the Puritan town apart. Page Smith's aphorism, "Honest values can only grow out of the shared experience of true communities," may be equally valid in reverse: true community can only grow out of the shared experience of honest values.[10] Sincere Puritan values were reflected in the everyday decisions of the New England home, marketplace, and political meeting, where they became internalized through practice.

In all these situations the town assumed the supremacy of the corporate life; the primary social value was that social value was primary. The town, for example, not merely was the sum of its citizens but held a meaning that went beyond them. It was Platonic in finding reality in an essence like the collective. When the covenanters of Dedham bound themselves to their fellows in everlasting love, the bond created a new entity as unquestionable as the existence of God Himself. As the allusion to Plato suggests, this particular concept was an inheritance older and broader than Puritan theology. In fact, such an ideal has been typical of peasant societies everywhere, as Herbert Baxter Adams implied when he found the roots of New England towns in ancient Germanic peasantry. And if we think of the social cohesion of any peasant society, we can understand better the conclusion reached by Edmund Morgan when he found the crucial characteristic of Puritan family life to be clannish and tribal.[11] When that corporate

[10] Haller, *The Puritan Frontier*, p. 18. Rising population constantly pressed on these considerations. In the fifty years after 1686, Dedham, mostly by natural means, approximately doubled. In less than fifteen years after 1739, Kent grew from 42 to 129 adult males. Lockridge, *New England Town*, p. 94; Charles S. Grant, *Democracy in the Connecticut Frontier Town of Kent*, p. 99.

tribalism eventually declined in America, only then could individual competition be elevated to a virtue.

Harmony was a corollary, along with all its handmaidens: social order, continuity, stability. Their contrasts — progress, change, competition — stood close to original sin. When town meetings were found to be acrimonious and time-consuming — both forms of disorder — townsmen resorted to a more harmonious system of representation in the board of selectmen. When one trusted one's fellow man, the values of balloting and debating were minimal compared with their accompanying disruptions. The selectmen, after all, must answer to God, like everyone else. Democracy as later understood would have been shockingly inharmonious. The Puritans, remember, banished their dissenters rather than let them cause turmoil. "In the spaciousness of the North American continent," claimed Edwin Gaustad, historian of American dissent, "a favorite way to solve a social problem was to declare it 'off limits.'" As the simple cobbler of Aggawam, Nathaniel Ward, early said, dissidents "shall have free liberty to keep away from us."[12] The Puritan town evicted Baptists, Quakers, and anyone else who disagreed. And so the community pursued its ideal of harmony.

But discord was not easy to banish. There were always disruptive tensions within the society. "Neither the homogeneity nor the establishment," wrote Gaustad, "was maintained without strenuous effort," and one should not ignore the frequency of "litigation concerning unlawful assemblies, unauthorized preachers, intolerable opinions, improper promiscuity, and unthinkable tithe-evasion." When these activities were controlled, they might be seen as

[11] Smith, *City upon a Hill,* pp. 31, 234; Lockridge, *New England Town,* p. 19; Herbert Adams, *The Germanic Origins of New England Towns,* pp. 8–9; Edmund S. Morgan, *The Puritan Family,* p. 90.

[12] Edwin S. Gaustad, *Dissent in American Religion;* Nathaniel Ward as quoted in Michael Zuckerman, *Peaceable Kingdoms,* p. 5.

normal community tensions, the tests and temptations for community commitment; when they grew rampant, they were signs of change.[13]

Puritan social values were revealed in the town's control over the individual. The community held the unquestioned right to interfere in the lives of its members. The selectmen regularly visited households, checking on idleness, on religious worship, on how parents were doing their job. In Ipswich a man who lived a bit out of town became lax in attendance at worship. The selectmen sold his farm from under him and so required him to live closer to meeting. John Littlefield of Dedham misspent his time, running up and down, bringing possible ruin on himself and damage to the town. He was judged miscreant and required to live with Thomas Aldrige's family for at least a month. If Littlefield later settled down to a job, he may have found that the community regulated his wages, the prices he paid, and the interest on money he might borrow. Interest over 8 percent was legal only in "biting extremeties."[14] And if John tried but could not repay, his lender was enjoined by the community to forgive him.

The Puritan family was a minicommunity, and the Puritan community was an extended family. Like a morning glory growing on a grapevine, it was hard to tell where one left off and the other began. The community had religious

[13] Edwin S. Gaustad, *Historical Atlas of Religion in America*, p. 1. The values of mutuality and harmony were far less evident among the English of colonial Virginia. Edmund Morgan described the first society there as more like a boom town, more like a mining camp in the later Far West. Tobacco in Virginia, like gold or silver, spelled rapid change in bettering one's position in this life, if not in the next; Edmund S. Morgan, *American Slavery, American Freedom*, pp. 108–30.

[14] Morgan, *The Puritan Family*, p. 87; Zuckerman, *Peaceable Kingdoms*, p. 71; Lockridge, *New England Town*, p. 15; Berthoff, *An Unsettled People*, p. 68.

obligations, as in the church building, but so did the family, as in daily worship and religious instruction. The community provided a school, but the family also educated its young morally and vocationally. The community offered economic opportunities, but the father worked within the family, where the mother and children could help. The family was responsible jointly if not wholly for the elderly, the poor, the criminal, and the insane. It sometimes seemed that the community replicated the family like the lithograph of a pattern etched on a larger scale.[15]

Within the community wealth was distributed rather evenly. There were no idle rich, as in England, and few destitute. In Dedham the richest 5 percent, themselves no more than well-to-do farmers, owned only 15 percent of the property. When the communal nature of the society was in flux in the eighteenth century, the same upper class in many New England towns would own as much as one-third. In the seventeenth century, at the other end of the scale, the poorest 20 percent still owned 10 percent of the wealth. Although the spread was not wide, there were nevertheless economic and social distinctions. Inequalities of ability and station were assumed. William Bradford naturally spoke of "the better part" of those aboard the *Mayflower.* Time, too, brought increasing disparity of wealth. Sometimes riches came fast. Newcomers to Spring-

[15] The most recent scholars of the Puritan family claim that it was more nuclear than extended; that is, the household consisted of parents and children. But it was also true that the Puritans tried to model their families on earlier village patterns in preseventeenth-century England. Scholars agree that the family and the community were closely integrated and in this sense were particularly different from the later nuclear family which became so divorced from the community. See John Demos, *A Little Commonwealth;* Philip Greven, Jr., *Four Generations;* Morgan, *The Puritan Family;* Bernard Bailyn, *Education in the Founding of American Society* (New York, 1960).

field, Massachusetts, could become wealthy within a decade and then melt into the older establishment. But in the seventeenth-century New England town there was only limited upward mobility, especially compared with the economic revolution to come later. So, although there was a definite upper level, the prevailing difference was small enough to limit the attractions of upward mobility. Men were also willing to stay where they were because they believed that social inequality, properly understood and accepted, led to social harmony. Such doctrines were easier to retain in the early years, when hardships were submerging potential differences. Everyone then lived simply, and, as in the hornbook primer, "When Adam delved and Eve span, who was then the gentleman?" When money and social distinctions grew, class lines were drawn much less rapidly in covenanted communities than in the unplanned, cumulative type.[16]

By the end of the century barometers of community change were legion. The number of landless doubled as land in the towns became scarce. Families became less patriarchal except in the wealthy class. In Bristol, Rhode Island, where statistics are available, the eighteenth century saw a dramatic rise in the number of children born outside marriage. Furthermore, in some towns leaders assumed excessive power and so undermined faith in the whole system, and the society's worry over such authority was itself a symptom of the change.[17]

Restlessness increased, and mobility affected community "head on." By the third or fourth generation *Gemeinschaft,*

---

[16] Frisch, *Town into City,* p. 34; Berthoff, *An Unsettled People,* p. 66; Lockridge, *New England Town,* pp. 11, 141, 151; Smith, *City upon a Hill,* p. 175.

[17] Greven, *Four Generations,* p. 273; Demos, "Colonial Bristol," p. 56; Lockridge, *New England Town,* pp. 150–51, 179–82.

the heart and spirit of community, was withering, while new forms of association took its place. The inertia of tradition, local attachments, and the continuity of institutions like the militia and the volunteer fire department kept the old forms alive; but the internal tensions of class, family, and individual were no longer balanced by the counterforces of religion and tradition.[18]

The final commercialization of New England agriculture waited till the nineteenth century with its changing markets and the coming of the railroad. Then, as in earlier revolutions in agriculture, the social consequences would be deep. In time the farm towns of the Great Plains would know—to their joy and sorrow—similar implications.

The frontier, like water over sandstone, worked its effect. It shaped what Carl Bridenbaugh called "the physiognomy" of the town, the natural context that would dictate a commercial potential of the Connecticut River; the town's population exploded and its covenant became a memory. Leading Puritans from the beginning worried about the effects of the frontier on their community. Cotton Mather called it a heathen influence, and Joseph Easterbrooks looked on many frontier towns as "ruinous heaps of confusion."[19] The fears were justified. If nothing else, the frontier intensified the ubiquitous tensions that over-

---

[18] Demos, *A Little Commonwealth*, p. 181. Michael Zuckerman makes a strong case for the consciousness of community remaining as a prime value, "an abiding core," of Puritan life at least three-quarters of the way through the eighteenth century, though he does admit that consensus through that century was increasingly based on compromise rather than conviction; Zuckerman, *Peaceable Kingdoms*, p. vii.

[19] Carl Bridenbaugh, *Cities in the Wilderness*, p. 3; Frisch, *Town into City*, pp. 15–19; Percy W. Bidwell, "Agricultural Revolution in New England," *American Historical Review* 26 (July, 1921): 683, 701–702; Easterbrooks, *Abraham the Passenger*, p. 3.

turned the balance in favor of individualism. The Puritan
men of God were indeed prophets of modulations to come.[20]

[20] New France built a community along the Saint Lawrence, but in
stringing its manorial estates along the watery stretches, it became far
easier to succumb to frontier pull. Samuel Champlain, long before the
seventeenth century ended, realized that Frenchmen would not remain
in the community of landed estates while the interior lured with furs
and Indian trade. New Spain too built communities—pueblos and *en-
comiendas*, as we shall see later—but these were built on the values
of exploitation. The Spanish missions perhaps held communitarian
values more similar to those of Puritan New England, yet the missions
on the Spanish frontier were so focused on conversion and imperial
expansion and their life so embroiled in racial overtones that comparisons are difficult. In none of these other situations, however, do
the holistic and harmonic values seem as commanding as they do in
Puritan New England.

The most comparable communities to those of New England were
probably the German ones. We shall look later at the migrations of all
the Pietists—Mennonites, Amish, Hutterites—in the eighteenth and
nineteenth centuries. Their communities seemed impervious to time
and change, even into the twentieth century. One offshoot of that experience was an early colony of French Huguenots which had fled to
the German Palatinate and later migrated to the Hudson River at New
Paltz. They brought the German village system of land divided by
family and redistributed each year. Unlike the Puritans, they divided
crops equally. There were common lands, common fences, and common
decisions on crops. Herbert Baxter Adams could have used these
Huguenots to expand his idea of Germanic origins for New England
communitarianism; Irving Elting, "Dutch Village Communities on the
Hudson" in Newall L. Sims, *The Rural Community,* pp. 80–94.

Of course, all these groups had more in common than direct or in-
direct Germanic roots: they were all religious dissenters from an established church. Their story would confirm Edwin Gaustad's contention that "only dissent makes genuine community possible, only
dissent transforms equality from a slogan into an experience"; Gaustad,
Dissent in American Religion, p. 152.

Chapter Three

Nomadic Communities of the Trail

[The members of the train should] obligate themselves
to aid each other, so as to make the individual interest of
each member the common concern of the whole company.

Randolph B. Marcy, *Prairie Traveler* (1859)

LANSFORD W. HASTINGS WAS twenty-five years old, dark-
complectioned like an Indian, and eager for adventure
in the West. He had left his small Ohio town in 1842 to
join the Oregon migration. He was a lawyer and politically
ambitious, which may explain his election as captain of
the wagon train. His legal training at least opened his eyes
to the nuances of social relations that might be called
community as people plodded their way across the continent. In his guide for emigrants Hastings told of an un-
named man in his train who neglected his communal turn
at night guard. His peers sentenced him to a punishment,
presumably of walking all the next day, which he refused
to accept. Ten armed men were sent to banish him, but
now thoroughly frightened, he was able to cajole the leaders into allowing him another chance. Thereafter he was
a model member of the company. Never again failing his
obligation, "day or night, rain or shine, he was always to
be found at his post."[1]

[1] Lansford W. Hastings, *Emigrants' Guide to Oregon and California*, p. 18.

Here the individual was reacting to community pressures in a mobile situation. The social effect of the overland experience, Josiah Royce contended, was "rather to
discipline than to educate."[2] Hastings's young man was disciplined to the ways of the trail, but we cannot conclude
that he was transformed in his values. The nomadic community—Jew, Bedouin, or Sioux—must always indoctri-
nate its people, molding habits so that the community can
survive. But nomads can forge lasting community only
through embodying their values in traditions, talismans,
and symbols persisting through time. Instead, on the American continental crossing the pressure was practical and
immediate.

Of course, the nomadic circumstance was a continual
happening on the frontier. It influenced for a time such
disparities as trains of peripatetic settlers, caravans of
freight handlers, bands of stream-working trappers, and
droves of cattle herders on the open range. Such was the
American community in transit. Settlers' "notions of community," according to Daniel Boorstin, were "shaped by
the group life which brought them safely to their destina-
tion."[3] Boorstin emphasized settlers, but everywhere—
among trappers or cowboys or freighters—the trail taught
similar lessons. There were external threats from Indians,
especially to long, unwieldy, slow-moving caravans; trans-
port problems like fording wide rivers; internal dangers
from accident or illness; and the risks of political breakdown. These prompted a communal response to reduce
the hazards. The process was the discipline of the trail;
the education came when the values of the group were
found to supersede the temptation of separateness.

The American fur trapper, above all, was charged and
sustained by that impulsion toward separateness. His occupation had selected him, a social renegade perhaps, a

[2] Josiah Royce, *California*, p. 193.
[3] Daniel Boorstin, *National Experience* (New York, 1965), p. 52.

"On the trail," about 1895
Keystone-Mast Collection, University of California, Riverside

Itinerants, about 1865
George E. Anderson Collection, Harold B. Lee Library,
Brigham Young University

pursuer of loneliness, one who craved "roving in the wild license of the forest"; the spirit probably suffused young Lewis Garrard when, celebrating his eighteenth birthday on a rain-drenched plain, he shrugged, "There is something refreshing in variety." Jedediah Smith admitted to a "love of novelty common to all which is much increased by the pursuit of its gratification."[4] Yet, paradoxically, even in his attachment to variety the trapper may have known a deep love of place, a longing for the changing forms of sage and juniper and spruce, for the cedared snow fields of one season and the castellated rocks of another. This infatuation with wilderness expressed itself in the "waghs," "hurraws," and hair-raising "damns" yelled to the heavens when the trapper left society and hit the lonely trail again. Whatever the attitude—in search of change, in love of wild place—it was an invitation to separation. And, even more important, the beaver hunt itself was better handled in a sparsely peopled environment. The animal was easily frightened by footsteps, and the larger the group of men, the smaller the catch.

But the trail also demanded larger numbers for security. According to Alexander Ross, a Scot working for the British Northwest Company, trappers should travel with twenty-five others for safety. He admitted, however, that if efficiency were the criterion, six would be the maximum.[5] The American fur companies generally solved the dilemma between the efficient few and the secure many by setting up base camps. From these tents and fires the hunters would fan out, somewhat like Puritan farmers walking from New England village to farm field or like Mother

[4] James O. Pattie, *Personal Narrative*, pp. 122–23; Lewis H. Garrard, *Wah-to-Yah and the Taos Trail*, p. 277; Dale L. Morgan, *Jedediah Smith*, p. 237.

[5] Alexander Ross, *Fur Hunters of the Far West* (Chicago, 1924), pp. 220–21. For William Ashley's detailed organization of an American trapping expedition, see Morgan, *Jedediah Smith*, pp. 177–79.

Lode miners tramping from camp to claim. Whenever dangers threatened, as with Indian or bear, the trapper could head for the bivouac to find refuge, ammunition, or medicine. These peregrinating cantonments moved only when the beaver of a region grew scarce.

The British were unusually cautious, and their fur brigades roved in what Don Berry, the novelist, likened to small villages, organized and relatively secure.[6] The American companies and their base camps were smaller and more casual. Still, Americans like Jedediah Smith frequently worked with twenty to thirty men, Jim Bridger trekked up the Madison River with sixty, and William Ashley keelboated the Missouri with ninety. When they acted as free-lancers, without company connections, they trapped in pairs or teams of under half a dozen.

In all these groups the trail planted seeds of community through the shared experience of hardship. Together men watched fires sizzle down in endless rain. They felt joint hunger as their flour and coffee dwindled. They sympathized with the pain of one another's bear-claw lacerations. Their lives were wagers on the limits of endurance. A challenge bound them rather as the harsh environment would later unite settlers on the plains. Intertwined with that challenge was the sociability with which to stock the collective memory—hours of gab while pines swallowed the firelight and walled out the world; winter recitations of *Robinson Crusoe, The Arabian Nights,* or *Pilgrim's Progress;* political arguments in what was jovially called "the Rocky Mountain college." There was a sense here of belonging to a unique trade with its own language and life-style. When trappers met on the trail, the greetings were unself-conscious, and the conversation could assume common knowledge and take the shortcuts of understanding.

The chief manifestation of the trappers' fraternity came

[6] Don Berry, A *Majority of Scoundrels,* p. 110.

in the rituals of the annual rendezvous. For four or five
days along the banks of the Green River or under the racks
of the Tetons, trappers encountered their larger society.
The rendezvous as an institution lasted for only a decade,
but that was long enough to weave through and around its
debauches the rudiments of community—a past and a
future in a known environment, face-to-face relationships,
and some sense of the group. No matter that the institution
stemmed from company shrewdness. Certainly the Saint
Louis and New York partnerships were keenly aware of
the stability the rendezvous secured for the trade. Its economic marketplace, its whisky and Indian women, kept
the men together and centered the society in identifiable,
if changeable, places. Otherwise the community would
have been diffused among distant frontier emporiums like
Saint Louis or Santa Fe.

In a normal society such solidarity would have been
strengthened by subunits of family. Some trappers reached
in this direction by taking Indian wives. Joe Meek, partner
of Kit Carson and Jim Bridger and later a leader of Oregon
territorial government, married into native society three
times, the third union producing seven children and a
reasonably happy marriage. A trapper's Indian mate offered him a dry lodge, hot meals, companionship, sex, and
an entrée into Indian culture, without raising a barrier to
his own trapper friends. Osborne Russell, in what is probably the most careful and perceptive of trapper journals,
described his winter lodge on the Weber River with its
evenings of food, games, and conversation; it sounded like
a family in Peoria except that all the participants but
Russell were Indians. Some lodges were less idyllic. Martin
McLeod, a Minnesota trapper married to a Sioux, described another man's Indian marriage with a "squaw
b——h of wife and two d——d noisy rude children." The
discrepancies only make the picture seem more normal.
Yet these were not the kinds of family involvements upon
which community was readily built. Serious cultural cleav-
ages in Indian-white marriages were likely. Most trappers

realized that the offspring of such unions would find little acceptance in white society.[7] And it must have been hard for mountain men to discard the cultural suspicions of faithlessness and dishonesty, to reject the stereotypes of filth and ugliness. While Russell was living with an Indian wife, he was writing of her race, saying that a rifle "is the only pen that can write a treaty that they will not forget."[8]

Group consciousness and potential community were further diminished by conditions of the trade. It was a cutthroat business for both individuals and companies. This morality was part of what historian Francis Prucha meant when he divided trappers between unprincipled free traders and hired trappers working for unprincipled companies. When Washington Irving scrutinized the fur trade, his key word seemed to be "competition." The rubrics of the trade were "to forestall and outwit each other; to cross each other's plans; to mislead each other as to routes."[9] Jim Bridger was willing to decoy other trappers into what he knew was an Indian snare, where one of the rivals was eventually killed.[10] Russell told of moving with thirty trappers in the Wyoming country when "I found myself with only one Companion. All had turned to the right or left without once hinting their intentions for it was not good policy for a Trapper to let too many know where he intends to set his traps." Added to the roving urge, this competitive spirit could raise barriers of personal insensitivity.

[7] Frances F. Victor, *River of the West*, pp. 175–76, 253; Osborne Russell, *Journal of a Trapper*, ed. Aubrey L. Haines, pp. 114–16; Martin McLeod, "Diary," ed. Grace Lee Nute, *Minnesota History* 4 (August–November, 1922): 350–439; Lewis O. Saum, *Fur Trader and the Indian* (Seattle, 1965), p. 207.

[8] Russell, *Journal of a Trapper*, p. 60.

[9] Francis Paul Prucha, *American Indian Policy in the Formative Years* (Cambridge, Mass., 1962), pp. 72–73; Washington Irving, *Adventures of Captain Bonneville* (Norman, Okla., 1961), p. 9.

[10] Kenneth W. Porter, *John Jacob Astor, Businessman*, 2:768; Bernard De Voto, *Across the Wide Missouri*, p. 72.

Joe Meek told a story of four trappers using the dead body of a friend for a temporary card table. True or not, the tale was used by one trapper to describe his colleagues. Later in his life Meek was asked by an interviewer about compassion among mountain men; he answered, "That war [sic] not our business. We had no time for such things."[11]

The consequent community was no more than collected individuals sharing a few attributes and experiences and cooperating only enough for survival. James Ohio Pattie, the Kentuckian who so egotistically embroidered the narrative of his five or six years in the Far West, was probably accurate when he described his trapping party engaging in a death-punishable covenant to stick together; in only a few weeks, though, the majority claimed they were no longer bound by it and slouched off. Pattie ruefully concluded that the splitting would go on and on.[12]

Similar tales of separation and realignment are scattered throughout the journals. George Simpson, the grand old man of the Hudson's Bay Company who had already spent nearly ten years in the trade, recognized this tendency when he wrote in 1829 that the Americans were "never sufficiently organized to hold together for any length of time." The British in Simpson was condescending, but he was nevertheless pointing to an influence of the trail on American trappers, and in that sense his perception of the fur community was accurate.

The trail conceivably could have bound cowboys into more cooperative units than those of trappers. Since cattle drivers could not move the great herds with fewer than six or eight men, the temptation to split off and compete by ones and twos was less likely. During the 1860s and 1870s the drives from Texas cattle spreads to the railheads in Kansas consumed up to three months, long weeks of riding

[11] Russell, *Journal of a Trapper*, p. 83; Victor, *River of the West*, pp. 249–50.

[12] Pattie, *Personal Narrative*, pp. 122–23.

and living together through heavy tedium and acrid dust. In the words of their historian Joe Frantz, cowboys "drew close to each other from the constant, enforced companionship."[13] On occasion the cohesive energy could even unite such heterogeneous elements as Anglo derelicts, derided Mexicans, and black former slaves. The feeling could penetrate and transcend the dull routine of ten miles a day that might stretch all the way from a Texas savannah to the lights of Wichita.

The cowboy trail, however, was only one unit in a larger system—an economic and ecological organism of ranch, range, and roundup of which the trail was the ultimate thrust. The same men were thrown together through the entire cattle operation, and their environment tended to be of one piece. The trapper had been a temporary adjunct of a distant company and had little face-to-face daily contact with his employers. But the cowboy might be surrounded on his ranch with owners or managers, including their families, and hence could function in more of a community. So, not on the trail alone but in the whole ranch experience, as we shall see later, would the roots of any cattle community spring.

At best, trapper and cowboy trails witnessed sex-role anomalies. Whereas the prevailing outside society rested on families and male dominance over women, on these trails women's work had to be allocated among men, a thorny assignment for a budding community. Taking an Indian wife might avoid the male rancor, but squaws were not universally available or acceptable. In contrast, the emigrant trail allowed a more normal society in which the traditional spheres of men and women could be perpetuated.[14]

[13] Joe B. Frantz and Julian E. Choate, Jr., *The American Cowboy*, p. 46.

[14] John M. Faragher, *Women and Men on the Overland Trail*, p. 112. The ensuing section relies heavily on Faragher's seminal study.

For a few years after 1848 the sexual mix of the trail population was skewed by male parties bent on mining. But these abberations aside, the typical wagon train during the three or four decades of the overland trail was composed of families seeking new land for new homes. Numbers in the train could be low, like a single family or a small clump of former neighbors; but as far as community was concerned, the long, lumbering caravans stretching and creaking their way west were the ones that wrestled with communal possibilities. Their people shared high hopes for a successful joint venture, expressing the optimism of the young. Most of them were newly married or married only long enough to have realized that their farms in Illinois or Indiana were doing poorly.[15] Yet they were old enough to cherish the memories of rural village cohesiveness, a legendary unity that presumably would continue to support them on the trail.

Gearing for the crossing, they could demonstrate their political acumen. In home villages and counties they had practiced local electioneering and now remembered the candidates on the stump and office seekers buttonholing their way to cracker-barrel leadership. Once they were on the hither edge of the prairie, the political bugle would bring together encampments of fifty or a hundred people. Here the men would forge a body politic in a process not unlike election day in Gopher Corners or Jefferson County. Sometimes conditions called for minor adaptations. Without paper ballots, for example, adherents would simply line up behind their favorite candidate, the longest lines quickly identifying the winner. Whimsical or not, through these political mechanisms strangers and friends alike hoped to form "an acquaintance with each other, to last, in all probability through good or evil fortune, through the rest of their days." It was the same communal dream that had motivated the Mayflower Compact and covenants

---

[15] Ibid., pp. 25, 191.

Wagon train, Echo Canyon, 1866
Nebraska State Historical Society

of Puritan towns. In each instance the dream was encased
in a mold of practicality. Likewise, the newly chosen cap-
tains of the trail held little abstract power, only obligations
to determine the hour of departure, the sites of the camp,
and the level of preparation for danger. Their good judgment in such matters was required to earn respect and
continuity in office.[16]

The rules, like the leaders, were quickly chosen. Regulations embodied what little specific lore had come through

[16]Matthew C. Field, *Prairie and Mountain Sketches* (Norman, Okla.,
1957), p. 26; Randolph B. Marcy, *The Prairie Traveler*, p. 23.

written guides or word of mouth—divisions into platoons, night formations for security, and rotations in the wagon lines to spread around the discomfort of the dust. Thus these companies tried to be practical and to profit from the experience of others. Yet at the same time the situations were frighteningly new, and the organization to cope with them was constructed in a day. As Edmund Burke once worried about the French Revolution, these pioneers might wonder if what was too quickly created might be as swiftly swept away.

Even in the harmonious days of roseate anticipation there were signs that unity might be precarious. The constituent assemblies often took time to bicker over travel on the Sabbath. This kind of issue could rankle for the entire journey. The Sabbath debate even split families, the men against the women. The women were, of course, upholding religious tradition, but also as the weeks wore on they came desperately to need a day of rest from constant work. The men, in contrast, found more daily respite, more time to sit around and talk.[17] During the days of formation, a faction in the Hastings party contended that the only law the train needed was "the moral code enacted by the Creator of the universe, and . . . found recorded in the breast of every man." These people lost, and the train wrote a strict set of regulations. Hastings saw the disagreement as an augury, concluding that this community was "determined to govern, but not to be governed."[18] What the splinter group could have been expressing was the community's need for a general will, a common set of values in which the group at least on occasion takes precedence over the individual. A body thus unified requires few written laws; disunity, on the other hand, demands careful codification.

Francis Parkman, the aristocratic Tacitus of the trail,

[17] Faragher, *Women and Men,* pp. 95–96.
[18] Hastings, *Emigrants' Guide,* pp. 6–7.

looked on the embarking emigrants of 1846 and found them hounded by indecision. As he bid adieu to the settlements and to the principles of Blackstone's *Commentaries*, he expected to find no reverence for law west of the Missouri. All his summer contact with immigrants confirmed his judgment on their inabilities to conform, to enforce their own regulations, or to accept their own discipline. Actually there were exceptions to Parkman's bleak picture, notably associations of neighbors formed before arriving at the brawling organization points.[19] These prior agreements between known friends occasionally assumed the trappings of solemn compacts only slightly more limited in time and purpose than Puritan town covenants of the seventeenth century.

Interestingly enough, high economic stakes seemed to work better than families as the base for cooperation. At least such seemed true with the great freighting caravans on the Santa Fe Trail. There dry plains and hostile Comanches posed serious risks to sizable capital investments. A single train in 1843, for example, was capitalized at $200,000 in merchandise—blankets, bolts of gingham and calico, iron pans, and steel knives.[20] Accordingly there followed a militaristic preoccupation with order and security. The wagons rolled in divisions of about twenty-five, each under a lieutenant and on occasion protected by the fire power of cannons. These caravans were abnormal communities because, like trapper's parties, they included no women except as infrequent passengers. Railroads or joint stock companies would make better comparisons than communities. In addition, frontier disruptions worked on the Santa Fe Trail as elsewhere. Captains were elected

[19] Francis Parkman, *Oregon Trail,* ed. E. N. Feltskog, p. 29; Owen C. Coy, *The Great Trek,* pp. 98–99, 115.

[20] Josiah Gregg, *Commerce of the Prairies,* ed. Max L. Moorhead, pp. 31, 80; Seymour Connor and Jimmy Skaggs, *Broadcloth and Britches: The Santa Fe Trade,* p. 70.

in the same ad hoc manner, but on the march their orders were "obeyed or neglected at the caprice of the subordinates." Still, these companies tended to stick together, and most settler's trains could have profited from a larger dose of their corporateness, their collective response to the risks involved. Randolph Marcy, frontier soldier, escort of emigrant trains, and trail expert for the army, realized that need and suggested that trains should contribute to a common supply of animals or a joint pool of replacement parts for wagons. Such incorporation among settlers, except for purely defensive purposes, was extremely rare, however.[21]

Alonzo Delano, whose prodigious nose and tendency to exaggerate make him a kind of Cyrano of the trail, was nevertheless reasonable when he observed a sense of community, not in separate wagon trains, but among all the people of the entire trail. The dirt and the hail and the desert bound them all together in the way hardship so often unites people. In busy seasons panoramas would suddenly open, eastward or westward, and the sight of hundreds of wagons like lines of emphasis under the hills would inspire a feeling of involvement in a larger enterprise. Contacts were frequent enough, as trains traveled together for a time, parted company, and then met again. "The high incidence of cooperation," wrote John Unruh in an overview, minimized the tragedies "as the emigrating community pushed westward together." Delano was probably typical when he expressed a thrill of participation in a mighty movement of comrades holding "one pursuit in common." He saw communal clues in little things, like a "post office" by the road consisting of a dusty rock guarding a few newspapers from the wind and bearing an invitation to read and leave for those to come. Messages were left for friends and relatives coming along. Forked sticks

[21] Marcy, *Prairie Traveler,* p. 23; Faragher, *Women and Men,* pp. 29–30.

waved frail but thoughtful warnings of bad water or harsh terrain. One Kentuckian backtracked for miles to leave a warning against a twenty-mile desert. And there were neat piles of castoffs with suggestions to use if needed.

But Delano, with that sense of ambiguity of a true Cyrano, also found evidence of selfishness, possessiveness, and meanness. There was another "post office," a pretense, taking money from the gullible. There were other categories of castoffs—deliberately burned wagons, sacks of sugar with turpentine poured over them, flour with dirt thrown in it, and clothes torn as if to say, "If I can't use it, I'll be damned if anyone else will."[22] Delano undoubtedly was forgetting the worries over confiscation by Indians, yet his thoughts on the psychology of spite are not to be overlooked.

Inasmuch as community radiates from its smaller to its larger units, the microcosm of the wagon train should have evidenced more group attachment than the macrocosm of the trail. Such would seem to be true. Diaries tell of women nursing the sick of neighboring wagons, then washing the clothes of the afflicted family; of men carrying injured to shelter in spite of danger to themselves; of parts donated for the repair of one another's wagons; of posses swiftly organizing to pursue thieves; of men walking because they had given their wagons to families in trouble; of whole trains traveling only a few hundred yards a day because the combined group assisted each wagon over an obstacle; of blacksmiths, wheelwrights, and barbers offering their services. Personal as they were, these acts must have been infused with some spirit of the group, like the salt of the loaf. It was the spirit that was sensed on rare occasions of frivolity in singing and dancing.

The women more than the men nurtured those intimate

[22] Alonzo Delano, *Life on the Plains and Among the Diggings,* pp. 46, 63, 70, 95, 110, 156; John D. Unruh, Jr., *The Plains Across,* pp. 133, 137.

exchanges that give flesh to the cooperative life—close eye contact, the easy conversation, the friendly touch. In coming west, most women experienced feelings not of buoyant opportunity but of great loss. The common plight of separation from home and friends, Susan Magoffin noticed, induced a bond of sympathy "that makes each other's society agreeable." Josiah Royce, his mother's reminiscence of prairie travel fresh in his mind, commented on the attribute of woman's intimacy on the trail. His observation has been reaffirmed in a recent study based on hundreds of trail diaries. Where men's journals might dwell on violence, aggression, and conflict, women's were occupied with the values of family, friends, and getting along with the group.[23] Ministering to the sick was perhaps the highest expression of such values, but these priorities spilled over into lesser moments, into the sisterhood of coffee, recipes, and concerned gossip about husbands and children.

But, alas, that is not the whole picture. Among the wagons a lack of cooperation and a rejection of the group was at least as evident as was the reverse. Fighting was endemic, over the "ten thousand little vexations continually recurring," usually inconsequential matters.[24] Bitter words flared frequently. Trains failed to wait for their own members after they had agreed to do so. Deception, feuding, and bickering were common and often ended in holding jury trials along the trail or in dragging offenders before army officers en route. On the way to Santa Fe, in spite of the economic pressure to stand together, quarreling was serious, and gambling left some men "next to

[23]Susan S. Magoffin, *Down the Santa Fé Trail and into Mexico,* pp. 80, 126; Royce, *California,* p. 193; Faragher, *Women and Men,* pp. 132–33; Christiane Fischer, ed. *Let Them Speak for Themselves,* p. 13; Unruh, *The Plains Across,* p. 140.

[24]Peter H. Burnett, *An Old California Pioneer* (Oakland, Calif., 1946), p. 60; John M. Faragher, *Women and Men,* p. 173.

nudity." A short-term captain of the 1843 Oregon migration, Peter Burnett, former Missouri lawyer and later governor of California, recalled how he had tried to enforce the rules "but found much practical difficulty and opposition." He doubted that large bodies of emigrants could be kept together on such journeys. The ill-humor, the annoyed murmurs, the curses, the ruptures over leadership reflected fatigue, drained energy, and anxiety—difficult hurdles for community. It was hard to be sick on the trail, Delano sadly remembered, "with the feelings of those around you so blunted by the weariness that they will not take the trouble to administer to your comfort."[25]

Splinterings and dissolutions punctured the trail experience. Before they crossed the plains, most parties held mass meetings that ended in expletives and a decision to separate. Occasionally sound reasons lay behind the breaking, like a divided train's easier foraging for its smaller herd. More often, disagreements over command incited the turmoil, producing what Parkman called "the extraordinary perplexity and indecision that prevailed."[26] Another point of crisis came at the forks of the trails in the Salt Lake region, associated with the necessity of a final choice between Oregon and California. By this time the train was usually charged with so much friction that even cooperative, positively motivated women like Sarah Royce or Tamsen Donner breathed sighs of relief watching parts of their company take the other route.

"I never saw a more discontented community," wrote that restless, sun-bleached trapper James Clyman of a wagon train just arrived in Oregon. This was in 1844, early in the history of the Overland Trail, when the perceived dangers of the crossing, which should have impelled

---

[25] John Bidwell, *Echoes of the Past About California* (Chicago, 1928), p. 47; Magoffin, *Down the Santa Fé Trail*, p. 66; Burnett, *An Old California Pioneer*, pp. 62–63; Delano, *Life on the Plains*, p. 158.
[26] Parkman, *Oregon Trail*, pp. 57, 114–15.

cooperation, were at their height. Through the years, as the Indian hazards and fears of the unknown diminished, the number of helping hands on the trail likewise declined.[27] Thus, as Clyman's comment implied, even in the most cooperative times there was little evidence that a momentum of community carried over from trail to settlement. If community had been implanted during the passage, it should have persisted after arrival. Instead, settlers went their individual ways, assumed that the purpose of trail association had been accomplished, and apparently remained uninfected by any deep desire for a continuing cooperative life. Thus rarely was ongoing collective action the outgrowth of the Overland Trail. If farmers' communities were to develop, they would have to be the offspring of differently perceived dangers and freshly shared hardships.

The trail offered no sense of place on which to rest the foundations of community, no sanctuary of memory, no repeated contact with a known environment. That was its most serious deficiency. In the face of similar difficulties gypsies and Bedouins have reared strong communities. But they have reacted to continually hostile environments, like deserts or social prejudices, which operated over a long period of time, time that the dwellers of the American trails did not have. Also, as Sarah Royce said, people of the trail shared little "mutual interest."[28] Although they all sought security and the efficient bridging of distance, group values were largely missing. There was little intention to live the collective life, few transcendent ideals of brotherhood, and little commitment to the mini-body

[27] James Clyman, *James Clyman, Frontiersman;* ed. Charles L. Camp, p. 119; Faragher, *Women and Men,* pp. 29–30. Unruh, *The Plains Across,* pp. 120–22, 380–81, stresses the change between the 1840s and 1850s in the overland-emigration experience, referring to support facilities, traffic security, and trail improvements.

[28] Sarah E. Royce, *A Frontier Lady,* p. 9.

politic. Cooperation seldom went beyond the immediate demands of the trail, and it was generally believed that whenever possible such demands should be met with individual effort or family action. The fundamental concern lay with the person and the family, not with the group. No matter how much Hastings's reformed young man was disciplined on the trail to social responsibility, no matter how much belonging the trapper and cowboy felt as the night walled in the firelight of their circle, these men remained temporary nomads, seeking safe transit and little more.

In the Bobtail Mine, Black Hawk Canyon, Colorado, 1898
Keystone-Mast Collection, University of California, Riverside

Chapter Four

The Frustrated Community
of Camp and Claim

They began at once to create new bonds of human
fellowship. The most interesting of these was the social
and spiritual significance given to the partnership idea.
It soon became almost as sacred as the marriage-bond.

Charles Shinn, *Mining Camps* (1884)

ANNE ELLIS WAS the "good angel" of a Colorado mining
camp. She had come when Bonanza counted its population
as thirty-six saloons and seven dance halls instead of
people. Slender, blue-eyed, alert, she kept a bunch of
wild flowers pinned above her apron. She read a great
deal and seriously — *Camille, Hamlet,* Plutarch's *Lives.*
She cooked for a living and understood miners. "Give me
a well-cooked, well-served meal, a bouquet, and a sunset
and I can do more for a man's soul than all the cant ever
preached. I can even do it without a sunset!"

Anne's father had dragged the family from Missouri to
Colorado in 1879. "We will go west where there are
chances for a man," he said. In fact, he sought quick
riches. During working hours he claimed headaches, but
he sprang to life with his banjo when the sun went down.
In Anne's first years they made three trips by oxcart
across the plains between Missouri and Colorado. Anne
was weaned on the trail and reared in transit. In Colorado
the father was continually chasing new booms. Later
Anne's stepfather led the same life of boom and bust.
"There he goes and we are alone again," the women
sighed. The second husband was a hired company miner.

71

Although he had not paid his dues, he wore his Masonic pin, cherishing the status it gave him.[1] All in all the Ellis family typified much about mining camps—courageous individualism, uprooted restlessness, rapid economic fluctuation—elements with which mining camps would have to cope in order to succeed in building their new communities.

In 1860 not far west of Bonanza a chill, barren valley was convulsed into what became California Gulch. Here, along the Great Divide, the days of California's forty-niners reverberated as they had at Washoe, Cripple Creek, Fraser River, and elsewhere throughout the West. The same magnetics drew men like Horace Tabor, who within thirty-five years would rise from a poor prospector and groceryman to a millionaire United States senator and then back again to penury. The town's story was equally dramatic. In the first spring and summer over five thousand people swarmed into the makeshift "bough town" of California Gulch. By 1865 the canyon was deserted by all but a few hundred hangers-on. Twelve years later and a few miles up the valley another town sprang up. More stable than California Gulch, Leadville too had its ups and downs, often as abrupt as the peaks that broke its western horizon. The cycles of California Gulch and Leadville were not unique. Nearly twenty years before, Prentice Mulford, a bright Down Easter sloshing around the California gold fields, reported laying out three new towns. "There is a sepulchral and post-mortem suggestion in that term 'laid out' which is peculiarly applicable to all the 'cities' which I attempted to found, and which 'cities' invariably foundered."[2]

Fluidity, E. Gould Buffum would have called the Mulford town phenomenon. Buffum was a Quaker, and such fluidity should have bothered his religion's hope for calm

---

[1] Anne Ellis, *Life of an Ordinary Woman*, pp. x, 8, 11.
[2] Prentice Mulford, *Prentice Mulford's Story*, p. 91.

consensus. He had already abridged Quaker principles, however, by volunteering for service in the Mexican War, which is how he got to California. He mustered out in Los Angeles and with a few other veterans headed north for gold. Three months later in camp on Weaver's Creek life already seemed monotonous. Men would descend on a new strike, and in a few days it would be dug out. So it went over and over again. Buffum was tired of his present ravine, tired of the creek and the pines and the hills with men everywhere. He tramped off alone and discovered a lovely stream bed, plump with golden gravels. The first day he panned $150 dollars in dust. The next day he was no longer alone; twenty men moved up along his creek. In three days the whole place was turned upside down, and the ravine given him from the hand of creation was now a shambles. The land, the creek, the folding hills came to be "a battlefield where primal forces and giant passions have wrestled."

A sense of place requires some hope of permanence. The men who came from New England with Mulford expected to be gone longer than a whaling voyage, three years, but no more than five. Buffum felt that the whole mining population was volatile, with no more feeling for the land than they might have held for a goose plucked to a few feathers and then forsaken. The early miners thought of themselves as Bedouins tramping far from civilization or as sojourners on a strange planet. They lived in caves, bivouacs, or "calico-shirt houses." They were prepared to be strangers to the land, which they could therefore gouge and litter with impunity. Although Buffum was generally a sensitive man, he was willing to join with others on a Sacramento River boat to light fires on the banks for the fun of watching the countryside burn.[3]

In spite of graves without graveyards, in spite of lives

[3] Edward G. Buffum, *Six Months in the Gold Mines*, pp. 71–72, 112, 20; Charles H. Shinn, *Mining Camps*, p. 144; Mulford, *Prentice Mul-*

without beginnings or endings, miners often expressed sentiment for their first diggings. "It was no common affection they entertained for these places," Mulford said, and they made yearly pilgrimages back as long as the camp lasted. It is not hard to imagine such feelings for a place like Meadow Lake, where in winter the entire camp was literally buried under snow. People dug tunnels from house to house, shared their food, and came up for ski races on sunny days.

Deeper commitments to place, however, waited for women to turn bivouacs into settlements. It was like the cattle towns described by Robert Dykstra, where the arrival of feminine influence coincided with the first efforts at reforms such as prohibition. More important in the mines, the women were likely to infuse the surroundings with sentiments that come with memory. Anne Ellis recalled playing on the mesa that would eventually be the site of the graves of her mother and brother. Pines encircled the quavering aspen. Daisies and honeysuckle followed the primroses in spring. And in Anne's town there was Nellie Smeltzer, who had gone with her husband from camp to camp until she planted herself and said "no more moves." Her husband went on. Through the years she got a little strange and once was charged with insanity because she kissed her cow. Long afterward she died, alone but still proud in her place.[4]

ford's Story, p. 2; Ernest A. Wiltsee, The Pioneer Miner and the Pack Mule Express, p. 15; Henry De Groot, Recollections of California Mining Life, p. 12; Ralph Mann, "The Decade After the Gold Rush," Pacific Historical Review 41 (November, 1972): 486; Rodman Paul, California Gold, p. 80.

[4]Mulford, Prentice Mulford's Story, p. 46; Clarence Wooster, "Meadow Lake City and a Winter at Cisco in the Sixties," California Historical Society Quarterly 18 (June, 1939): 152; Ellis, Life of an Ordinary Woman, pp. 61–62, 89, 94, 168; Robert R. Dykstra, Cattle Towns, p. 253.

The statistics support Mulford's mobility, not Nellie Smeltzer's entrenchment. Grass Valley and Nevada City, California, were among the mother lode's richest camps, their production steadily rising as they changed from placer to quartz operations. Yet of every one hundred people there in 1850 only five remained in 1856. Merchants, craftsmen, and attorneys were the most stable, but even among them four out of five moved on. Consequently, wrote Ralph Mann, the demographer, the most obvious characteristic of these years was transience, both physical and social. This itchiness to shift about was, in part, related to the age of the population — over 60 percent were between the ages of twenty and thirty. On the other hand, mining itself was unstable because it could not restore what it removed from the ground.[5]

Mulford once sat beside a stove in winter with lonely, silent, miners making little pasteboard figures with moving grindstones. Glued on the flue, the paper grindstones turned in the rising heat. Before the day was over the flue was covered, all the paper figures moving frantically. Mulford's picture caught the boredom, the lack of purpose, the ephemeral quality of a mining camp. A year hence where would all these men be? Sagging resources or surging restlessness spurred by disappointment could decimate their town. Mulford often reflected on abandoned mining communities. He once stumbled upon the ruins of Dry Bar, where a booming camp had given men a "local habitation and a name"; the world had then seemed so much younger. In another place he mused, "What solitude of ancient ruined cities equals this?" He had once known practically everyone here, and now there was nothing.

The same forces that compelled men to move also dispersed them over the landscape, resulting in very small

[5] Mann, "Decade After the Gold Rush," pp. 486–87, 493–94; Rodman Paul, *Mining Frontiers of the Far West*, p. 9; John W. Caughey, *Gold Is the Cornerstone*, p. 168.

mining camps, and, ironically, consequent situations that drew them together. Typically each valley or watershed would have its own camp where the miners would live and from which they would go out to work on their claims. In this way it functioned like a New England farming village, besides providing supplies, news, a stagecoach station, and mail. Each night when Mulford walked the three miles from his claim, he thought of his camp as a nerve center, his one link with civilization and the outside world. "Everybody at these camps knew us," said Mulford, "and we knew everybody and were pretty sure of meeting everybody we knew." He spoke of the "receptions" every evening at the store and the ease of dropping in for a chat.[6]

We might be suspicious, though, of the depth and breadth of relationships throughout a camp. There were frequently inner barriers of race and nationality. From the first great rush to California came a welter of commentators like Bayard Taylor of the *New York Tribune* stressing the polyglot nature of the population. Dame Shirley called it "a perambulating picture gallery, illustrative of national variety." Charles Gillespie, less well known but likewise on the scene, underscored the same "antipodes of color, race, religion, language, government, condition, size, capability, strength and morals." At Treasure Hill south of Elko, Nevada, three years after the discovery, the foreign-born ranged from 40 to 50 percent of the population. Agreed, the racial mix was not a universal phenomenon. Colorado mines, for example, attracted a large number of middle-western farmers. Generally racial tensions should have been mitigated by contributions of the foreign-born to the entire community; there was ready adaptation of Cornish methods and Spanish-Mexican laws and practices. But even in these small camps miners tended to congregate according to their roots. Men from

[6]Mulford, *Prentice Mulford's Story,* pp. 58, 64, 78, 133, 135.

the same families, the same regions, the same state, or
even adjacent states lived together.[7]

Some cohesion was born from the experience of the
trail. The routes to the mother lode, to Washoe, to Leadville, to Coeur d'Alene, to Helena were all at one time
cluttered with men moving in groups, cooking and riding
and bedding down together. Whether they came carrying
a carpetbag, pushing a wheelbarrow, or driving a spring
wagon, few traveled alone. Expenses and dangers were
thereby minimized. The smaller the band the more likely
it would stick together after arrival in the mines, but not
many lasted more than a few months. Other groups would
form, though, to travel to new strikes. John Steele's journal, which he kept for three years in California before he
returned to Wisconsin to become a Methodist minister,
reads like a catalog of groups beginning and ending. Each
party formed for some specific purpose and split when the
goal was achieved. Their agreements might spell out
amounts of work expected, percentages for donated tools,
coverage in case of sickness or injury, prohibition of liquor,
and sometimes a pledge to stand by one another regardless
of what happened.[8] The trail stayed alive, at least for a
short time, in their thinking.

As time passed, the shovel and the pan were replaced
by long tom and cradle, long boxes on rockers into which
gravels were shoveled and water channeled. Josiah Royce
termed these improvements "social agents," because they
demanded greater cooperation. Three or four men could

[7] Louise Amelia K. Clappe (Dame Shirley), *The Shirley Letters*, p.
121; Charles B. Gillespie, "A Miner's Sunday in Coloma," *Century
Magazine* 42 (June, 1891): 259; Paul, *Mining Frontiers*, p. 45; Don L.
Griswold and Jean H. Griswold, *The Carbonate Camp Called Leadville*, p. 96; Mann, "Decade After the Gold Rush," p. 487; W. Turrentine Jackson, *Treasure Hill*, p. 27.

[8] Mann, "Decade After the Gold Rush," p. 489; John Steele, *In Camp
and Cabin*, pp. 19, 44–45; Shinn, *Mining Camps*, pp. 113–14.

now work together far more advantageously. Thus wherever large amounts of water had to be diverted from stream beds through ditches or sluices or flumes, joint labor became necessary. "When the hills are to be torn to their very bases," as Buffum put it, "individuals must retire from the field, and make room for combined efforts."[9]

In all these fragile collaborations small size made compassion more evident. When Anne Ellis's mother lay dying, not only the doctor but a whole troop of people came tramping up the hill, and she wrote, "Nowhere on earth are neighbors so good as in mining camps." An Idaho man talked of many "homestakes" raised for broken miners. And there was the penniless boy, dejectedly sitting on the riverbank, not realizing that the men of the ravine had agreed each to work an hour to set him up with a claim.

In bands of friends, relatives, and partners shared hardship brought out the best in people. Men nursed the sick and raised funds to send the seriously ill home. They risked their own lives to dig others out of avalanches. They volunteered to fight fires. They shared books and papers. Almost every man in Leadville contributed labor or money for the first church.[10]

The existence of such cooperation is clear; its typicality is not. When food ran low in the severe winter of 1865, hoarding in Alder Gulch, Montana, reached threatening proportions and required rationing. In the relatively well organized camp at Meadow Lake, California, arson of neighboring mills and destructive acts on the plaza suggested divisiveness, not cooperation. Sarah Royce, mother

[9] Josiah Royce, *California*, p. 223; Paul, *California Gold*, pp. 50, 64; Buffum, *Six Months in Gold Mines*, p. 86.

[10] Ellis, *Life of an Ordinary Woman*, p. 167; Shinn, *Mining Camps*, pp. 111, 156; Steele, *In Camp and Cabin*, pp. 126, 184; Griswold and Griswold, *Carbonate Camp Called Leadville*, p. 78. For others see Shinn, ibid., p. 119; Jackson, *Treasure Hill*, p. 226.

Corporate hydraulic mining, Alma, Colorado, 1887
Western History Department, Denver Public Library

of the philosopher of community, having recently arrived
with her husband and baby in the mines, needed help in
building a cabin. On all sides, she wrote, "the goldpans
were rattling, the cradles rocking, and the water splash-
ing," but no one would help them. Later, in the big flood

of January, 1850, though Mrs. Royce admittedly observed much generosity, she also told of a man who extorted twenty dollars from a miner before rescuing him. Apparently more was needed than the smallness of the group to evoke cooperation.

Sarah Royce looked into the faces of a congregation of miners—earnest and intelligent, she said—and thought she saw the glow of new values rising from the mining experience, infused meanings, recharged power from spiritual truth.[11] Could she have been right? Could mining camps nurture the values that might transcend uprootedness, capitalize on their small size, and transform limited cooperation into community?

Miners certainly seemed to want community. They were known to collect town libraries of fiction, poetry, science, and reference works. They jointly constructed roads and water supplies. They quickly organized chapters of their old fraternal lodges—notably Masons, Odd Fellows, and the Knights of Pythias—institutions that carried from home the echoes of a summer ball game and a band on the Fourth of July.

The most powerful values of the mining camp, however, were pragmatic. The social contract was pared to the bare bones. Nuances and complexities that dwell in custom, like the "frills" of due process and procedures of appeal in the law, were swept aside to grapple with needs of the cabins and hills. In the bitter barrenness of the Yukon, for example, the theft of food brought automatic banishment into the deadly cold. The men who kept that law had stood close to the painful swellings of scurvy and the bloatings of hunger. In the face of such immediacies, the niceties were suspended for pragmatic ends. In a much

---

[11] Dorothy Winner, "Rationing During the Montana Gold Rush," *Pacific Northwest Quarterly* 36 (April, 1945): 115–20; Paul Fatout, *Meadow Lake: Gold Town*, pp. 47, 93–94; Sarah E. Royce, *A Frontier Lady*, pp. 84, 96, 104.

lighter vein the same was true for an assembly of miners gathered in California on outdoor benches to hear a traveling preacher. Rather than sit meditatively while waiting, they dealt out a few hands of euchre, retiring the cards as casually as any Huck Finn when the preacher arrived.[12] Custom gave way to the wants of the moment.

Only when the pragmatic became less insistent did the manners of neighborliness and sociability thrive. Of course, Sunday in the camps, as the familiar drawings of Charles Nahl have etched in our minds, was always a combination of necessary marketplace, trapper's rendezvous, and religious revival. The occasion was indeed sociable and a kind of common denominator for all. But as women began arriving and the camp became a town, the expected subtle complication in circles of sociability arose. Two events in Leadville will illustrate. The first notable social, organized by the ladies of the town, was a Christmas party to which everyone was invited. Seven months later the celebration of the Fourth of July had a very different flavor. The Episcopalians led an excursion to Twin Lakes; several Sunday schools went to Soda Springs; the Catholics sponsored a special fair; the Odd Fellows held their own grand ball. Circles of sociability had segmented the community, and, without realizing it, the city fathers contributed by eliminating the town parade.

Cooperation and sociability were undoubtedly overarched by what Thorstein Veblen, a contemporary, would call cupidity—the desire to get quickly rich so well exemplified by Anne Ellis's father and stepfather. As the historian Duane Smith put it, "The community existed for one major purpose, to make money." This pecuniary drive explains much of the competitive dissatisfaction,

---

[12] Daniel R. Mortensen, "Process of Community Development in a Frontier Town, Sonora, California, 1848–1860" (Ph.D. diss., University of Southern California, 1977), pp. 15–16; William S. Greever, *The Bonanza West*, p. 332; Steele, *In Camp and Cabin*, p. 207.

the lootings after fires, the burials at night so that newcomers would not be discouraged—the seldom-exposed
seamy undersides of the history.[13]

This cupidity was an individualistic trait, undermining
group values. Mulford eventually found that all the men
with whom he had once lived cooperatively preferred to
live apart like hermits, each in his own cabin. They were
unwilling, he said, to accept one another's peculiarities.
"The neat man couldn't abide the slovenly man; the
economic man couldn't sit patiently by and see his partner
cut potato parings a quarter of an inch in thickness."
These were natural differences, always present in human
relations, but a strong community vision can keep them
from driving men too far apart. In spirit miners remained
as "solitary as grizzly bears." Perhaps it was because they
could not own and consequently feel settled on their land,
being able to claim by law only mineral rights.[14] But more
likely they and their communities were victims of their
values.

In 1850 only three in a hundred Grass Valley and Nevada
City men were married and living with their families; in
1860, only ten. These may indeed have been "golden
seasons of masculine domestic tranquility." But from the
standpoint of a community built upon the blocks of family,
it was a dismal scene. Isaac Baer would have agreed,
advertising for a wife in Leadville, unmarried in spite of
what the reporter described as a handsome physique,
French beard, deep baritone voice, gentlemanly bearing,
and a good income as a liquor dealer. But even when the
families came, the desire to go home again, especially
among women, had to be quenched before that family

[13] Griswold and Griswold, *Carbonate Camp Called Leadville*, pp. 73,
232; Duane A. Smith, *Rocky Mountain Mining Camps*, p. 105; Buffum,
Six Months in Gold Mines, p. 47; Greever, *The Bonanza West*, pp. 189,
206.

[14] Mulford, *Prentice Mulford's Story*, pp. 61–62; Shinn, *Mining
Camps*, p. 155; Paul, *Mining Frontiers*, pp. 168–69.

could be a vital catalyst in the community. The Ellis family, for instance, might superficially assume before a camera the most coherent "blest be the tie that binds" effect, yet the mother would still at night drop her sewing and quietly cry—the sweet long ago, the golden shore of lost home, friends, and familiar faces now traded for the hope of gold in the pocket.[15] As always, women were less fearful than men of succumbing to the weakness of longing.

Although only one in thirty-three of the working miners of Grass Valley lived with families, one in six of the professional men, members of the wealthier, more stable group, were so favored. Thus, in a curious way, the coming of the women and families helped in the separation and identification of class differences. While families were increasing, the economy was stabilizing, and commercial interests were being forged, leading also to the solidification of class. No mining camp was ever devoid of class distinctions. Even the egalitarianism of the earliest days included recognition of former status. The judge from Plainville, Missouri, remained a judge even though he might temporarily tend bar. People like Sarah Royce would always know the difference.[16] As time went on and the incipient urban quality of all mining camps became more apparent, the emergence of in-groups and out-groups was natural. The rise of "bit" and "two bit" saloons, separating out the poorer miners, was a clue to what was happening in the society.

In 1879 in the town of Leadville, then less than a decade old, the incredible number of 146 freight wagons arrived

[15] Mann, "Decade After the Gold Rush," pp. 487, 500; Mulford, *Prentice Mulford's Story,* p. 46; Griswold and Griswold, *Carbonate Camp Called Leadville,* p. 251; Ellis, *Life of an Ordinary Woman,* pp. 82–83, 86.

[16] The professionals were six percent of the population, but they had 24 percent of the families; Mann, "Decade After the Gold Rush," p. 500. Royce, *A Frontier Lady,* p. 86; Gillespie, "Miner's Sunday in Coloma," pp. 268–69.

Chestnut Street, Leadville, Colorado, about 1881
From Eduoard de Laveleye, "Excursion aux Nouvelles

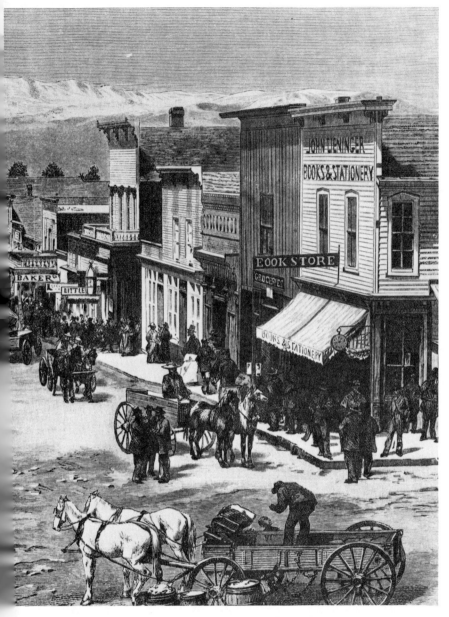

Découvertes Minières du Colorado," in *Le tour du Monde,*
2d Semestre (1881)

on May 18 alone. Merchants that year more than doubled the gross from the mines. Large commercial operations with permanent wage earners were developing fast. As changes in mining technology made small group cooperation advantageous, so the shift later brought large corporations. Heavy hydraulic and quartz mining, tunneling, crushing mills, and smelters made corporate investment more and more desirable. In most areas these changes had begun within two years of the first rush. Ten years after the first comers in a town like Grass Valley, although most men might still live in male groups, their cabins now clustered around corporate mines.[17] It was a long way from those individual claims worked by independents. Still, the bushy-tailed miners, so transitory, men who had left the mines shortly after the corporations settled in, continued to be celebrated by the Mark Twains and Bret Hartes.

One such corporation in the Black Hills of Dakota, the Homestake Mining Company, was almost as old as its hometown, Deadwood. Within fifteen years it was employing fifteen hundred men. The owners of corporate mines and mills, unlike their eastern counterparts, were sons of small farmers or small businessmen. They arrived in the mines young and worked up. But their eventual employees would not have the same opportunity. These wage earners turned instead toward fellow workers and organized unions. In Virginia City as early as 1863, just after twenty-eight-year-old Mark Twain left town, the new Miner's Protective Association paraded the streets protesting low wages. Strikes came to Grass Valley in 1860 and to Leadville in 1880, leaving raw wounds in the community. In 1869, two years after the ore discoveries around Treasure Hill, Nevada, one thousand miners joined the newly organized union. The battles of the Western

[17] Griswold and Griswold, *Carbonate Camp Called Leadville*, pp. 204, 228; Mann, "Decade After the Gold Rush," p. 502.

Federation of Miners at Cripple Creek and Coeur d'Alene lay just ahead. Labor unions themselves exposed other rifts in the society, as Cornishmen, Irishmen, and Anglo-Americans struggled for power within their ranks.

Anne Ellis expressed the community frustrations as she looked back over forty-five years of opening up and closing down the mines. With each shutdown came hard times —cornbread and milk for dinner, along with bitterness. Once the butcher shop was raided. Her stepfather had not been the thief, but he gratefully hid a fresh chunk of meat under the bed.[18] Such discord measured how far and how quickly the community had evolved from its more cohesive days.

No one doubts that the Americans had a remarkable gift for practical politics. They deftly appropriated forms at hand, as they did for a short time with the alcalde system in California. Elsewhere they adopted familiar patterns, like the small town meeting. Ad hoc handfuls of men were quickly organized if formal political services were not available. Raising a group to search for a missing man was never difficult. For laws regulating claims, no more than a day's meeting was required to produce a code. These were practical acts, and occasionally they were original. Sonora, for example, declared its land common property, sold lots, and with the proceeds ran a hospital specializing in the treatment of scurvy. Because of the political deftness Josiah Royce worried that overconfidence in creating government retarded rather than hastened "the voluntary and loyal devotion" required for a "truly significant social order." Without this deeper commitment government was merely a shell, and it was easy within

---

[18] Greever, *The Bonanza West*, p. 308; Richard H. Peterson, "The Frontier Thesis and Social Mobility on the Mining Frontier," *Pacific Historical Review* 44 (February, 1975): 63, 67; Paul, *Mining Frontiers*, p. 69; Jackson, *Treasure Hill*, p. 129; Richard E. Lingenfelter, *The Hardrock Miners*, p. 6; Ellis, *Life of an Ordinary Woman*, pp. 30, 40.

it to court litigiousness. If the Puritan town had preferred
social sanctions to courts, the mining town came to prefer
legal actions. Old-timers frequently complained about lawyers. "We needed no law" they said, "until the lawyers
came."[19]

In time high levels of lawlessness would encourage a
traditional frontier response. The community needed puri-
fication, the romantic historians would say, for often order
was not easy to maintain. For example, the men of Meadow
Lake, one of the calmest of mining communities, were
said to be ready to fight over most anything. In some
areas, chiefly in California, racial and ideological heterogeneity caused conflict.[20] In any case, vigilante activity
initially walked hand in hand with local self-government;
ideally the community was protecting itself from disruption.

Very quickly, however, vigilantism became itself a measure of social disintegration. In the first place, the townspeople had failed to provide services and facilities like
jails or to elect adequate officials; they consequently
abetted crime. Second, the continued use of the vigilante
device exposed one group of the community at odds with
another. The classic and pivotal example was San Francisco
in 1856, where vigilantism became a thinly veiled weapon
against Australian immigrants and Irish politicians. After
that, the victims of vigilante action increasingly became
"the little people," in John Caughey's words, "the sub-
ordinate, looked down upon or despised." The frequent
intimacy between the Masonic lodge (the self-appointed
elite) and vigilantism (the self-appointed law) was a clue
to what Richard Maxwell Brown called "the struggle of

[19] Greever, *The Bonanza West*, p. 41; Royce, *California*, p. 217;
Michael Zuckerman, *Peaceable Kingdoms*, p. 90; Shinn, *Mining Camps*,
pp. 120–21.
[20] Fatout, *Meadow Lake: Gold Town*, p. 64. Robert Redfield refuses
even to discuss mining camps because of their heterogeneity; *The Little
Community*, p. 5.

groups in conflict." Upper-class mining townsmen rallied around their interests, as later lynchings in the South would protect the established way. The San Francisco elite in 1856 was threatened economically by financial erosion, and their violence spoke as much to that worry as to any political or social concerns. Thus it was in Montana in 1883 when the merchants and entrepreneurs of Virginia City stood against the transients. It was Masons and the "better people," a surprising number of whom were Harvard graduates, against the Catholic immigrants, usually described as riffraff. Likewise, the first vigilance committee in Leadville was organized by those who felt that certain elements were smudging the town's reputation and hurting business. Eventually two more committees were formed, and two men were lynched.[21] Here as in San Francisco more than business and order were involved. The community itself was being ruptured.

Whenever a miner professed a poetic strain, he cast himself as an Argonaut. The cliché became apt enough for individuals bringing back the fleece of the golden ram, wandering and longing. But even the literate of the latter-day Argonauts chose to forget that their Homeric analogy held implications beyond the individual. The first Jason in his pursuit sowed the dragon's teeth of discord, and heterogeneous miners often planted social irresponsibility. Jason achieved his goal only with the help of a woman, Medea, who would become his wife, and miners were helpless to mold a rounded society until women and families joined them. Jason was ultimately

[21] John W. Caughey, *Their Majesties the Mob*, p. 18; Richard M. Brown, *Strain of Violence*, p. 5; Griswold and Griswold, *Carbonate Camp Called Leadville*, pp. 170, 171, 177. The economic threat to the elite vigilantes is discussed in Peter Decker, *Fortunes and Failures*, pp. 138–43; he concluded that 80 percent of this group either maintained or improved occupational status as a result of the vigilante activity.

The dominance of the fraternal lodge, Masonic Temple,
Central City, Colorado, 1868
Western History Department, Denver Public Library

The fraternal subcommunity, Knights of Pythias, Leadville,
Colorado, about 1900
Western History Department, Denver Public Library

condemned to a life of roaming, and the social psychology
of miners regularized their rootlessness. Jason died pin-
ioned under the rotting prow of the ship that had once
carried him so far afield, and the frontier mining community long suffered the effects of its initiation. Its size
was propitious; its values were not, largely because it was
so hard for these descendent Jasons to nourish a sense
of place. Mobility was inherent in mining; the requisite
disturbance of the terrain took from them the comfort of
a stable environment. These neo-Jasons lived in the pres-

ent, almost without a past. As a group they were oppor-
tunists, adapting their values to the pursuit of wealth.
They would compete or share, whichever served best.
The bonds of unity were not absolute principles or lasting
ideals. Because the camps were small, their close-knit
cooperation could be impressive. When miners realized
the need for law, they buckled down to self-government
in actions that were pregnant with true community. But
in the end the values of exaggerated individualism were
their nemesis.

Many mining camps grew into mining towns. In some
ways the camp was always the germ of a city: it was urban
in its associations for specific goals, in its inward-looking
nuclear families, in its class distinctions, in its service as
a mercantile center for wide areas, and especially in its
cosmopolitan and transient population. Thus it is not surprising that whenever the camp became a town, it was
well advanced in segmenting the lives of its people into
associative groups.

Mining camps were morally and socially tried, said
Josiah Royce, "as no other American community ever has
been tried." The trial was actually a regrouping, a reassign-
ment of priorities. Bancroft floridly implied the same:
"The social heart . . . lay so embedded in gold that it could
not throb."[22] Although the blood of Prentice Mulford and
Anne Ellis pulsed as warmly as any since Jason's and
Medea's, the heart of the community not only suffered
but was in the process of mutation.

[22] Smith, *Rocky Mountain Mining Camps*, p. 57; Royce, *California*,
p. 175; Hubert Howe Bancroft, *California Inter Pocula* (San Francisco,
1888), p. 303.

Chapter Five

Solitude and Society:
Farm Cooperation
on the Plains

In no civilized country have the cultivators of the soil
adapted their homelife so badly to the conditions of
nature.

Virgil Smalley, *Atlantic Monthly* (1893)

"I WAS ALONE all the daylight hours with the cattle, and
all around me the prairie was dying. The sound of death
was in the wind that never stopped blowing across the
whitening grass, or rustling the dead weeds at the edges
of the fields. There was a forlorn, lonely note in the bawl
of a calf for its mother and in the honking of wild geese
down the pale sky." Grace Snyder's thoughts were the
aftermath of death, the obliteration of a distant neighbor
boy who had died while hurrying through his noon dinner.
She and her family had walked the half mile to the funeral,
where the glass-topped coffin exposed the bloated face of
John, as lonely in death as the prairies were in life. Grace
had known solitude playing among the bleached bones in
the buffalo wallow, she and her sister alone because the
Snyder farm was so far from neighbors. Grace's father
had migrated with his proud wife and three daughters
from Missouri to the Platte River Valley in Custer County,
Nebraska. That was 1885, and Grace was three. Their
father had preceded them and prepared housing, but
Grace later remembered her first sight of "two naked
little soddies" on a bare, wind-swept ridge. Nothing else.
The flatness of the prairies threatened her with a child's

unconscious fear of abandonment, perhaps of lost identity, perhaps even of oblivion beneath that unbroken sky.[1]

The prairies and plains demanded cooperation. At the same time the land system and the traditions of isolation acted on a sense of community as do hot winds on autumn fields. The necessity for cooperation began here, as for the Puritans, with a harsh wilderness. Jonathan Edwards was no more eloquent about the wilderness than twenty-year-old Seth Humphrey, speaking of the Dakota Territory: its unrelieved vastness, its utter silence, its appalling rigidity, "as of an enormous thing long dead." Seth had come from Minnesota to the shacks of Aberdeen about the time that Grace Snyder had been frightened by the Nebraska prairie. Seth's young eyes stared at the "limitless vacuity," and it was hard for him to grasp how those hordes of home-steaders tramping through Aberdeen could cope with "that trembling horizon." These homesteaders were his people. In the 1850s his New England father had moved to Min-nesota after several previous steps, "always settling, never settled." In the midst of the Minnesota wilderness the father had come across a fellow Yankee from whose cabin no one was ever turned away "while there is room to lay his head on a blanket."[2] Here was the trust and the shar-ing, like the Puritan New England community struggling to find a foothold in this limitless vacuity.

Seth Humphrey became a mortgage collector, traveling across the Great Plains in the early 1890s. Everywhere he found abandoned claims, shacks pulled apart and used by others, the winds and the horizon taking their toll. Guy Divet, an Irishman who had come to Dakota with his family in the 1870s and prospered, told the story of another couple who had not. Ned and his young, pregnant wife moved into the neighborhood, and in their first winter

<hr/>

[1] Grace Snyder, *No Time on My Hands,* ed. N. S. Yost, pp. 13–15, 126.

[2] Seth K. Humphrey, *Following the Prairie Frontier,* pp. 9, 20, 131.

Margie was "sick and out of her mind with loneliness and fear." So the warm, caring Divets took them in for the winter, putting up a bed in their living room.

That spring Mrs. Divet helped with the birth, but the young mother remained half-crazed, and the young father grew more and more depressed. So they left with Margie still ill. The neighbors raised thirty-six dollars to help them. The baby died on the journey, and the mother shortly after. Ned sold the wagon and team to pay for the burials. "Grist for the prairie mill," the Divets said. Ned's claim was jumped, but before that the Divets rode over to see his cabin. There were unwashed dishes and a homemade crib. The Divets piled dry weeds, lit them, and watched reverently as the cabin burned to the ground. It did not take long.

But the fire could not erase the memory, and the prairie continued to stare. Mrs. Divet herself developed a goiter, and when her husband offered a visit to her family in Wisconsin, she refused, sadly pointing to her straggly hair and sagging body and "this hideous bag than hangs at my throat." "No," she cried, "it's too late now. I don't want to go." The Divet manuscripts are memorials to "the frayed ends" of these lives, "the heartstrings broken in the process of uprooting never to be brought together again."[3]

The lives of the Snyders, the Humphreys, and the Divets were in many respects full and rewarding. Nevertheless, as with all settlers on the Great Plains between the Civil War and the close of the century, the fact of isolation underlay all other facts, social, economic, and political. Isolation was the environment in which the structure of community must grow. Shortly after the turn of the century, when the President's Commission on Country Life asked over 100,000 rural inhabitants what could improve

[3] Hiram M. Drache, *Challenge of the Prairie*, pp. 28, 240, 244.

their lives, an overwhelming response was better roads, or, in other words, a way of overcoming isolation.[4]

Eugene Virgil Smalley spelled out the central problem in similar terms. A newsman, he had lived and worked from Ohio to Minnesota, served in the government, and traveled abroad. "In no civilized country," he wrote, "have the cultivators of the soil adapted their homelife so badly to the conditions of nature." He saw only one solution: to draw farmers together into village communities. He knew that it would be difficult because of land laws and, even more important, American ways of thinking. There is an old western saying, he quoted, that the prairies would not produce until the Indian was beaten out of them, something savage wrested from the land by individual struggle. Smalley told of four farm families who, like many others, had decided to work more closely by building their houses and barns on the adjacent corners of their claims. But in a few years they had all moved to the far corners because, they explained lamely, when they were together their chickens had gotten mixed up. Such was the "crusty individuality" that Smalley felt had produced the inheritance of isolated lives.[5]

But it takes time to beat the Indian out of the soil, and how could that typical pioneer tame the land if he was always moving on, always settling, never settled! He seemed to love his land so little that he was willing to sell or leave at the drop of a hat. One observer of the West, a man from Scotland where land was cherished, found Americans without qualms in abandoning their land. Richard Weston traveled through the Old Northwest in

[4] U.S., Congress, Senate, Country Life Commission, *Report*, 60th Cong. 2d sess. (1909), Sen. Doc. 705, pp. 27, 38.

[5] "The Isolation of Life on Prairie Farms," *Atlantic Monthly* 72 (September, 1893): 378, 382. Another example of farmers building houses on contiguous corners is in Ada B. Clarke, "Pothook Pioneer: A Remembrance," *Nebraska History* 29 (March, 1958): 46.

the 1830s, and he disliked much of what he saw. He concluded that America was a country fit only for hermits
and cynics.[6] Weston was himself too cynically anti-Ameri-
can to be taken without corroboration, but he did see the
connection between mobility and isolated lives.

Sources of plains history are records of mobility. The
Snyder family, for example, moved four times after arriving in Nebraska. William Gregory, who died in Iowa in
1858 after fathering at least twenty-four children, had
moved six times westward. In the Dakotas, when Seth
Humphrey began his rounds as a mortgage collector, he
was appalled by the number of abandoned farms. Of the
first forty-one he visited, eight were occupied by original
mortgagees and three by squatters; all the rest were
deserted. There were often fresh reminders—young weeds
not yet crowding out the heliotrope. Humphrey ran across
one farmer who was profiting from the restlessness. He
had been dragging abandoned shacks over the level plains
to his own place, where he was already using one for
chickens, one for pigs, one for corn, and one as a lean-to
extension of his own house.[7] Elsewhere in a typical Wisconsin county only 21 percent of the families who lived
there in 1880 remained fifteen years later. In Wapelo
County, Iowa, only 33 percent of the farmers of 1850
remained after ten years. The persistence rate in Kansas
in the decade following 1860 was usually under 30 percent
and in no cases higher than 42 percent.[8]

Such was the mobility which the Country Life Commis-

[6] Richard Weston, *A Visit to the United States and Canada in 1833*,
pp. 113, 123.

[7] James E. Davis, *Frontier America, 1800–1840*, pp. 35–36; Humphrey, *Following the Prairie Frontier*, pp. 164, 172.

[8] The county in Wisconsin appeared on the surface to be stable; the
manuscript census revealed the enormous influx and outflow; Peter
Coleman, "Restless Grant County: Americans on the Move," in *The
Old Northwest*, ed. Harry Scheiber (Lincoln, Nebr., 1969), p. 283. See

sion saw undermining the farm as a home. There were even less stable transients at the bottom of the community's social scale. These were the drifters, moving into the orbit of the larger society only on occasion. One Minnesotan called them "wandering Willies." They were migrants, and they supplied vital labor at crucial times of the year. Between periods of living on handouts, they might buckle down to a winter as timber men or in the late summer join a harvest or threshing crew. They slept in the hay-mows, drank a lot of whiskey, and were tolerated by the farming community only because they were so much needed.

What community there was among plains farmers, how-ever, revolved around those who settled and stayed. For them the environment was harsh, but it could also be loved. Grace Snyder, by now grown into a young tomboy, hair a mop and clothes in tatters, undoubtedly meant it when she spoke fondly of "every hill and canyon, every plum thicket and currant patch." She would have shared the satisfaction of John Muir when as a boy he thrilled to the Wisconsin spring. It is hard to know how widespread such sentiments were. The Country Life Commission must have thought them infrequent, for it pointedly challenged farmers to "learn to love the country."[9] In any case, how-

---

also Mildred Throne, "Population Study of an Iowa County in 1850," *Iowa Journal of History* 57 (October, 1959): 310, 316. James C. Malin, "The Turnover of Farm Population in Kansas," *Kansas Historical Quarterly* 4 (November, 1935): 344. Geographical mobility in America was, of course, widespread; in Boston, for example, figured annually, one-third of the population of 1890 had moved there since 1880; Stephan Thernstrom, *Other Bostonians,* p. 16. See also Thernstrom and Knights, "Men in Motion." *Journal of Interdisciplinary History* 1 (Autumn, 1970): 7–35.

[9] Snyder, *No Time on My Hands,* pp. 25, 27; John Muir, *The Story of My Boyhood and Youth* (Madison, Wis., 1965), p. 54; U.S., Congress, Senate, Country Life Commission, *Report,* p. 60.

Coyote Hunt, about 1885
Nebraska State Historical Society

ever much these personal attachments encouraged rootedness, they were not the cement of community.

Some cultural identities, however, did stem from the
use of, if not love of, the land. Sometimes one part of the
ecology, one feature of the natural environment, can become the center of the culture, the heart of the community,
like corn for the Latin-American natives or the buffalo
for the Sioux.[10] Thus on the plains cultural differences

[10]Robert Redfield, *The Little Community*, p. 22.

arose between wheat and corn farming. Corn cultivation spread into the plains following the watercourses, and carrying a certain life-style. The cornhusker reflected his "corn-belt mentality" when he spoke of huskings, cribs, and fodder, topics irrelevant to the wheat grower. And, more basically, he and the wheat farmer would argue over proper use of the upland plains. Each wave of newcomers to Nebraska between the 1850s and 1880s brought new and conflicting concepts of land use. In time attitudes would change, but before the late 1870s two potential cultural communities existed.[11]

Separate crop cultures, however, did not really develop on the plains, partly because the environment was a common hazard, a common hardship, and it dictated fast, cooperative action from cornhusker, wheat grower, or cattle grazer alike. Prairie fires, for example, were a threat to all. And wolves, jackrabbits, and rattlesnakes, like fires, were more effectively controlled by cooperative drives. Cooperative coyote hunting in pioneer Nebraska was probably the only occasion when farmers, cattlemen, and sheepmen worked in concert — although afterward, eating cold pies with their wives in the nearest barn mow, in their conversations they dwelled on only safe topics like past hunts.[12] Natural disasters such as floods could be better withstood by groups. The common threat of the environment is suggested in the tall tales and weather jokes. Why did the western farmer so love to tell of the drought when the fish in the river kicked up such a dust that the volunteer fire department had to sprinkle them

[11] Martyn Bowden, "Desert Wheat Belt, Plains Corn Belt," in *Images of the Plains,* ed. Brian Blouet and Merlin Lawson (Lincoln, Nebr., 1975), pp. 194–98.

[12] Mari Sandoz, *Old Jules,* pp. 225–26. Snyder, *No Time on My Hands,* p. 384, tells of one Nebraska fire in which farmers protected their individual houses for so long that they could not collectively extinguish it.

Prairie rabbit hunt, about 1900
Keystone-Mast Collection, University of California, Riverside

Barn raising near Rainy River, Minnesota, about 1900
Minnesota Historical Society

down? Or why did he like to repeat the details of the well that ran so dry that a tornado lifted it from one county to another? Perhaps because the common experience welded them in a psychic community. That same drought of the tall tales, for example, brought the farmers of Roten Valley, Nebraska, to act in concert regarding their suffering livestock.[13] Thus the environment bred cooperative action.

Prairie farmers followed a long tradition of frontier cooperation. In colonial New England all nonfarming artisans and laborers were required by law to help with the mowing and reaping. In western Pennsylvania in the eighteenth century neighbors would donate three days to build a newcomer's house, including furniture. In Kentucky about 1810 an observer described a cooperative "bond of amity." "In no other part of the world," he wrote, "is good neighborship found in greater perfection."[14] Everywhere the tradition was built on the problem of getting big jobs done, tasks too large for the individual — clearing acres of land, house and barn raising, road building, threshing before the rains. These were situations in which men were grappling most desperately with the environment.

On the plains cooperative house raising retained its full vigor. Howard Ruede, a thin young Pennsylvania Moravian who went to Kansas in 1877, explained that neighbors would gather from miles around to construct a settler's house, and they would finish in a day. Eleven men had helped a neighbor shortly before, though Ruede was sure six could have done the job. Houses were raised frequently

---

[13] Snyder, *No Time on My Hands*, pp. 163, 165.

[14] For the text of the Puritan law see Herbert Adams, "Common Fields in Salem," in *The Rural Community*, ed. Newell L. Sims, pp. 99–100; John E. Wright and Doris S. Corbett, *Pioneer Life in Pennsylvania* (Pittsburgh, 1940), pp. 44–46; John Bradbury, "Travels in the Interior," in *Early Western Travels*, ed. Reuben G. Thwaites, 5:283.

enough that men fell in accustomed roles based on their skills. Such raisings were not always signs of stability, for many a house soon needed moving, sometimes for long distances, as to a new homestead. More often, though, the move for which the neighbors would gather would be short, like putting Percy Ebbutt's cabin on rollers to relocate on a hilltop or dragging Faye Lewis's house on skids to a site nearer the well.[15]

Hospitality itself was largely an exchange of goods and services. A farmer, for example, would sometimes have to ride for days to round up stray cattle, but he would never want for lodging or provender. Some distant, lonely neighbor could be found for roof, a meal, and hay. "You'll do the same for me," he would hear, "when I'm in your parts." It was an outright exchange, the neighbor expecting reciprocity. When the farmer moved on main-traveled roads, he would more likely pay for his lodging. In such a situation the Snyders were once amazed to be charged a whopping eight dollars.[16]

The height of cooperative work came at harvesttime. In those autumn days of thronging threshers and aching backs, the traditions of cooperation prospered. Crews made the rounds from farm to farm, and men sweated together over one another's fields. The men talked at dinner, cooked by women whose backs also ached. Later there was talk in the barn as the men waited for a squall to pass. One Iowa farmer described these moments as "inner neighborhood." Such was the conversational stuff of community, and it grew from simple but universal topics like the weather—the breeze from the east, the nervous-

[15]Howard Ruede, *Sod House Days*, ed. John Ise, p. 196; Albert Greene, "In Remembrance," *Kansas State Historical Society Collections* 11 (1909–10): 484; Percy G. Ebbutt, *Emigrant Life in Kansas*, p. 83; Faye C. Lewis, *Nothing to Make a Shadow*, p. 43.

[16]Ebbutt, *Emigrant Life in Kansas*, p. 165; Snyder, *No Time on My Hands*, p. 222.

Cooperative threshing, Walsh County, North Dakota, about
1890
Minnesota Historical Society

ness of the horses, the "sun dogs" in the west that portended storm.[17] Or it could be the state of the crops or the advantages of this country over another region or another land.

The threshing crew was a mixed lot. In addition to the local neighbors exchanging work, there could be a few leftover hired hands, some unemployed seasonal workers like timbermen in Minnesota, perhaps a hobo, and a schoolboy or two. The nonneighbors were paid. A band cutter got $1.50 a day in Minnesota in the early 1880s. These men slept in haymows and were fed plenty of chicken and pumpkin pie. Ebbutt thought they "lived off the fat of the land."[18]

The cooperative element in threshing should be placed in the context of a rather large, extensive operation that was partly local cooperation and barter, partly capitalistic investment, and partly involvement in wider economic markets. The threshing machine itself, for example, was usually owned by one or two of the neighbors, who would assemble the crew, arrange the schedule, and bring the rig around for a cash fee or a portion of the crop. If the machine was owned by a Swede and you were the only non-Swede in the area, your turn might well come last. But you probably had little choice, for the cost of a thresher in 1851 was $175. Few farmers could afford that, since most had already invested a minimum of $400 just to begin farming.[19]

The rental for a thresher in 1877 was five dollars for

[17] Gary Koerselman, "The Quest for Community in Rural Iowa: Neighborhood Life in Early Middleburg History," *Annals of Iowa* 41 (Summer, 1972): 1010, 1013.

[18] Humphrey, *Following the Prairie Frontier*, p. 76; Ebbutt, *Emigrant Life in Kansas*, p. 215.

[19] Snyder, *No Time on My Hands*; Paul W. Gates, *Farmer's Age*, p. 288; Paul W. Gates, "Frontier Estate Builders and Farm Laborers," in *Turner and the Sociology of the Frontier*, ed. Richard Hofstadter and S. Martin Lipset, p. 106.

Cooperative harvesting in Utah, about 1895
Utah State Historical Society

less than a hundred bushels of wheat; otherwise, five cents
a bushel (plus fodder for the team). Such costs were kept
low because of the exchange work. Other, smaller items
helped reduce the expense, like the cooperative use and
reuse of sacks. Threshing was typical of other mixes of
cooperation, barter, and cash. If you exchanged work and
brought along a team for a day, you got three days' work
from a man without a team. In exchange for sporadic labor
over many months as a hired hand, Howard Ruede received help in breaking three acres of his own land, 11½

Threshing at I. Newton's place, September, 1894
Iowa State Historical Society

bushels of wheat, a few bushels of rye, and five dollars.[20]

Reciprocal labor resulted far more often from an absence of capital than from a desire to cooperate. Anyone could offer labor, but few could offer cash. Even Old Jules Sandoz, probably the least cooperative curmudgeon Nebraska ever produced, exchanged labor. In return for

[20] Ruede, *Sod House Days,* pp. 120, 126; Charley O'Kieffe, *Western Story: Recollections,* p. 86. One woman thought that it would be cheaper to hire out such work completely; see Dee Brown, *The Gentle Tamers,* p. 156.

digging his well, two men received his services as land
locator; for plowing or harvesting his crops, he cut gun-
stocks or castrated pigs. Howard Ruede's Kansas neighborhood in the 1870s circulated a paper seeking help in
building the school, either work or money. Eighty-one
hours were pledged, but only eighteen dollars in cash.[21]
Pockets then were empty because of hard times following
1873; but in depression or not, reciprocal work expanded
the cash supply. The neighbors were a reservoir of cooperative labor that assumed the nature of capital.

Exchange work was a form of barter and was thus a
precapitalist method. As soon as the farmer became firmly
entrenched in the larger economy, as we will see later — as
soon as he became enmeshed in the railroad system, for
example — exchange work and the barter system became
far less important.

So the plains environment and an immature economy
spawned cooperative activities that could become community. Irrespective of economic forces, however, the
isolation of farms called up a strong psychic yearning for
companionship. Starved emotions cried for nourishment.
Certainly the community was small enough in numbers,
but the distances reduced practical contacts to the level
of acquaintances in a large city. Neighborhoods in Kansas
are measured in miles, not blocks, wrote Charley O'Kieffe,
adding sadly if not typically that there was little social
intermingling, and only two dances a year.[22]

Edgar Watson Howe had an explanation for the kind of
gloomy picture O'Kieffe drew. Howe thought his neighbors
in Missouri in the 1850s were so habituated to isolation
that they could socialize for only a short time, as in church,
and then they would immediately head for their farms to
resume their lives of misery. It was an immature or ar-

[21] Sandoz, *Old Jules*, pp. 41, 89–90; Ruede, *Sod House Days*, p. 217.
[22] O'Kieffe, *Western Story*, p. 59.

rested social life. Richard Weston had earlier described
a frontier party in which forty couples engaged in "puerile
and frivolous sport," like kissing games, and usually in
silence because the art of conversation was so little
known.[23] Of course, the preponderance of accounts of
social life on the plains frontier is of vital, engaging, lively
times, but the more grim commentators would say that
the happier descriptions were reflections of the infre-
quency of the contacts, etching them in memory and
exaggerating them in reminiscence.

Still there is abundant evidence of pleasurable social
life among prairie farmers. In North Dakota in the 1870s
a ring of eight families rotated their dances every Friday
night. Even Grace Fairchild, a big woman whose strong
face reflected her hard life, recalled that the dances were
so popular around her house that in rapid succession they
outgrew the parlor, the machine shed, and the barn. These
parties were usually open, nonselective affairs. At least
Percy Ebbutt always assumed that if anyone had a party
everyone else was invited.[24]

There were quilting bees, husking bees, apple bees,
and "fulling bees" (for the fulling or thickening of cloth).
To be sure, all these had practical ends, but they skillfully
blended play with cooperative work, "a means of enliven-
ing the spirits of old and young." As in any other true
community, these occasions sparked tension. Hamlin Garland remembered Mrs. Whitwell's ostracism from the
quiltings because she was too loud and told vulgar stories.
There were limits to which loneliness would compel acceptance, but Garland understood as well as anyone else
the gratifying cohesive force in this cooperative socializa-

[23] Edgar W. Howe, *Story of a Country Town*, p. 36; Weston, *Visit*,
p. 97.

[24] Drache, *Challenge of the Prairie*, p. 210; Grace Fairchild, *Frontier
Woman*, ed. Walker Wyman, p. 85; Ebbutt, *Emigrant Life in Kansas*,
p. 56.

Quilting bee, Minnesota, no date
Minnesota Historical Society

tion—the vigor, the laughter, the rejoicing. Imagine what
it meant even to children playing together under the frame
with adults chattering and stitching on the quilt above.[25]
At least two holidays embraced the whole community.
Decoration Day combined spring with a communal me-

[25] Merrill E. Jarchow, *The Earth Brought Forth*, p. 191; Hamlin
Garland, *A Son of the Middle Border*, pp. 21, 30, 34.

morial. Everyone picked flowers, decorated the graves, and remained for the picnic. But no community event pulled together the straggling farms as did the Fourth of July. At some nearby fort or crossroad there were flags and speeches and cold chicken, and the day was full of horse races, foot races, sack races, and baseball. There were greased pigs, greased poles, and gallons of cold drinks. At Fort Scott, Kansas, in 1859 it took four horse-drawn wagons to draw ice for the lemonade alone. Faye Lewis, a shy adolescent in South Dakota, was taken to the celebration her first year on the plains. She feared that, for families like hers, farmers who could not afford the expense or time, it would be an "irresponsible and reckless binge," but she later understood the "immeasurable benefits" from the three days, from the four-hour wagon ride, the parade, the singing, the merry-go-round, the popcorn, the fireworks. For similar reasons Friday night "literaries," often sedate enough, occasionally reverted to nonsense: Resolved that pigs are smarter than sheep; or, Resolved that it is better to be kicked by a mule than bitten by a rattler.[26]

Between special occasions and formal gatherings, there was always visiting. In Oklahoma in the 1890s, Allie Wallace thought that her house enjoyed so many visitors because her mother owned a sewing machine; but the need being met was deeper than practicality. Grace Snyder observed an increase in visiting during a period of extended drought.[27] The relief of tensions through social intercourse was well expressed by Grace's father, who,

[26] Charles S. Reed, "Life in a Nebraska Soddy," *Nebraska History* 39 (March, 1958): 70; George Meltzer, "Social Life and Entertainment on the Kansas Frontier, 1854–1890" (master's thesis, University of Wichita, 1941), p. 44; Lewis, *Nothing to Make a Shadow*, pp. 6, 48–56, 74.

[27] Allie B. Wallace, *Frontier Life in Oklahoma*, p. 44; Snyder, *No Time on My Hands*, p. 172.

Community picnic near Cedar River, Iowa, about 1900
Iowa State Historical Society

even when weary, wished to go visiting. He took his family, weather permitting, as often as once a week, jolting over the miles, bearing a few gifts of flowers or fresh eggs, hoping for a sip of wine and a face. For a time isolation would thaw in the warmth of human contact.

Worship services, prayer meetings, evening sings, and especially camp meetings were social events too. Small groups of neighbors could always pray together in farmhouses, but the outdoor revivals, lasting from three days to a week, provided the most highly charged release of emotion. Families came from dozens or hundreds of miles.

Religion in wagons, Charles Reed called it, and like most other farmers he happily welcomed any preacher who stopped at his sod-house door. The word flew. Soon there would be "tenting tonight" in the old grove at the forks of Clear Creek. Preachings and bonfires and a few true conversions there were, but the serious reclamation of souls was overlaid with the spirit of the Fourth of July. Everyone came — Baptists, Mennonites, Catholics. The circuit rider preached to a heterogeneous congregation. Most people went, even when they had to sit under clumps of hay on poles for shade. At least, Allie Wallace said, it "broke the monotony." Whatever their backgrounds, they joined or witnessed members of their community publicly confessing sin or publicly accepting the Lord. The camp meeting, in its power to answer the religious and emotional needs of a varied population, was what Page Smith called a substitution for the fragmented covenant.[28] Its public confession was an assertion of public values. In those days of tenting and praying, the Puritan community was conceived anew, regenerated in hope on the plains of the West.

The place as an ecological system demanded economic cooperation, and the size of the group, small but scattered, shaped the need for social gatherings; but neither would bring community without the values of sharing and caring. Such values were once held aloft by Fred Shannon as a distinctive culture revolving around cooperative rural life.[29] Such a cooperative culture based on values might indeed be a community, but, on the other hand, group cooperation does not necessarily mean community. Was it evidence of cooperative culture when, during a measles epidemic,

[28] Reed, "Nebraska Soddy," p. 69; Ebbutt, *Emigrant Life in Kansas*, p. 124; Ruede, *Sod House Days*, p. 32; Wallace, *Frontier Life in Oklahoma*, pp. 15, 35; Page Smith, *As a City upon a Hill*, p. 67.

[29] Fred A. Shannon, "Culture and Agriculture," *Mississippi Valley Historical Review* 41 (June, 1954): 3, 19–20.

Recess time at a rural schoolhouse in Kansas, 1899
Keystone-Mast Collection, University of California, Riverside

neighbors fed stricken families and took in their healthy children to stem the spread of the disease? Or when neighbors banded together to help the surviving families of two murdered men? Or when settlers shared the cost of a school teacher by rotating her residence among them? Or when, after a disastrous fire, the farmers near Torkel Fugelstad threshed his crop while he was away?[30]

Was, for example, Mrs. Lockhart living the cooperative life when, unpaid, she brought her "little kit and some tools" either to deliver babies or to prepare bodies for burial? Or the "angel of mercy," who came to the smallpox house to nurse the sick while others whipped their horses to get by faster? Or Mollie Sanford, who was always feeding wanderers? Or the bachelor nursing a neighbor through a long illness? Or the neighbors in North Dakota who walked to one another's farms after severe storms to make sure everyone could get out? Or the boy in Iowa who hunted daily to feed an entire area stricken by a grasshopper plague? Or Mrs. King, who, after caring for her own twelve children, nursed the neighborhood sick, carrying their chamber pots and wet-nursing their babies?[31]

Like exchange work, altruistic acts embodied the techniques of survival. Mollie Sanford once said that she took care of others but also expected others to care for her when she needed help. In this sense charity is individualistic, and its arena may more realistically be called the neighborhood than the community. A neighborhood is a loose collection of people, informal, unofficial, with no

[30] Snyder, *No Time on My Hands*, pp. 73, 208; Ebbutt, *Emigrant Life in Kansas*, p. 150; Drache, *Challenge of the Prairie*, p. 163.

[31] Drache, *Challenge of the Prairie*, p. 261; Garland, *Son of the Middle Border*, p. 76; Mollie Sanford, *Mollie*, pp. 35–37; Ruede, *Sod House Days*, pp. 79–80; Drache, *Challenge of the Prairie*, p. 157; John E. Briggs, "The Grasshopper Plagues in Iowa," *Iowa Journal of History and Politics* 13 (July, 1915): 366; Wallace, *Frontier Life in Oklahoma*, pp. 43–44.

binding force over its members. It is reflected in many simple acts like the willingness to stop and talk over the fence.[32] The altruism of the plains farmer, the aesthetics of the cooperative life, may have stopped at the level of neighborhood.

Of course, if there was a community on the plains, individual tensions would rise within it. There is no paucity of evidence for individualism. When John McConnell, for example, distilled from his lifetime on the Illinois prairie a composite pioneer settler, his figure was not cooperative but proud and solitary. This farmer might welcome a stranger, but he would not want him to stay long. "It was but little assistance that he ever required from his neighbors, though no man was ever more willing to render it to others in the hour of need." These were types like Jules Sandoz in Nebraska, egotistical and even antisocial. They were not likely to keep memoirs. But their figures emerge in the accounts of others. They were smudges on the record of community building. When the Wares, dirty but proud, were kindly offered some potatoes to help them over a hard time, they went to the cellar and took a bushel of the biggest and best. The Cogills, when offered chicken feed, took fine seed corn. The Fairchilds once failed to tell a neighbor that he had eaten carbolic acid in their house because they were afraid they would be blamed if he died.[33]

A strong competitive spirit was a boon to individualism and a bane to the furthering of community. "They were always racing in those days," Garland said. Holiday rivalries were perpetuated in shooting matches and tugs-of-war. At log rollings men struggled to build the largest piles. Harvest crews raced to the ends of the rows. And those

---

[32] Sanford, *Mollie*, p. 139; Koerselman, "Quest for Community," pp. 1008, 1015.

[33] John L. McConnel, *Western Characters*, p. 115; Fairchild, *Frontier Woman*, pp. 40–41, 46.

who did not win could still tell a tall tale, for the language was peculiarly braced with competitive exaggeration. Behind the bragging was often severe privatization. Some subjects were retained for the individual or family alone, topics into which the community had no entry. Curiously, for example, bedbugs, known to be legion and battled by all, could not be discussed.[34]

The vigorous individualism of the plains farmer has been overemphasized in the annals of the West. But it should not be dismissed. Carl Becker, one of America's most perceptive historians, would agree, and he once tried to analyze that individualism in terms of the Kansas he had come to know and love. He too distilled a pioneer type as McConnell had done, but Becker saw a more complicated phenomenon, what he called "an individualism of conformity."[35] Among pioneers there was a common bond, so ingrained that conformity to it was assumed, and nonconformists were instinctively ostracized. The essence of the bond was endurance, the triumph over a hostile wilderness. Although the end might be a common tie, the beginning was not in the ethics of the group but in the supreme value of the individual.

Walter Prescott Webb claimed that the 100th meridian, symbol of the passage to the Great Plains, shook to the foundation the culture of those who crossed it. In one respect Webb was wrong—the plains did not change the institution of the family. This social unit remained unusually vital as population pushed over prairies and plains. Recent demographers point clearly to this conclusion.[36]

[34] Garland, *Son of the Middle Border*, p. 21; Dan Clark, *Middle West in American History*, p. 216; Lewis, *Nothing to Make a Shadow*, p. 97.

[35] Mody Boatwright, "The Myth of Frontier Individualism," in *Turner and the Sociology of the Frontier*, ed. Richard Hofstadter and S. Martin Lipset, pp. 44–45; Carl L. Becker, *Everyman His Own Historian*, p. 9.

[36] Blaine T. Williams, "The Frontier Family," in *Essays on the American West*, ed. Harold M. Hollingsworth, p. 60; John Modell, "The

The pattern of frontier family life was remarkably nuclear and similar to patterns elsewhere in the nation. James Davis, for example, in a study of ten thousand pioneer households between 1800 and 1840, found practically no one living alone. Even the few hired hands resided in the households. On the northern plains families were small — at any given time the largest number of children was only one or two, owing to birth control (abstinence), the young age of the couples, and the absence of economic incentives for large families.[37] The pioneer farm family was nuclear in the sense that it was isolated from the community, a separate unit not subject to community controls. Of course, there were exceptions where the family appeared to be intimately linked with the community. In the Dakotas in the earliest days baptisms, weddings, shivarees, and funerals were often community affairs. Weddings in Kansas dugouts often brought so many neighbors that they had to move outside for the feasting and dancing. At Bell's Lake, Iowa, worship was held in homes before the public services, reminiscent of Puritan family prayers, but Bell's Lake was an unusual community with a religious base. Elsewhere most cases of community-oriented families came from the earliest dugout times. In the great thrust of the plains experience "the hearth of the lonely farm" was the center, with otherwise only kin and a few neighborly connections binding people together.[38]

In fact, the family persisted through desperate circum-

Family and Fertility on the Indiana Frontier, 1820," *American Quarterly* 23 (December, 1971): 615; Jack E. Eblen, "An Analysis of Nineteenth-Century Frontier Populations," *Demography*, no. 2 (1965): 412–13; Davis, *Frontier America*, p. 179.

[37] Davis, *Frontier America*, pp. 37, 58–59, 64–67.

[38] Drache, *Challenge of the Prairie*, pp. 255, 286; Koerselman, "Quest for Community," p. 1018; Jeff Jenkins, *The Northern Tier*, p. 154; Redfield, *The Little Community*, p. 6.

stances. Children sometimes retained the family unit long after parents had died. A seventeen-year-old girl in early Texas, for example, maintained a house of seven brothers and sisters. A sixteen-year-old boy alone supervised two siblings. The community did not intervene in these situations unless the arrangement proved absolutely impossible.[39]

Although often enough denied, social and economic class lines were always evident on the frontier. Some people lived in dugouts, and some in houses of pine boards. There was never any doubt in the mind of Allie Wallace that the Stewarts, who had built the biggest house in the area, were in a "different" category from the Germans and Russians in the neighborhood. She drew her "class" lines by means of the shawls of the immigrant women, their unshapely bodies from bearing babies, and the strict discipline their children received.[40] These were hardly satisfactory guides to class distinctions, but they existed. Class consciousness was blurred, of course, by the proud equality stemming from shared hardships.

Still the community of endurance could not last indefinitely. For one thing, it was subject to invasions from outside. Think of land agents, "the wool hat people," as Grace Fairchild called them, filtering into a community's space. Mrs. Fairchild would give them a bed, meat, potatoes, and "spud varnish" for twenty-five cents, but the presence of these speculators did not please her, as if they embodied a vaguely threatening force. Seth Humphrey was playing a similarly invasive role when he came into Nebraska as a mortgage agent. He lodged with farm families but always left fifty cents on the table, symbol of the gulf between them. He noted too that as soon as a house was identified as a foreclosure the settlers quickly stole the movables. The same property was safe for months if

---

[39] Williams, "The Frontier Family," pp. 60–62.
[40] Wallace, *Frontier Life in Oklahoma*, p. 22.

the owner was only temporarily away. Humphrey told of a man named George who had combined with a fellow homesteader to build one house squarely across their common section line. Inside the house they dutifully slept and lived each over his own land. But the friend gave up and let the mortgage company foreclose. When Humphrey arrived, George was hitching a team to the house to pull it entirely on his own land. Humphrey protested. The man firmly explained, "I'm not touching yours; I'm pulling mine and yours is following." Knowing the climate of opinion, the mortgage man did not interfere.[41]

But land-agent tensions were minor compared with those aroused in the community by the railroad. Of course, without the railroad the plains probably could not have been settled, at least not in the mold of large farms linked to a wider economic market. It might be remembered that Max Weber on his 1904 tour observed that on the plains the market economy blocked the older forms of community, just as it had destroyed the rural village community in his native Germany. In this viewpoint the plains farmer was destined never to experience *Gemeinschaft,* but was thrust from the beginning into a fragmented and limited kind of community. Even his cooperation was for particular and restricted ends, and increasingly so as class division grew. The more he became geared to the business system the more "calculation was substituted for custom." A recent exploration of American agriculture by Walter Goldschmidt implied a similar idea: an industrialized sowing of the soil reaped an urbanized rural society.[42]

The national economy intersected the local. Prices for farm products fluctuated mysteriously. Higher freight rates were determined in Omaha or New York. Interest on borrowing was fixed in the East. Quotations rose and fell

[41] Fairchild, *Frontier Woman,* p. 53; Humphrey, *Following the Prairie Frontier,* pp. 124–26.
[42] Walter Goldschmidt, *As You Sow,* p. xxiii.

because of world markets, and the farmer unwittingly was forced into competition with foreign lands he little knew. At the same time his machinery was manufactured elsewhere, and to bring it to his fields he needed cash or credit. He even had to buy some consumer goods once made on his own farm or at least nearby. With his capital no longer merely an extension of his labor, a farmer felt himself succeeding or failing not so much as a farmer but as a businessman. He began to see distant tyrants with local representatives. Railroad agents, grain operators, and equipment salesmen became petty despots, especially since, unlike the old store owners, they could not "respond to tales of a bad year, family illness, or other such problems."[43]

Underlying these basic changes was the farmer's uneasiness over his position, his waning voice in the councils of state and nation. He felt helpless that the manufacturers of the machinery he now required were assuming his former significance, especially as he saw the disparity between his share of the bounty and that of others. Manufacturers were building fortunes on those threshers he needed even to begin his cooperative life. In the 1870s some farm literaries began debating less often the relative merits of pig versus cow and instead discussing steel and railroad monopoly. That was the decade too in which Oliver Kelley founded the Grange. Kelley was a thirty-second degree Mason, keenly aware of the fraternal needs of rural people. His organization was crammed with symbols and signs, passwords and hierarchical degrees. Both men and women studied and progressed through the

---

[43] Carl C. Taylor, *Farmers' Movement*, p. 89; Anne Mayhew, "A Reappraisal of the Causes of Farm Protest in the United States, 1870–1900," *Journal of Economic History* 32 (June, 1972): 468, 474–75. Mayhew includes an excellent critique on the interpretations of Douglas North and Allan Bogue.

elaborate ceremonies, accompanied with singing, picnics, and feasts for the seasons.

Mary Mayo came through the Grange rituals, starting as a neophyte Maid and advancing through Shepherdess, Gleaner, and Matron. Once as an adolescent she had been told that all she ever needed was to "work hard and make good butter." Many a farm girl would have smiled and toiled on, but Mary Mayo was incensed that making butter should be the measure of a human life. The Grange became a marvelous outlet for a woman of her spunk. For years she led the women of the Grange in countless activities of mental sweep and social joys. But she came to realize that farm community was being seriously attacked—if indeed it had ever been a community. "Because of this pioneer life," she said, "of its struggles, anxieties, and cares, I want to tell them that these things should only bind them close together."[44]

Like the literaries, the Grange too began to discuss marketing and "consumer protection." Locals identified swindling firms and listed them in permanent blue books, like blacklists, and they kept a red book for honest merchants, a roll of honor. Talk rose of fighting the harvest and plow "rings." They tried cooperative buying and selling. They entered politics. But in none of these efforts was the Grange notably successful. The National Farmers' Alliance, organized in Chicago in the 1880s, was better at politics, and some of the Grange cooperative buying was incorporated into the rising Rochedale movement. But even the awareness of the tyranny of industrial monopoly, a sense of hostile invasion of their precincts, did not engender sufficient loyalty in the farm community to produce effective results.

The failure of the Grange to combine social, economic, and political messages illustrated again the extent to which

[44]Jennie Buell, *One Woman's Work for Farm Women*, pp. 9, 60.

the plains farmer created no more than a community of "limited liability." He was good, as Turner said, at informal combinations, extralegal voluntary associations, and he was endowed with an extraordinary "power to join together for a common end."[45] But the causes were limited, specific, partial. And no commitment, no loyalty, no *Gemeinschaft* was deep enough to hold a man from pulling up stakes and moving on. Personal investment was minimal to keep mobility maximal.

The environment, the place, inspired a community of hardship, but it also injected a constant dilution of community caused by separation. Even the cooperation of exchanging work and the emotionally warming social events and revivals seemed to be measures of separation rather than cornerstones in community. Altruism, heroic and soul-stirring as it was, remained individualistic, not group-oriented. The family, dominant, vital, clung to itself. Growing class distinctions, especially after the community of hardship was suspended and national economic forces pushed in, worked against unity. Thus the total experience was of limited associations, not genuine community. Grace Snyder's brooding throughts of death as a child on the Nebraska prairie had foreshadowed the unusual difficulties faced by community on the plains.

[45] Morris Janowitz, *The Community Press in an Urban Setting*, pp. 210–13; Frederick J. Turner, *The Frontier in American History*, p. 343.

Chapter Six

Our Town
in the Middle West

The country town of the great American farming region is the perfect flower of self-help and cupidity standardised on the American plan. Its name may be Spoon River or Gopher Prairie, or it may be Emporia or Centralia or Columbia. The pattern is substantially the same, and is repeated several thousand times with a faithful perfection which argues that there is no help for it, that it is worked out by uniform circumstances over which there is no control, and that it wholly falls in with the spirit of things and answers to the enduring aspirations of the community.

Thorstein Veblen, "Absentee Ownership" (1923)

As the MIDDLE-WESTERN SMALL TOWN blessed the ties that bound its hearts, it was cherishing and perpetuating the vision of a stable, homogeneous society, rich in humane face-to-face contacts. A small-town son from Wisconsin, Thornton Wilder, saw "our town" persisting through birth, adolescence, and death, from love recognized in the glow of neighboring windows to love felt at the graveside for the dead. The town quietly bore the hope of continuity, and in its dusty streets lay the dreams of brotherhood inherited from colonial New England. It carried too the universal attraction for smallness, for "simple and common things" rather than "rich and divisive things," for a "native warmth of heart, not cooled by convention and competition."[1]

[1] Wilbert L. Anderson, *Country Town*, p. 207.

The model of the New England town had moved inexorably westward, south of the Great Lakes, down the Ohio River, inspiring counterparts like Marietta, Worthington, and Oberlin. After the Civil War such replication of New England ideals continued in the Mississippi Valley and Great Plains—from Denison, Indiana, to Longmont, Colorado, and from Amenia, Dakota Territory, to Atchison, Kansas. This covenanted community became the archetype and the ideal of all American small towns, self-contained, close-knit, and highly colored by its agricultural environment.[2] Indeed, the centrifugal effect of western farming might have been mitigated by the centripetal communitarianism of the Puritan tradition. The historical timing, however, was wrong. Land policy and economic theory moved in other directions. The small town could function like a compact, seventeenth-century village no more easily than the American farmer could become the European peasant. Instead, the western small town wrestled with its own forms of community, and in the end succeeded weakly, if at all.

Thorstein Veblen, like Thornton Wilder, grew up in rural Wisconsin, but while Wilder loved the small town, Veblen found it repugnant in perpetuating the Puritan model. As a boy Veblen had known the cohesiveness of Norwegian immigrant settlements. But he was an unexpected product of that life—eccentric, cantankerous, ill-mannered. At Carlton College he recognized his intellectual bent and eventually entered the academic world. Through his life he wandered from place to place—Johns Hopkins, Yale, Cornell, Chicago, Stanford, Missouri, and

[2] Edmund Brunner defines the community to include the area that avails itself ot the services of the town: *Village Communities*, p. 27. Malcolm J. Rohrbough, *The Trans-Appalachian Frontier*, draws a clear distinction between trans-Appalachian communities and those in the Far West; the former imported more traditional forms and lost frontier status more quickly.

the New School in New York. The result was a tired, lonely man, far from his original ethnic community. In his writing he bitterly criticized American business values, beginning with *The Theory of the Leisure Class* in 1899. In 1923, near the close of his life, he wrote and included in his final book an essay on the small town, a spiritual return to his Wisconsin roots.[3]

Most important to Veblen was the interrelation of the small town with its agricultural surroundings, those fields of wheat and corn that gave the town a place in life's vast food chain. The town always felt itself both separate from and close to those prairies and farms. Young William Allen White, for example, described his Kansas playground as "everything west of the schoolhouse to Denver."[4] But where the boy was seeing the open space and the soft clouds of summer, the elder Veblen was picking up the sad dependence of those widespread farms on the village businessmen.

There were others like young Willy, gentle commentators on the town, such as Harlan Douglass, the midwesterner who left the ministry to supervise rural schools about the time Veblen went to Stanford. Douglass described the town in a symbiotic relationship to agriculture and "in the service of the countryside."[5] By contrast, Veblen excoriated the town as the flowering of cupidity, spreading over the entire West. The "spirit" of the town was the greed of its merchants in exploiting the farmer, Veblen said, mulcting the hinterland by charging what the traffic would bear and amassing unfair profits that ran annually into ten or twelve digits. The town acted in the name of princely

[3] Thorstein Veblen, *Absentee Ownership and Business Enterprise in Recent Times,* pp. 142–65.

[4] William Allen White, *Autobiography,* p. 38.

[5] Harlan Douglass, *The Little Town,* p. 10. For other discussions of the relationship see Arthur Vidich and Joseph Bensman, *Small Town in Mass Society,* p. 7; Merle Curti, *Making of an American Community,* p. 29.

corporations and predatory masters and piously camou-
flaged its avarice as self-help. Local bankers busily convinced townsmen and farmers alike that what was good
for business was good for the whole community. At the
same time the farmer's illusion of his own independence
blinded him to the real drive of the merchants: "indefinitely extensible cupidity," not good workmanship or self-
reliance.[6] Large-scale credit and national advertising turned
the town, even before it turned the farm, into a deception
rather than a community. Veblen was obviously out of
sorts with the world, but he was, nevertheless, a hard
thinker and a firsthand source regarding the farms and
towns of which he wrote. His general conclusions do not
go unsupported. One recent commentator, Ronald Tobey,
wrote, "The town is where the country and city meet."
In the town arises a dualism in which individuals are required to face in two directions, rural and urban, in turn
producing a peculiar anomie more pervasive than the anxieties and confusions of the city.[7]

Towns in their founding and purposes varied widely.
The covenant at Amenia was very different from the real
estate speculation that gave birth to Jacksonville, Illinois,
in 1825.[8] Amenia sought the brotherhood of man; Jacksonville inflated land values. Jacksonville lots were planned
on a New England grid, not from the ideals of Congre-
gational equality but for convenience in sales. The first
common action was not to ensure against temptation but
to secure the county seat. But time and growth mix purposes. As boosters came to Amenia, so religion came to
Jacksonville. A few years after the first churches a "Yale
band" arrived, a group of Yankee families intent on saving

[6] Joseph Dorfman, *Thorstein Veblen and His America*, p. 473.

[7] Ronald Tobey, "How Urbane Is the Urbanite?" *Historical Methods
Newsletter* 7 (September, 1974): 263, 268.

[8] The following section relies heavily on Don H. Doyle, *The Social
Order of a Frontier Community.*

the West from its structureless ways by founding schools
and seminaries. These were the kinds of people who carried west the practiced behavior and ideals of town life.

The Jacksonville Yale band, however, never worked
with a homogeneous society. Even as early as the 1830s
signs of social discord and conflict were abundant. A cholera epidemic in 1833 convinced a new teacher in town that
"the wild, vague terror of a disease . . . kept men aloof
from each other." In the pale, tearful faces he read the
disintegration of society. "The people, gathered from all
quarters, had not coalescense [*sic*] enough for mutual helpfulness."⁹ Four years later a bitter fight erupted over the
location of the railroad tracks. The winners happily
watched the route run straight through the town square,
like an arrow through the heart of the New England ideal.

Homogeneity, if the Yankees had ever hoped for it,
slipped further and further away, but the boosters did not
worry. In general they assumed that diversity was acceptable and might even encourage its own kind of community.
In fact, however, in early Saint Louis the confrontation between the established French and the upstart Americans
produced "a democracy of innovation, competition, conflict, and compromise, often to the undermining of community." In Jacksonville neither the Yale band nor the
boosters wished to stop land speculation, and they held
no power to block immigration. By the 1850s immigrants
had brought other visions of community, not the New
England version. Irish laborers sought Catholic churches
and grog shops. Southerners looked for large landholdings
and slaves. And transients continued to drift through,
seeking temporary shelter and odd jobs. Half a century
later in Oklahoma the same rapid diversity continued to
insert itself. Angie Debo saw it in terms of a foreign influx.
When enough German settlers reached his town, the furniture dealer learned to stock pictures of the kaiser, and

⁹ Truman Post, as quoted in Doyle, *Social Order,* pp. 41–42.

"the hard, narrow face with its absurd mustaches looked down strangely upon this new American scene."[10]

So the towns that grew also changed. Take Aberdeen, Dakota Territory, which Seth Humphrey, the mortgage agent, entered as a young man in 1884. It was one street, two banks, and two little hotels, a few boarding houses, swarms of cheap lawyers and loan sharks giving advice to the land seekers, and just outside of town "a bright red light" in a cluster of frame shacks where the "diseased discards" operated. Five years later Humphrey returned to find Aberdeen a different place. The bustle was gone. The only hum was of the lonely cricket. The town had gained "a painful respectability." After the frontier moved west, Humphrey said, the average border town became a country village, "its population shrunken and shifted and devitalized." It settled down to living off the surrounding farms for the next hundred years or so.

Veblen could not have put it more succinctly. Aberdeen was saved from that ultimate fate, however, Humphrey said, by the coming of railroads that transformed it into a distributing center. The hum of the land seekers and the hum of the cricket were replaced by the cry of the locomotive. In his Eldorado, Will White saw the same process. When the railroad came, it seemed "to shrivel and wither its little industries," contracting their importance, shrinking their independence, changing the whole economic ambience.[11] Aberdeen and Eldorado were passing through two unstable periods, the early and the late, separated by a settled one. Here as elsewhere the middle period would witness little growth, and then a canal or a railroad and industrial development or a new flush of immigrants

[10] Ronald Davis, "Community and Conflict in Pioneer St. Louis, Missouri," *Western Historical Quarterly* (July, 1979): 355; Angie Debo, *Prairie City*, p. 104.

[11] Seth Humphrey, *Following the Prairie Frontier*, pp. 80–81, 97–98; White, *Autobiography*, p. 66.

would upset the balance and destroy one kind of community while creating another.

Or nothing might happen; the town could die, the hum of the cricket signaling the beginning of the end. The frontier was as wasteful of towns as it was of human fulfillment. The Ohio Valley by the 1820s was, as Richard Wade said, "littered with ambitious towns that never grew." Jeff Jenkins, that agent of the land office, looked around his Doniphan County, Kansas, in the 1880s and found fifteen towns that had simply given up, "relics of lost opportunities for greatness." Edgar Howe, the Kansas editor, assumed that Twin Mounds would have grown regardless of the meetings and the debates; all it took was accretion, he said, but he was wrong.[12]

"Different places on the face of the earth," wrote D. H. Lawrence in New Mexico, "have different effluence, different vibration, different chemical exhalation, different polarity with different stars." On the fabric of place rested the small towns that lingered and lived. Soil, topography, the climate were vital influences on the growth of any community, said Merle Curti in a classic study of a Wisconsin county. In his detailed examination of early towns he could identify a pride of place motivating political behavior. Past affinities played a part. Anglo-Americans were attracted to prairies, and Norwegian immigrants to timber.[13]

A love of place nurtures pride. It is a reinforcement of belonging. Each sighting of familiar surroundings adds to the larger experience, like a ritual elevation of the host of collective memory. The western town echoed these feelings when it sought to insulate itself from outside ideas, from penetration of the veil of its uniqueness by doctrines

[12] Richard Wade, *Urban Frontier,* p. 33; Jeff Jenkins, *The Northern Tier,* p. 34; Edgar W. Howe, *Story of a Country Town,* p. 194.

[13] D. H. Lawrence, *Studies in Classic American Literature* (Garden City, N.Y., 1923), p. 16; Curti, *Making of an American Community,* pp. 11, 32, 325.

of evolution or socialism. But these were later manifestations of town insularity; earlier, pride took the form of
dressing up for community events and especially bragging,
boasting, and boosting.[14] Local expressions of tall talk,
however, were probably motivated as much by salesman-
ship and speculative addiction as by simple pride in place.
Pride should have been stabilizing, encouraging people to
remain in their chosen environment long after economics
would warrant.

Yet western townspeople refused to stay put. The throb-
bing frontier drumbeat of mobility sounded in the small
town no less than in the farmlands. Willie White in the
1870s watched scores of former soldiers and their wives
pour daily into little Eldorado, Kansas, and called the influx into the western Mississippi Valley unbelievable. The
"haughty aristocracy" of his schoolmates could be only
ephemeral. In a few days the newcomers would join the
regulars in lording it over still newer arrivals. The historian
of Jacksonville, Don Doyle, estimated that the persistence
of such western town populations was at best 20 to 25
percent. Accordingly, fewer than one in four people stayed
in the town. In 1860 and 1870 only one in eight people
had been in Jacksonville ten years or more. Even in predominantly ethnic Holland, Michigan, between 1850 and
1880 the out-migration of labor amounted to 40 percent
of the in-migration. The same flux was reflected in institutions. One Missouri town in one ten-year period saw six
newspapers come and go. Crawford County, Kansas, between 1870 and 1900 had eighty-nine newspapers, their
editors, like tramp printers, publishing for a while, then
moving on.[15]

---

[14] Carl Withers, "Plainville, U.S.A.," in *Psychological Frontiers of
Society*, ed. Abram Kardiner, p. 55.

[15] Don H. Doyle, "Social Theory and New Communities in Nineteenth-Century America," *Western Historical Quarterly* 8 (April, 1977):
p. 155; Doyle, *Social Order*, pp. 95, 261; Withers, "Plainville, U.S.A.,"

Whole towns were known to pick up and move. In Washington Territory in the 1880s, Colfax and Palouse City abandoned old and took up new sites. A *Harpers' Magazine* reporter wrote: "It never occurred to any of these persons that there was any sentiment to hinder their pulling up stakes and moving a town about in this fashion." Turning philosophical, he went on, "The owner has not planted hopes along with his orchard, and therefore has none to uproot in the abandonment of his trees."[16]

In addition to a sense of place, the people of a small town must have frequent, face-to-face contact. If 1,000 people live together in reasonably stable conditions, such contacts can be maintained. Beyond 1,000 they become increasingly difficult. Accordingly, students of the nineteenth-century small town have tended to focus on places of that size. They could be recalling the Puritan practice of hiving off into new communities when growth reached about two hundred families, the equivalent of 1,000 people. Carl Withers, the anthropologist, looked only at such populations when he sought a typical middle-western small town, and Wheatland, Missouri, his final choice, had only 275 people.[17] In a Colorado town, given the fictitious name

---

pp. 208–209; Kenneth C. Bronson, "The Local Press and the Changing Community," *Kansas Historical Quarterly* 42 (Spring, 1976): 51; Gordon W. Kirk, Jr., *The Promise of American Life*, pp. 42, 43.

[16] Anonymous, "Wheat Fields of the Columbia," *Harper's Monthly* 69 (September, 1884): 510.

[17] Withers, "Plainville, U.S.A."; the identification of the fictitious Plainville with Wheatland, Missouri, is an extrapolation from internal evidence. And for further demographical discussion, see Tobey, "How Urbane," *Historical Methods Newsletter*, pp. 259–75, in which a range of 1,501 to 7,200 is established; this high level refers largely to a later period and excludes the village. Brunner, *Village Communities*, p. 14, uses a range of 250 to 2,500. Walter Burr, *Small Towns*, p. 94, attacked the question through distance: a small town should be no larger than a "team haul," about eight miles. According to the U.S. Census Bureau

Fourth of July celebration, Tucson, Arizona, about 1900
Arizona Historical Society

Mineville, numbering 1,410, each adult knew an average of nine-tenths of the other adults by "sight, name or reputation." There was no need in Mineville for street names or artificial designation of house numbers.

Intimacy was thus the return from small size. By word

in 1870 all the units in Dakota Territory and in Idaho, almost all in Montana and Oregon, and an overwhelming majority in Minnesota were under 1,000; in Illinois, Iowa, and Kansas there were healthy majorities under 1,000.

of mouth people absorbed one another's histories, becoming "walking chronicles of past and present." They acted as a collective memory, an incarnation of the many in the one, so that the chief meanings of life were experienced through others. Gossip was the medium of this personal history, as well as the tool of the collective conscience. It was "the invisible policeman." A person who had been "talked about" was avoided. In one Indiana town these social controls worked on recent arrivals who rode ponies on the Sabbath. In another town it curtailed a man from spending more money on a second wife than he had on the first. Sharp eyes and sharp tongues could tether the unruly in an intimate society.[18]

If a community is small enough, its social events will continually refurbish the collective memory. There were ball games in which practically all the men from one town played all the men from another with dozens on the field at a time, proudly bearing their colors or tags or horsetails. The women sat in lines of wagons and buggies. "The men stood on the ground, yelling, crowding the players until they had to run in curves to reach the bases."[19] The coming of the circus, a high school graduation, even the weekly market day could be the material for the collective memory.

Looked at realistically, however, the collective memory seldom spoke for the entire community. Certainly by the end of the century the small town recognized that its power to direct the lives of its people had become illusory. For one thing, too many kinds of voices spoke. A welter of voluntary associations bore off the individual's allegiance,

[18] Albert Blumenthal, *Small-Town Stuff*, pp. 23, 124, 103, 105; see also Lewis Atherton, *Main Street on the Middle Border*, p. 181; Newell L. Sims, *A Hoosier Village*, pp. 53, 55.

[19] Debo, *Prairie City*, p. 66; George Meltzer, "Social Life and Entertainment on the Kansas Frontier, 1854–1890" (master's thesis, University of Wichita, 1941), p. 106; Grace Snyder, *No Time on My Hands*, p. 173.

Town baseball game, Douglas, Arizona, about 1900
Arizona Historical Society

and these organizations kept alive the spirit of the entire
community only in superficial ways. This process was well
along even in the frontier small towns. Factions and rivalries split Jacksonville, Doyle observed, even in its first
decades. The community's search for nonfactional meeting
grounds, which had begun with the town's founding, became desperate in the 1850s with the large influx of
foreign-born. As elsewhere it was concerned with order in

The face-to-face community: a Mercur, Utah, saloon, about
1895
Utah State Historical Society

a frontier society, and it often answered that need through
voluntary associations and fraternal lodges.[20]

In some communities fraternal orders thrived almost
from the moment of birth; in others the secret lodges came
twenty and thirty years later, as if waiting to see whether
the town would meet its communal obligations. One of
Curti's Wisconsin towns started fraternal organizations

[20] Doyle, *Social Order,* pp. 178, 180; Robert R. Dykstra, *Cattle
Towns,* pp. 212, 218, 365.

within five years, while another held back for twenty-two. As with the Grange the West led in promoting lodges; by the 1920s an average town in the East counted four, in the Middle West eight, and in the Far West ten. By then there were at least seventy-six orders to choose from. By the 1890s there were Freemasonry, the Independent Order of Oddfellows, the Improved Order of Red Men, the Benevolent and Protective Order of Elks, the Loyal Order of Moose, the Good Templars, the Knights of Columbus, the Ancient Order of Hibernians, the Woodmen of the World, the Foresters of America, the Brotherhood of American Yeomen, the Ancient Order of United Workmen, and the Knights of Pythias. Most of them nurtured auxiliaries — the Order of the Eastern Star, the Daughters of Rebekah, the Mooseheart Legion, the Women of Woodcraft, the Companions of the Forest, the Degree of Honor, and the Pythian Sisterhood, to mention a few. Mineville had sixteen but felt a bit overextended. In the small town these clubs offered the joys of fellowship within the myths and rituals of community. They were particularly comforting at times of bereavement, many specializing in insurance plans to cover burial costs. Though there were many overlapping memberships, each lodge tended to serve a different constituency. The Masons and Red Men were for Protestants, the Hibernians and Knights of Columbus for Catholics, the Templars for temperance reformers, and the United Workmen for nonradical laborers. They were not community organizations in the total sense; they were institutionalized neighborhoods. Despite Jacksonville's modest size, Doyle wrote, it had become through a variety of voluntary associations largely a collection of political and social subcommunities.[21]

---

[21] Curti, *Making of an American Community*, pp. 125–27; Brunner, *Village Communities*, p. 85; Blumenthal, *Small-Town Stuff*, pp. 264–65; Vidich and Bensman, *Small Town in Mass Society*, p. 34; Doyle, *Social Order*, pp. 156–57.

Volunteer fire department, O. K. Hose Co., Prescott, Arizona,
about 1890
Sharlott Hall Museum, Prescott, Arizona

Part of the Mercur Fire Department, June, 1903
Utah State Historical Society

The volunteer fire department, too, was close to the heart of small-town life, yet like the fraternal lodge it was not necessarily an indicator of strong local community. Though it originated as and continued to provide a common service, it soon evolved into a social club, suggesting the need for subgroupings. It was selective, often drawing on "the best people" and furnishing its rooms like clubhouses. Uniforms identified members of each enginehouse before admiring citizens. The twenty men of one Iowa City brigade wore red stockings, blue trousers, white shirts, and skullcaps. Later in the century volunteer fire departments began proudly to compete in regional tournaments, and in so doing they subtly derogated their independence. The tournaments were devices of statewide associations to improve efficiency and standardize methods. Iowa's State Fire Association was organized in 1886, one more step away from community self-sufficiency.[22]

If the subgroups could ever work together, it was for town progress, for material advancement, for commercial success. The fight to become the county seat, for example, could rouse a town into virtual battle array. Indeed, in Butler County, Kansas, on a gray dawn in 1870, armed men from Augusta attacked a hundred Eldorado defenders, old Civil War muskets in hand, for possession of the county records. Willie White's father, a "fussy, pudgy man" in a white Nanking suit, successfully commanded the Eldorado defense. His strategy had also included building a courthouse free to the county and hiring a man to subvert the election. Frequently the battle was less overt, but vituperation and mud-slinging were rampant. Ravanna, Kansas, called its rival "a nondescript collection of bug infested huts," with an editor who slept by choice on a

[22] Carl B. Cone, "The Iowa Firemen's Association," *Iowa Journal of History and Politics* 42 (January, 1944): 228, 231, 240; Atherton, *Main Street*, pp. 217–18. Debo, *Prairie City*, pp. 67–68, shows the local horse thief association becoming a similar social club.

manure pile. Jocular words, perhaps, but they aimed at
the energy and funds thrown into the struggle. Ravanna
flourished in its hope. Its stone buildings would make excellent forums for county affairs. But the solons of Emi-
nence, three miles away, were equally eager. They hired
Bat Masterson to protect their interests in the election of
October 18, 1887. Ravanna won by thirty-four votes. It
boomed anew. But Masterson had not prevented fraud, for
after two years of fracas the courts voided the election,
and Ravanna was disinherited. Decline followed rapidly.
Its stone walls fell into ruins.[23]

There were a few, very few, other campaigns that might
also unite the town. Agreement could usually be reached
on the enticing of a private college or seminary or, perhaps,
a state institution like a school for the handicapped or an
asylum.[24] Above all, farmer, businessman, laborer, fraternal order, church, or whatever—all would agree that the
town should be linked with the railroad and it should have
as many rail connections as possible. Ironically these ends
would ultimately destroy the stable community. They
would push the community into wider orbits where the
controls over its life and economy would be removed from
the local scene, curtailing self-sufficiency. Every new railroad station, every new state institution turned eyes outward and propelled the town along a path leading beyond
the optimum size for community.

Progress was a town value, as immutable as the Dox-
ology. Curti found it so in his Wisconsin towns. Here was

---

[23] White, *Autobiography*, pp. 21–22; Kenneth C. Bronson, "The
Local Press and the Changing Community," *Kansas Historical Quar-
terly* 42 (Spring, 1976): 50; W. M. Richards, "Some Ghost Towns of
Kansas," *Heritage of Kansas* 5 (February, 1961): 9–11.

[24] That Nebraska by 1865 already had chartered 23 colleges and
seminaries suggests the pressures; Orville H. Zabel, "Community Development: Another Look at the Elkhorn Valley," *Nebraska History*
54 (Fall, 1973): 393.

a local manifestation of the nineteenth-century worship of growth and technical achievement. But westerners saw such advancement as the peculiar domain of the frontier, and the small town was a precious instrument of progress. These were the values of the booster, but they went beyond the businessmen. Veblen-type cynics saw all other values as camouflages for real estate speculation. The universal game of the West, speculation, was far dearer to the town's heart than baseball or poker. Even interest in one another could by then be interpreted as the salesman's competitive strategy, as it was with George Pendleton in Ed Howe's town. On the surface Pendleton typified the liberal, community-minded citizen, but in reality he sought only to advertise his business. As Dykstra found in cattle towns, once the entrepreneur risked an investment, he thereafter identified the community's well-being with his own.[25] From this viewpoint property was the town's common bond, inflation its good and deflation its evil.

Religion was the bearer of the town's values, and the Protestant churches their physical reminders. Life was punctuated with Sunday school, prayer meeting, monthly preaching service, ladies' aid, youth club, and, once a year or more, a revival. Here the community came together — at least the Protestants within it, essentially as equals, with an earthly disregard for denominational differences. Just as he could with the farmers, a forceful traveling preacher could bind villagers with song and word. In fact, revivals usually included both farmers and townspeople. Their strength was not statistically measurable, but even Edgar Howe, who delighted in pointing out the surreptitious whiskey sales and the fights just outside the tent, would not underestimate their significance to the values of the

[25] Curti, *Making of an American Community,* p. 116; Veblen, *Absentee Ownership,* pp. 143, 163; Howe, *The Anthology of Another Town,* p. 114; Dykstra, *Cattle Towns,* p. 115.

community. To early Cheyenne, Wyoming, rough and heterogeneous, came young Josiah Strong, fresh from the seminary and still unknown. He grew into an integrating force on the frontier by preaching local issues like libraries, parks, and temperance rather than theology.

Behind the hallelujahs and the temperance, however, there was more than whiskey to disturb the religious community. The Catholics were never included in the Protestant unity. And, in spite of the revival's suspension of hostility, there was plenty of denominational friction among the Protestants. Though Strong felt that conflict in Cheyenne was constructive to the community process, in general the more churches in a town the greater the social cleavage. There was even a minor crack between boosters on one hand and religion in general on the other. The temperance movement and the quiet Sabbath were brakes on business progress.[26]

Frictions and fractures in the values of the total community were like seepages on a marshy plain. Where the community was slipping from its responsibilities, new institutions would sometimes be rising. Buildings, often erected in distant cities, began housing the poor, the insane, the criminal. It was, in the phrase of one recent historian, David Rothman, a discovery of the asylum, a common sense of relief that an agency would assume those burdens. The mental asylum, the orphanage, the penitentiary removed problems from the community's vision. Many middle-western towns built almshouses before the number of poor would warrant the expenditure, overly eager to see those worries removed. Of course, the almshouses were soon filled, not so much with native-born

[26] Calder M. Pickett, *Ed Howe*, p. 6; Brunner, *Village Communities*, p. 69; Withers, "Plainville, U.S.A.," pp. 163–64; Dorothea R. Muller, "Church Building and Community Making on the Frontier," *Western Historical Quarterly* 10 (April, 1979): 193–94.

Americans as with immigrants, which suggests again the loss of a homogeneous community.[27]

The internal rifts were often related to the town's ambiguous stance, courting the wider world and at the same time hating the consequences. Townsfolk were fearful that self-sufficiency was lost forever. The gap was blamed on a host of evils lurking outside their borders—trusts, Wall Street, international bankers, systems of political influence, corrupt machines. Railroads, immigration, and labor unions were all frightening, alien forces.

Perhaps these fears strengthened patriotism. The federal government could balance those threats better than the small town. As the bitterness of the Civil War subsided, as the local chapter of the Grand Army of the Republic sang "Marching Through Georgia" more and more softly, national pride became the universal value professed. It too was unifying—a Niagara of emotion at Decoration and Independence Day parades or at reviews of the local militia. This small community would stand with the nation, and that fact was unshakable. Yet love of country is not a substitute for community; patriotism is not a local value; it is not primarily focused on the near-at-hand. It may and should be based on local attachments, as Josiah Royce late in the century was pointing out. As a substitute for community, patriotism becomes harsh and hollow.

Reclusive temperaments create tensions in community life. There will always be Emily Dickinsons who cannot tolerate neighborliness and who prefer the hermitage. "You have the inclination to be alone, and to dream, and you are afraid of dreams." So Sherwood Anderson captured the torment of one individual in Winesburg, Ohio. And how many other novelists of the frontier town, like

[27] David Rothman, *Discovery of the Asylum*, pp. 185, 29; a similar point has been made for the law by David J. Bodenhamer, "Law and Disorder on the Early Frontier," *Western Historical Quarterly* 10 (July, 1979): 335–36.

Willa Cather in Nebraska, have evoked the smothering of artistry and intellect.

The more the town lost its center, the more it went off in different directions, the more difficult it became for some individuals to accept the town's continuing efforts at communal ways. It was then that gossips became busybodies. It was then that life became "slow and heavy. It drags. It does not readily take the stimulus of new ideas." Attendance at funerals remained widespread, but the practice became a morbid obsession rather than a profound participation in communal life.[28]

The values of progress, however, were apt to be more fundamental than the desire for commercial success. They were closely allied to independence, hard work, sobriety, simplicity, and all the other prudential virtues from the Puritan tradition. When New Englanders like the Yale band in Jacksonville moved into small towns, their zeal usually transcended growth and real estate. They saw the town as a buttress against the anarchy of the frontier, supporting community values and preventing the ascendance of Catholicism. Their social virtues were mutual helpfulness, generosity, sociability, and neighborliness. Curti in his minute study cited innumerable examples of behavior expressing these deeper values. He also found, however, that such examples were often associated with references to the hardships of a new country, as if the values might not be permanent.[29]

Commitment to the family remained firm in the towns as on the farms. Kin took advantage of kin in sharing work, especially child care. But in the frontier years these kin

[28] Sherwood Anderson, *Winesburg, Ohio*, p. 27; Nathaniel Egleston, *Villages and Village Life*, p. 34; compare Michael Lesy, *Wisconsin Death Trip* (New York, 1973).

[29] Withers, "Plainville, U.S.A.," p. 55; Vidich and Bensman, *Small Town in Mass Society*, pp. 36–39; Doyle, *Social Order*, pp. 27–28; Curti, *Making of an American Community*, p. 139.

relationships were usually male because men so often determined the move and the settlement. They were correspondingly tenuous and not the cement of community. Nor were they the strong extended families of tradition. Society was too fluid. In the 1860s in Jacksonville the median age of all males over twenty years old was under thirty; about one-third of those were unmarried. The figure was high because of the influx of immigrant laborers without their families, but that condition was frequent enough to unsettle many a frontier town. Towns under one thousand in Nebraska in 1870 contained almost 20 percent foreign-born.[30] In the context of continuing immigration and mobility, the nuclear family was all that could be expected.

Patterns of conflict highlighted and foreshadowed the changing commitment to community. There were always resentments between individuals, feuds between families, rifts between groups. These jabbing points of contention can strengthen the community that mutes and transcends them. Otherwise they are signals of danger. Furthermore, when conflicts congeal around single commanding issues, like slavery in the 1850s, it may be too late for muted transcendence; then the community becomes rigid and can be split into separate compartments.

The more close-knit the community, the greater the impact when lines of conflict coincide and reinforce one another like the meeting of wave crests. Class consciousness can emerge from such clashes, as Sorel and Marx long ago pointed out. Yet often the existence of discord matters less than its context. A Flagstaff saloonkeeper dynamited a rival shop in a price war between the two. The antagonism would appear severe, but since the saloonkeepers

[30] Doyle, *Social Order,* pp. 265, 269; Withers, "Plainville, U.S.A.," p. 58; U.S. Bureau of the Census, *The Statistics of the Population of the United States* (Washington, D.C., 1872). Brunner, *Village Communities,* p. 21, says 10 percent in agricultural villages.

were equally aspiring capitalists, it probably had little effect on the commitment to community. On the other hand, the two men might have represented different class interests. One could have owned his property and ridden regularly with the local vigilance committee of business-men. The other could have been a tenant and a recent Irish immigrant. The dynamiting would then be a har-binger of social collapse and mirror emerging class con-sciousness. It could become like the "one horse town" in Arkansas where Huck Finn watched drunken old Boggs, poor and feeling victimized by the town merchants, storm up to the biggest store in town and pour out vilification on its owner. Colonel Sherburn demanded cessation in cool, pure language and, when unsuccessful, calmly shot Boggs. The businessman then proceeded to shame threatening townsmen into inaction in a tight little drama of class prerogative and tension. As a matter of fact, most towns saw their local council become the arm of the boosters rather than the ally of church and family, as it had been in colonial New England. The wealthy began sending their children to outside schools. Marriages were made from the elites of a region of towns rather than between classes within one town. Class, historian Robert Wiebe said, took the place of the old community.[31]

The myths of the classless society, however, continued to run swift and clear. Few believed that there were rigid classes in the small town; to point them out was un-Ameri-can. Any description of poverty was bad for business. Yet the same man who would vehemently denounce social or economic division could readily identify the better sort, the average workingman, and lower elements. That was

[31] Lewis A. Coser, *The Functions of Social Conflict*, p. 76; Platt Cline, *They Came to the Mountain* (Flagstaff, Ariz., 1976), p. 294; Doyle, "Social Theory and New Communities," pp. 158–59; Mark Twain, *Huckleberry Finn,* in *The Portable Mark Twain* (New York, 1946), pp. 368–75; Robert Wiebe, *The Search for Order*, pp. 11–112.

the way it was in Wheatland, even though courtship had become restricted to class lines, and social movement upward had virtually ceased. Caricatures could even be drawn between inferior and superior by the frequency of their shaving. Billington added, "Class divisions occurred in the most primitive communities [and] deepened as the social order matured."[32]

In Wisconsin towns, according to Curti, class distinctions were firm only fifteen years after the area was opened for settlement. Upper strata were easily identified, though geographical mobility continued high. The newspapers were expressing hostility toward local elites, calling them "dough-heads getting rich doing nothing." Everywhere the columns of the local *Gazettes* and *Tribunes* revealed increasing social differentiation. Even the fraternal lodges could trace the class lines. In Angie Debo's Prairie City, for example, the small farmers joined the Odd Fellows while the businessmen and most prosperous farmers rallied to the Masons. In these towns separate neighborhoods were growing where the field workers and the section hands on the railroad lived in little houses, sometimes with one cow in the back. Indigents were already there. By the 1870s in Wisconsin there was even a political battle between town and county over who would support paupers."[33]

The depression following 1873 not only intensified poverty but caused the townsmen to wonder about their dependence on the wider economy. The railroad, for example, had made some men very rich, and immigration

[32] Withers, *Plainville*, pp. 133–37; Ray A. Billington, *America's Frontier Heritage*, pp. 97–98; Dykstra, *Cattle Towns*, p. 193.

[33] Curti, *Making of an American Community*, pp. 113, 122, 283–84; James C. Malin, *Grassland of North America*, pp. 316–17; S. Anderson, *Winesburg, Ohio*, p. 169. Kirk, *The Promise of American Life*, pp. 140–41, in studying Holland, Michigan, confirms Curti's conclusions about frontier mobility.

had brought the poor to their doorstep. The town wanted neither the rich nor the poor. And they could be eliminated, according to one critic, by the great migration to the city. That was because only the rich and the poor, the best and the worst, the cream and the unfit dregs separated themselves out and went to Chicago or Omaha or Saint Louis.[34]

Of course, it was not just the town but America as a whole that was busily transforming itself. By the end of the century United States Steel and Standard Oil had tested the muscle of the corporate idea, the Progressive Movement was challenging government to exert itself, and labor unions fought for position with whiffs of socialism around the edge of the fray. The greater casualty of that turmoil, Robert Wiebe wrote, was "the island community." In the face of all these larger forces of modernity the small town struggled to preserve its old powers and its confidence in its own way of life.

Sometimes unexpected things happen. One New York small town evidenced more close-knit community after industrialization than before. "Any month of the calendar year now brought more Kingstonians together in group activity than had the entire year in pre-canal days."[35] But closer inspection reveals not intensification of the community as a whole but associative community, *Gesellschaft*, and the rise of more active subgroupings. These forms were perfectly appropriate to transiency in a world of strangers. But had the small middle-western town ever enjoyed much else? How long had it been since the townsman had become, as Veblen called him, "the toll-gate

---

[34] W. Anderson, *Country Town*, pp. 141–44.

[35] Wiebe, *The Search for Order*, p. 44; Stuart Blumin, *Urban Threshold*, pp. 216, 220–21. Another description of community disintegration in the late-nineteenth-century Middle West, from which the subsequent "invisible-roof" reference is taken, is Sherwood Anderson, *Poor White*, pp. 46–47, 210–11.

keeper" for the larger economic interests beyond their town limits, or, in other words, tools of transient strangers? Even in the covenanted community frontier restlessness allowed little of the intimacy with place and person that comes from stability. The community cooperated in seeking progress, which meant growth, which in turn meant the loss of small size, one hub of community. Growth too brought other values, other religions, and the end of the hopes for traditional homogeneity. The total community shared fewer and fewer occasions of common purpose.

Between extreme frontier restlessness and later booming growth came an "Our Town" period, a time when the whole community turned out for baseball games, when each member of the choir personally understood the tie that binds, when wagonloads of people still sang their way home from a church or town event instead of separating in buggies. Sherwood Anderson imagined an invisible roof arching these lives. But such years were short. Anderson's Main Street was gashed by sewer lines, while the workmen sat on piles of upturned earth eating from dinner pails and speaking strange tongues. The town's house was also being altered. The one room had been converted into many, the doors between were often locked, and most of the furniture inherited from seventeenth-century New England had been carried to the attic.

Chapter Seven

The Corralled Community:
Mexican and Anglo Ranches

> If I must be cast in sickness or destitution on the care of
> the stranger, let it be in California [on a *rancho*]; let it
> be before American avarice has hardened the heart and
> made a god of gold.
>
> Walter Colton, *Three Years in California* (1850)

THE WESTERN RANCH came to embrace two cultures, because
its Hispanic beginnings were fused with Anglo economics.
In the process came a subtle shift in the nature and definition of this mini-community, containing much of the function but not the complete machinery of a community.
Ranchers habitually thought of themselves as living in a
separate world, each ranch with its own name, self-contained, with its own life-style and identity, touching the
larger society of farmers and merchants only when the
animals, its products, were ready for market. Yet during
the nineteenth century within these corralled sanctuaries
the vaquero evolved into the cowboy, the *patrón* became
the rancher, and the *mesta*—the Spanish-style cattle
breeders' union—was replaced by the stockgrowers' association—all suggesting major changes in community.

Arnold Rojas, born near the end of the nineteenth century, carried on the traditions of the vaquero while astutely
assessing Anglo ranch life. "A skinny gangling kid on a
hip-shot hump-backed pinto mare," as he described himself, "rode into the southern San Joaquin Valley, looking

for a job."[1] He began work at the Tejon Ranch, whose pastures ran through four counties and then wandered from ranch to ranch, from the small San Emideo to the Button-willow, headquarters for the enormous Miller and Lux enterprises. In the shade of cottonwoods, rolling brown-paper cigarettes, he listened to old-timers like Lenardo Ruiz or José Jesús López, whose grandfather had marched into California with Anza. And even that grandfather could have sung ballads of Mexican cattle herds numbering tens of thousands and going back to the conquistadors. To Rojas the vaquero was distinct from the Anglo cowboy, revealing all manner of different methods and attitudes. His life was patterned on close contact: "It bred strong loyalties." Attached to his employers, the vaquero underwent "any hardship or privation, which he would never think of suffering when working for himself."[2]

Rojas and his friends represented a latter-day extension of the early-nineteenth-century Mexican rancho, an institution scattered with only moderate variations from Alta California to the Gulf of Mexico. Its medieval beginnings, echoing through terms like *mesta* and *patrón*, were evident on all sides. There was, for example, the ceremony of possession. Standing among a few neighbors, the new grantee tore up grass and threw stones while the little band shouted, "¡Viva el Rey!" This was the place! These were the grasses and the rocks on which another mini-community would be raised. Descendants of these founders would live in largely self-contained, isolated ranchos, long unruffled in their hierarchies. Secure in their sense of place, they lived intimately with the land, although it

[1] Arnold Rojas, *Last of the Vaqueros*, author's note, unpaged.
[2] Arnold Rojas, *California Vaquero*, p. 16; Arnold Rojas, *The Vaquero*, p. 13; Rojas, *Last of the Vaqueros*, p. 80.

spanned a thousand rolling hills, nestled between red mesas, or stretched across the Staked Plains.

Fabiola Cabeza de Baca was raised on such a rancho. Here in northern New Mexico her grandfather had first torn the grasses and thrown the stones. She remembered the Piñon plateaus and grassy draws, the haciendas and the *patrónes*. She walked in the sparse villages, like San Helario, whose chapel her grandfather had built, his wife's fine silks hanging beside the wood-carved *santos* of the common people.[3] Around the village *placitas*, with their walls of adobe, lived the *empleados*. Here cattle could be sheltered in emergencies, or vesper processions could march toward the chapel. *Bailes* and fiestas lasted till dawn. Itinerant workers acted as troubadors, singing ballads of unrequited love and lonely death.

Similarly, Cleofas Jaramillo recalled her young days along the Río Hondo as a granddaughter of a *patrón*. The ranch buildings ranged around an enclosure — "a combination," she said, "of family domicile, handicraft center, factory, and work shop for all the necessities of life." The chapel stood across the courtyard. Its bell had been cast in a nearby shed, all the people having thrown rings and golden trinkets into the molten metal to sweeten its tone. Now it rang for their weddings and funerals as well as for Indian alarms. When her grandfather died, the *patrón's* house was merely divided to accommodate the two families of Cleofas's father and his brother.[4] In such ways a world of continuity and stability was maintained.

---

[3] Marc Simmons, *Spanish Government in New Mexico* (Albuquerque, N.Mex., 1968), pp. 179–80; Fabiola Cabeza de Baca, *We Fed Them Cactus*, pp. 53, 68.

[4] Cleofas Jaramillo, "Shadows of the Past," in *The New Mexico Hispano*, pp. 14–15, 18. Outside Anglo observers were sometimes less happy in their descriptions: Susan Magoffin called these northern Mexican ranchos no more than "genteel pigsties." Susan S. Magoffin, *Down the Santa Fé Trail and into Mexico*, p. 90.

The familial pattern of the Mexican rancho was essentially hierarchical and patriarchal. The lines of deference and control began with the *patrón* and extended downward through his immediate and extended family and onward through all the employees. These *empleados,* Cabeza de Baca claimed, were as much a part of the family as were the sons and daughters of the *patrón.* She quoted the family cook as saying, "It was a very democratic way of life," by which he undoubtedly meant that everyone was cared for with equal affection. It was not an egalitarian system, and her journals reflect the distinctions—special serapes spread in the chapel for the *patrón* and his family, the men served their meals before the women. The role for the wife of the *patrón* was clear. She acted as the universal mother of the clan and was responsible for all the general welfare. Knowledgeable in herbs and remedies, she was the first called "when there was death, illness, misfortune, or good tidings in the family."[5] Her ministrations included the elderly and the poor of the community, for they were often related through baptismal vows. Those in need were in fact more present there than on Anglo ranches because the Mexican society was less mobile and longer established and hence a more rounded community.

The Mexican model, of course, varied from region to region. In Alta California, for example, land was granted in relatively smaller parcels to a larger number of rancheros. Ties between *patrón* and vaquero tended to be weaker there, influenced by the availability of cheap Indian labor. In New Mexico the ranchero was like the *hacendado,* grand as were the haciendas over which he ruled on the north Mexican plains. But these differences seemed not to have affected the basic extended family, which remained strong, devout in its faith, and eager to

[5] Cabeza de Baca, *We Fed Them Cactus,* pp. 31, 59–60.

exert its sway over the generations of *primos hermanos* and *empleados* alike.[6]

As with their Catholic peasant village forebears everywhere, the people of the rancho were cemented by religious ceremonies that carried meanings far beyond the immediate ritual. *Compadres,* for example, were linked through the baptism of a child. As the baby was admitted to the scheme of creation, his natural parents and his godparents were meshed almost into kinship. They became mutually responsible for the child and in the process much closer to one another, finding increasing reasons for contact and creating deeper mutual concern. They shared resources more often, helped one another, and closed grieving ranks when death took one of the circle. It was a net of security that bound conflicting classes, catching within it the seeds of community.[7]

The *compadre* idea was uncongenial to an ethic of personal accumulation. Each *compadre* was a potential drain on the resources of the others, hence a threat to individual gain. Consequently, as it did to all traditional culture, growing class consciousness would undermine a rancho society resting on *compadres.* Walter Colton's romantic impression of a ranchero class gently refusing to grind the face of the poor showed deep misunderstanding of the essential class structure. It was true, however, that the speculative Yankee, as Colton saw him, came from another world, another age, with far less acceptance of class responsibility and position. By Colton's time, with or without the Yankee, class aggravations had seriously intensified,

---

[6]Leonard Pitt, *The Decline of the Californios* (Berkeley, Calif., 1966), p. 11; Nancie L. Gonzalez, *Spanish-Americans of New Mexico,* p. 59.

[7]Sidney Mintz and Eric Wolf, "Analysis of Ritual Co-Parenthood," *Southwestern Journal of Anthropology* 6 (Winter, 1950): 351–52; George Foster, "The Dyadic Contract: A Model for the Social Structure of a Mexican Peasant Village," *American Anthropologist* 63:1173–92.

at least on New Mexican ranchos. The upper class was seldom entered except by pure Europeans and mestizos, usually of lighter skins. In this context the *patrón* would be considered not as a father figure but as the owner of the land, a wielder of political power, a force that maintained order. Far below him the *genízaro*, the common man or Christian Indian, had little chance for education, money, or political or social power. He was likely to be in debt to the town store, belonging, as he was well aware, to the *patrón*. Not until the late nineteenth century did a middle class of small herders and merchants appear in these areas. By then in the popular mind *el patrón* had become no more than *el rico*.[8]

Hardly surprising were the changes wrought in the rancho by contact with the Anglos. The military conquest of northern Mexico was the initial upheaval. But even more disruptive was the effect of industrialization. The expansion of railroads into the southwest after the 1870s hauled the rancheros into world markets and competition with other, more businesslike cattlemen. Isolation and self-sufficiency were inevitably doomed. On the other hand, as the Anglo cattlemen moved into the Southwest, they were in turn affected by earlier practices of the Mexicans. The traditional enclosed cowpens were abandoned in favor of the Latin American open range, an old Hispanic device. Moreover, Texans, most of whom were originally from the Deep South, added a few methods and postures from the cotton plantation, and so the changing cattle ranch spread across the Great Plains, until the new institution could be recognized from the mountains of Montana to the grasslands of Texas.

One of the ranch's common characteristics, at least till the 1880s, was its claim to the free use of the public domain. In that decade, for example, Walt Alderson and

[8] Mintz and Wolf, "Analysis," pp. 351–52; Walter Colton, *Three Years in California*, p. 359; Gonzalez, *Spanish Americans*, pp. 63–65.

Cutting cactus with an ensilage cutter, King Ranch, Texas,
about 1885
Keystone-Mast Collection, University of California, Riverside

Oklahoma cowboys, about 1900
Keystone-Mast Collection, University of California, Riverside

his bride, Nannie, were ranching near the Rosebud River in Montana when their "maverick shack" burned down. They could, however, rebuild almost anywhere, "since no one took up land in those days."[9] They were reflecting the ranchers' casual assumption that all of the open land was theirs for the using.

Both Mexican and Anglo ranchers claimed a special affinity to their land, whether public or private. They lived close to the cycles of the seasons. Most of the functions of the ranch community revolved around perennial rituals like calving, branding, trailing, and haying. The greening of spring meant the excitement of the rodeo or roundup. Ranchers knew that universal agrarian kinship with the environment. Grace Snyder, whom we have already met through her reminiscence of life on a Nebraska farm, later married a cattleman, Bert, and her subsequent journals of her cattle years were as aware of seasons and cycles as were her farm journals. On their vast Montana ranch even the burial of a stillborn child ("You are quiet, and forever. Though for us the silence is so loud . . .") was a part of becoming rooted to their land. "That's my mountain," screamed Agnes Cleaveland, while a child on a Colorado ranch, "and that's my cañon!"[10] It was a vigorous assertion of a sense of place quite unrelated to ownership. Also as with farmers, some of the attachments came from living through the initial hardships. Bert Snyder's gray eyes had to see beyond the prickly pear of the Nebraska sand hills, beyond the one sad little tree that survived beside their tin-roofed soddie, to a vision of his own locus, "a place where he intended to settle down and stay a long time."[11]

[9] Nannie Alderson as told to Helena H. Smith, *A Bride Goes West,* pp. 26, 110.

[10] Albert B. Snyder, as told to Nellie Snyder Yost, *Pinnacle Jake,* pp. 335–36; Agnes Morley Cleaveland, *No Life for a Lady,* p. 27.

[11] Snyder, *Pinnacle Jake,* p. 320.

When Charles Goodnight established his Palo Duro Ranch, his wife Mary was so depressed by its roughness that he was forced to build an irrigation system and plant apple trees to console her. Nannie Alderson's bridal house was an abandoned railroad workers' shack, furnished with elk antlers about the door and a human skull suspended from one prong. Her housing improved, but the isolation remained. The distance was like "a Chinese wall' dividing ranchers. Even the post office was twenty-five miles across the Divide. Agnes Cleaveland spoke of her "twenty-miles-away neighbors" and complained of being "marooned . . . on a desert island of cultural barrenness, with no means of escape." She felt that she was recapitulating the story of the Swiss Family Robinson.[12]

For Anglos as well as for Mexicans the ranch was indeed a frontier institution.[13] Because of the enormous size of most ranches, to say nothing of the public domain itself, loneliness was endemic and often endurable only because of the dream of wealth, the expectation of joining the fraternity of cattle kings.

By the 1870s, when the Anglo open-range ranch reached its zenith in size and significance, its people had become highly mobile. Geographical and occupational options were open to them in ways unknown to Mexican rancheros. "There was always a great deal of moving around in the West," Nannie Alderson said, "and a great deal of giving up and going back East when things grew hard." She was struck by the number of ranchers who "apologized for being in the West," wishing to be elsewhere.[14] Bert Snyder lived three places in Nebraska, and he worked shorter stands in Colorado, Wyoming, and Dakota. Bruce Siberts

[12]Mari Sandoz, *Cattlemen from the Río Grande Across the Far Marias,* p. 178; Alderson, *A Bride Goes West,* pp. 122, 50; Cleaveland, *No Life for a Lady,* p. 37.

[13]Sandra Myers, *The Ranch in Spanish Texas, 1691–1900,* p. 51.

[14]Alderson, *A Bride Goes West,* pp. 143, 109.

was a bachelor rancher, but his singleness only partly explained his frequent shifts from Iowa to South Dakota (which he called "that 11,000-acre pasture") to Chicago, and finally to Oklahoma. These men moved as if impelled by steel springs; no economic or social forces can fully explain their restlessness. It stemmed more from what James Malin, the Great Plains historian, assigned to "group behavior," the intangible circuits motivated not only by depressions and crises but also by conversations around the wood stove.[15]

As one response to this drifting, the larger ranch community fostered an unusually hospitable way of life. Of course, the tradition was strongest in the Mexican rancho. Walter Colton, the navy chaplain who lived in California during the 1840s, found the rancho a wellspring of hospitality. "Were the De'il himself to call for a night's lodging," he wrote, "the Californian would hardly find it in his heart to bolt the door."[16] Of course, *Californio* hospitality was unusually grand, based as it was on a high level of leisure, which in turn stemmed from the abundant, cheap Indian labor. But most ranchers throughout the Southwest expected their fellow ranchers to lodge with them whenever near. Exceptions like the business-minded XIT, which charged and limited the stay of "bona fide travelers," only proved the rule. In Nebraska, Mrs. Nate Trego explained that her baking chores were heavy because her family so seldom sat down alone at meals. "Such things as baking up a batch of biscuits for any bunch of cowhands who dropped by was part of the pattern of life for a ranch woman."[17]

[15] Walker D. Wyman and Bruce Siberts, *Nothing but Prairie and Sky,* p. 30; James C. Malin, "The Turnover of Farm Population in Kansas," *Kansas Historical Quarterly* 4 (November, 1935): 353.

[16] Walter Colton, *Three Years in California,* p. 194.

[17] Snyder, *Pinnacle Jake,* pp. 338–39; Charles L. Sonnichsen, *Cowboys and Cattle Kings,* p. 50.

In winter, "the season of repose," when the land rested, the work was over, and the larger ranching community celebrated. For a brief time long distances and weather conditions were negligible deterrents. At the end of the travel, however long, were the barn with corn meal sprinkled on the floor, fiddles in rhythm, and dancing till dawn. The Mexican rancho had saints' and feast days throughout the year, but no event on the calendar, Mexican or Anglo, was as cohesive as the festivities during roundup. Following the day's work—the roping, branding, and castrating that called for cooperation among ranches— the evenings were filled with food and dance and song. Neighboring women helped with the cooking, often feeding twenty or thirty people at a time.[18] It was all very like the barn raisings and corn huskings of farmers, when pleasure flowed so naturally from the necessities of working together.

Cattle raising as an occupation was as committed to cooperation as early farming on the plains. As with farmers, unwritten codes demanded immediate help with emergencies like fires. Roundingup and driving were counterparts to threshing and harvesting, and the spirit spilled over into other life activities. Cattlemen united against horse thieves and collaborated in hunting game or predators. Mexicans, of course, had set the whole pattern for the cooperative rodeo. Moreover, on the plains where rancheros together tracked the buffalo, the people of an area formed long caravans, including the poorest of each community, all planning to get their share of the meat. Though it cost precious time, ranch outfits worked "promiscuously together," Andy Adams put it, as when they helped one another over a ford. On such occasions coop-

[18] Jaramillo, "Shadows of the Past," p. 54; Cabeza de Baca, *We Fed Them Cactus*, p. 133.

eration came so naturally that Adams "never knew who was the directing spirit in the work."[19]

Only organization made an open-range cattle system function. At roundup time, for example, each ranch crew scoured its assigned district, moving in smaller and smaller circles toward a designated point. As the circle narrowed, the crews combined. Here, as on the trail drive, planning and strategy approached the military. Tedious, painstaking, based on a differentiation of skills, this task placed an appropriate premium on loyalty.[20] Charles Sonnichsen, in an extensive study, found the cowhand traditionally attached to the brand, the outfit, the men he worked with. He had to be a reliable part of the whole, and his employer had to be loyal and dependable too.

Unfortunately, the cooperative loyalties were overlaid by an imperious individualism, a spirit that insinuated itself in many shapes. Thus, though certainly not typical, the rancher of one South Dakota area watched a neighboring family meeting death and hard times reduced to living "on little more than what the cat brought in." The ranch community did nothing to help until the family eventually drifted away. Or the feeling could take the form of a fierce pride in the powers of oneself, the self-reliant one, the single organism denying the compelling nexus of the group, unwilling to seek the help of others. Sonnichsen compared cattlemen to "softer citizens in the settlement [who] might call a lawyer and start a damage suit to atone for affront or injury. On the range you handled it yourself." The next man must be willing to work out his destiny in the same way. Or, as Joseph McCoy said after eight years

[19] Andy Adams, *The Log of a Cowboy,* p. 297; J. Evetts Haley, *The XIT Ranch of Texas and the Early Days of the Llano Estacado,* p. 160; Cabeza de Baca, *We Fed Them Cactus,* pp. 39–41.

[20] Joe B. Frantz and Julian E. Choate, Jr., *The American Cowboy,* p. 35; Mody Boatright, "The Myth of Frontier Individualism," in Hofstadter and Lipset, *Turner and the Sociology of the Frontier,* p. 54.

of contact with southwesterners, the attitude could erode
public spirit "in manners pertaining to the general good."
He painted cattlemen as indifferent to the public welfare;
"it is extremely difficult to induce them to expend even a
small sum in forwarding a project or enterprise that has
other than a purely selfish end in view."[21]

Mari Sandoz used I. P. ("Print") Olive as her favorite
example of ranchers of this imperious persuasion. With
the air of a Genghis Khan he was moving his ranch from
Texas to Nebraska in an entourage of cattle, horses,
wagons, and people that stretched for ten miles along the
trail. Coming upon a destitute settler's family whose
wagons had collapsed, Olive surveyed the situation and
decreed paternally, "Come along, I'll adopt you." It was
the individual acting as a law unto himself, which is what
Olive became. Judges and sheriffs heeded his nod, and the
community at large could not touch him. Indeed, his freedom was destructive of the larger community. Like a
medieval baron, he had no desire to band together with
others to form what might be thought of as the cattleman's
counterpart of the modern nation-state. Later, in 1900,
when Print Olive was forced for economic survival to
join a cattlemen's marketing pool, he was sure that the
day of the real cattleman had passed. As Sandoz put it,
giving up individualistic ways was for these men as "hard
as a horse pill to swallow."[22] They ate their meat and
drank their coffee in silence and often with their hats on,
proud in their cavalier disregard for the community and
the public good.

These individualistic values paralleled the competitive
ethic of the Anglo cattle trade itself. In the 1870s, during

---

[21] Wyman and Siberts, *Nothing but Prairie and Sky*, pp. 60–61; Sonnichsen, *Cowboys and Cattle Kings*, p. 45; Joseph G. McCoy, *Cattle
Trade of the West and Southwest*, p. 145.

[22] Sandoz, *The Cattlemen*, pp. 189–90, 227–33, 219.

the heyday of the open range before the sobering results of overstocking and sagging prices, the race for market was keen, and the press to expand was heady. Expectations of a 25 percent annual profit goaded men on. Even around the corral the competitive nature of the roundup — the races, the timings, the challenges to muscle and endurance — were exhilarations that infused every dusty minute.

Little interfered with the ongoing business of an Anglo ranch — certainly not irrelevancies like an observance of the Sabbath. As with the men on wagon trains, the press of immediate business superseded sacramental distractions. On many ranches work never stopped seven days a week through a season of eight months. Again, the Mexican ranchero stood in striking contrast; he frequently stopped work for religious purposes. "Religion is his whole being," Cabeza de Baca said, and the ranchero's life was filled with solemn and reverential occasions, with saints' days, followed by midnight suppers and prayers.[23] Even on regular days there were often group devotions both morning and night. Though the priest could seldom visit for more than a few times a year, in the interim the rancho chapel was proudly polished and maintained.

As for most other communities, the hub of Anglo ranch society was the family. Ideally the whole ranch was included in a vaguely defined outfit, almost a kingroup, the main family taking the unmarried cowhands under its wing like a proxy for an extended family. The ranch house was its central symbol, and the hospitality of that house was its aura. Some women, like Lizzie Campbell of the Matador or Mary Goodnight of the Palo Duro, mothered their cowboys, offering meals, staging dances,

[23] Haley, *XIT Ranch*, p. 116; Lewis Atherton, *The Cattle Kings*, p. 129; Cabeza de Baca, *We Fed Them Cactus*, pp. 51, 53.

preaching admonitions, nursing the sick, and patching clothes. Agnes Cleaveland remembered dispensing the bitter universal medicine, Oregon graperoot. "We shared our home," Nannie Alderson said, "with our nice cowboys." She fed them favorite dishes as they loitered in her kitchen. She literally held the hands of the dying and was moved: "There was great good in these wild and homeless boys." Richard King acted the father to his hands, his "Kineños," protecting and disciplining and bailing them out of trouble.[24]

In fact, however, the Aldersons, Goodnights, and Kings were rare. Nannie Alderson admitted that few other ranchers welcomed cowboys into the big house. Most thought ranch hands wild and undesirable and would have little to do with them. The better people "would as soon have thought of inviting a rattlesnake into their homes as inviting a cowboy."[25]

Then, too, it was hard to keep even the owner's family intact on the ranch. Wealthier ranchers moved into town for the winter, seeking better schools for their children. Many of Lizzie Campbell's counterparts preferred to live in Fort Worth most of the year. Bruce Siberts found the same pattern around Pierre in Dakota.[26] Such moving did not necessarily break the family, though it did often separate husband and wife; but, more important, it weakened the bonds between family and community. It assumed the priority of family needs and goals over the unity of the ranch.

The literary image of lonely independence infected the cowboy himself and may also have hindered family attachment. In magazines and dime novels the bachelor cowboy,

[24] Atherton, *The Cattle Kings*, p. 97; Sandoz, *The Cattlemen*, p. 183; Cleaveland, *No Life for a Lady*, p. 146; Alderson, *A Bride Goes West*, pp. 72–73, 40–41, 118; Tom Lea, *The King Ranch*, pp. 127, 349–51.

[25] Alderson, *A Bride Goes West*, pp. 72–76.

[26] Wyman and Siberts, *Nothing but Prairie and Sky*, p. 130.

melancholy and singular, talked little of his past and often had no surname, which is to say no family. Owen Wister's prototype was known only as "the Virginian," "nor had his strong heart yet waked up to any hunger for a home." Peter Shaffer caught that symbol in the modern play *Equus,* where young Alan dreams of being a cowboy, swinging across the open prairie high in the saddle. "I bet all cowboys are orphans," he sighs. Richard King, a historical counterpart of the fictional Alan, fled the family to which he was apprenticed. Likewise, Andy Adams, in the guise of his fictional character Tom Moore, escapes an apprenticeship and "as a preacher's son takes to vice," and assimilates "the vagabond temperament of the range."[27]

Some of this lack of attachment was likely a function of youth, a wandering before marriage and responsibility. Alexander MacKay, inspecting his extensive ranch holdings in 1885, noticed that most cowboys were in their twenties and the bosses in their thirties.[28] Joseph McCoy, the founder of the Chisholm Trail, in his *Historic Sketches,* described forty-five cattlemen by name; one he referred to as older, for seven he made no mention of age, and thirty-five he described as youthful: "Such as appeared on the western markets were usually young men of energy." When he wrote in 1874, McCoy himself was only in his thirties.[29]

By the fourth quarter of the nineteenth century the Anglo cattle industry was maturing, and all of the cattle kingdom was changing, wrestling with the demands of a

[27] Owen Wister, *The Virginian* (Boston, 1968), p. 37; Peter Shaffer, *Equus* (London, 1973), p. 48; Adams, *Log of a Cowboy,* p. 7.

[28] Atherton, *The Cattle Kings,* p. 31.

[29] McCoy, *Cattle Trade,* esp. pp. 192–93. Erik Erikson theorized that frontier disengagement could stem from rejective mothers: *Childhood and Society* (New York, 1963), p. 292; Nannie Alderson, for one, thus thought it wise to send out her children early on their own: Alderson, *A Bride Goes West,* pp. 170–71.

more industrialized economy. In urban markets tastes grew for more tender meat, requiring scientific breeding and imported Hereford stock in the corrals. The greatest successes were market entrepreneurs like Henry Miller, who had begun as a butcher in San Francisco. If the ranch had ever seemed like a community, it now took on the color of a factory controlled by a corporation. Often it paid dividends to foreign investors like the English syndicate that owned Bert Snyder's 101 Ranch in Nebraska. A British manager supervised the seven hundred employees from his twenty-room townhouse. Foreign investment in trans-Mississippi cattle ranching by the mid-1880s reached as high as 45 million dollars. On the ranch a cowboy was vaguely aware that the owners sat in expensive offices in Kansas City or London.

In the case of the great Texas XIT, an extreme example, the Chicago proprietors held its three million acres primarily for speculation in land. In such a context attitudes were inevitably affected. In the 1890s the XIT was riddled with petty theft. The manager brought the situation under control, he proudly reported, "by fear."[30] It was a long way from Cabeza de Baca's grand *patrón* with his employee sons and daughters.

Then, too, much of ranch community had thrived on mutual hostility against settlers, a solidarity in defense of the open range. But by the end of the century the open range was little more than a dream. Bert Snyder in 1906 was one of the last to give in and file on his land to protect it from homesteaders. A modus vivendi was reached with farmers. Friendships grew, intermarriages occurred, and the sense of cattle-kingdom distinction weakened.[31]

[30] Snyder, *Pinnacle Jake*, p. 92; William G. Kerr, *Scottish Capital on the American Credit Frontier*, p. 48; Haley, *XIT Ranch*, pp. 6, 56–57, 206.

[31] Snyder, *Pinnacle Jake*, p. 352; Frantz and Choate, *The American Cowboy*, p. 106.

Horizontal class lines extending beyond the ranch became more important than ties within the ranch. The
commonality had reached out in layers and spread like
oil on water. It was reflected in the camaraderie of stock-
men's clubrooms in San Antonio, Denver, and Cheyenne.
The Wyoming Association, over three hundred members
by 1885, grew notorious imposing its will on cowboys and
small ranchers. Its counterparts from Texas to Montana,
intellectual descendants of the medieval Spanish *mesta*,
held heavy modern class and economic connotations.[32]
They tackled transportation, marketing, and rustling and
sent their men to the legislatures. Eventually, beyond
their regions, though torn by wrangling, they joined together at national conventions in Chicago and Saint Louis.

At the other end of the spectrum the independent spirit
of the cowboy, attached to nothing but horse and outfit,
was jogging along into oblivion, as Rojas put it. The cowhand now bore the stamp of wage earner; he could be
dismissed as readily as any factory worker and consequently lost much of his connection to the ranch community. He became a fluctuating labor supply facing
corporate impersonality. He often drifted from job to job.
At the Spring Ranch in Texas after 1885, 64 percent of
the cowboys stayed for only one season and only 3 percent
lasted for five years.[33]

If he tried, as many did, to save a bit from his wages,
buy a small ranch, and raise his own small herd, he was
frequently blacklisted as a rustler. Hiring such a blacklisted cowboy could cost up to three thousand dollars in

[32] Myers, *The Ranch in Spanish Texas,* p. 34; Donald E. Worcester,
"The Significance of the Spanish Borderlands to the United States,"
Western Historical Quarterly 7 (January, 1976): 6.

[33] Rojas, *California Vaquero,* p. 194; Terry G. Jordan, "The Origin
and Distribution of Open-Range Cattle Ranching," *Social Science Quarterly* 53 (June, 1972): 117; Atherton, *Cattle Kings,* p. 16.

forfeited bond.[34] As the cowhands sidled around, they picked up reputations: "burned out bad with whiskey and disease." Siberts in South Dakota described "the scrubby bunch" working for half the year and then filling in as pimps in town until ranch jobs opened up again. Most of the Texas kids coming through, he said, had malaria or hookworm. In this world of increasing rifts and distinctions developed the emotions of Robin Hood and social banditry. The small cowboy could take from the big ranch, could live off "O. P. [other people's] beef." It was not stealing, as far as the thief was concerned.

One historian described life on the large ranches as a framework of suspicion. To Siberts, "Everybody seemed on outs with everybody else." The ranch community was unraveling into its associative parts, sensing social distinctions, assessing class positions. Subgroups broke the old nets of attachment. Organizers for the Knights of Labor came around, signed up members among the old, loyal cowboys, and called strikes. An economic consciousness rose in cowhands. In March, 1883, punchers on the LX, the XIT, and the LS ranches handed to their bosses written ultimatums demanding a wage of fifty dollars a month. The result was a strike just before roundup time, when the men had the heaviest bargaining power, but the ranchers brought in Texas Rangers and won. Charles Siringo, the cowhand, said that the whole affair made a raft of enemies. A few years later in Wyoming the same pattern was repeated. Stockgrowers there in 1886 had banded together to cut wages, and as a consequence it was easy for the Knights of Labor to gain recruits. John Clay, Scottish agent for several cattle companies, described the strike with a tinge of bitterness, thinking of the strikers almost as bums. By the 1890s even New Mexican ranchos saw chapters of *Los Cabelleros de*

---

[34] Sandoz, *The Cattlemen*, p. 225.

Labor.[35] Indeed, as Rojas had said, the old vaquero was jogging into oblivion.

Richard King, like Arnold Rojas, wanted to bridge the cultures. An Anglo, he would have liked to have been the *patrón,* the *hacendado.* The New York boy turned Texan created the semblance of a Mexican rancho along the Santa Gertrudis River. He consciously patterned his foundations on the "primal outlines" of the Mexican model. Among his closest friends and managers were men with names like Patiño and Villa. Once he brought a whole Mexican town from Tamaulipas to the Santa Gertrudis: one hundred people, belongings, *carretas,* burros, and all. As on the Cabeza de Baca or Jaramillo ranchos, King built his *casa grande* in the midst of the adobes of the vaqueros, near the sheds and workshops, near the church with its bell and tall cross. But King and his partners, like Mifflin Kenedy and Legs Lewis, also built one of the most impressive business enterprises in western history. He ranged 600,000 cattle, and he made money, a lot of it. As he and his family grew wealthy, they constructed another big house in Brownsville, and the would-be *patrón* and his wife spent time among their kineños only in the pleasant seasons. Business feelings imposed on sentiment so that in 1881 King could write, "The Mexicans won't work and things are getting in a hell of a fix fast." His stockgrowers' association acted against thieves. For the vagabonds crossing his lands he posed as a "maneater," to avoid, he thought, being killed. While cowboys on ranches around him were beginning to join the Knights

[35]Wyman and Siberts, *Nothing but Prairie and Sky,* pp. 100, 142, 67; Atherton, *Cattle Kings,* p. 182; Gonzalez, *Spanish-Americans,* p. 92; Lewis Nordyke, *Great Roundup,* pp. 109–10; Ruth Allen, *Chapters in the History of Organized Labor in Texas,* pp. 33–40; Charles A. Siringo, *A Lone Star Cowboy,* p. 268; John Clay, *My Life on the Range,* pp. 122–24; Helena H. Smith, *The War on Powder River,* pp. 31–33.

of Labor, the proud Richard King died, not the *hacendado* in the midst of his lands and people, but far away in a San Antonio hotel room.[36] As an Anglo, like Rojas the Mexican, he had clutched at an older brand of community while living in a newer age in which only the symbols and rhetoric of the old ranch could survive.

[36]Lea, *King Ranch*, pp. 140, 351, 268–69, 348–51, 368.

Chapter Eight

The Ethnic Colony:
An Ark in a
Strange Land

When I was a boy [in Dannebrog, Nebraska], I often
thought the sun shone a little brighter on our community than upon other communities in our country. I am
sure that some of the old Danes felt that these strangers
lived in the great darkness.

Alfred Nielsen, *Life in an American Denmark* (1962)

THE MEMBERS OF THE GERMAN AMANA SOCIETY, unhappy in
New York State and seeking another home, were attracted
by the cheap lands of the frontier, the fertile soil they found
in Iowa at $1.25 an acre. Communitarian ventures have
always delighted in the frontier pledge of cheap land. When
two or three people were gathered together in the name of
any cause or category, the frontier beckoned. Its seclusion
encouraged hopes for untrammeled beliefs and for closer
group attachments unfolding within the walls of wilderness.
Such colonization on the frontier was a constant note in the
cacophony of settlement.

Supporting such colonization, ethnicity was surely the
most effective force. The ethnic bond was drawn from the
precious attractiveness of the familiar—the language, the
habit, the taste of food and drink, the color of skin and hair,
the nuance of creed, the tempo of living, and the shape of
roof and wall. In Ole Rölvaag's novel, *Giants in the Earth*,
a knot of potential colonists, five Norwegian families facing
the hostile prairies, agree to stay together and not let "anyone

get in between us."[1] The ethnic bond—racial, national, cultural—had to be strong enough for identity, strong enough
to separate the colony from those who might "get in between
us." Those outside were the aliens, the gentiles (the Latin
equivalent of the Greek word for ethnic). The colony stood
alone in a foreign field. What to the outside world was heresy
was to it catholicity and truth. It was a magnetic situation,
pulling a community together.

These colonies could recruit from a pool of compatriots
on the frontier. Of the Nebraska population in 1870, 25
percent was foreign-born; of the Dakota Territory population, 34 percent. In Henry County, Illinois, between 1828
and 1846, of the thirty-eight colony settlements, nine were
of European ethnics. By 1860 non-British immigrants were
noticeable throughout the Far West in groups and compact
settlements.[2] There were Polish and Russian, Bohemian,
Jewish, Roman Catholic, and black colonies. Examining
frontier community without looking at ethnicity would be
like studying the frontier without recognizing the availability of land.

In assessing community among ethnic colonies, the fit
between the colony and the prevailing culture would ultimately determine persistence. The larger the ethnic colony, the higher were the barriers raised around it; the
more distinct the cultural differences between colony and
prevailing society, the greater its longevity. Hardship generally aided the cooperative community, but sometimes

[1] Ole E. Rölvaag, *Giants in the Earth,* p. 33.
[2] Frederick C. Luebke, "Ethnic Group Settlement on the Great
Plains," *Western Historical Quarterly* 8 (October, 1977): 405–406.
Among foreign-born the largest group was German, the British second,
the Scandinavian third. Southern Europeans tended to stay in the East;
Ronald E. Nelson, "The Role of the Colonies in the Pioneer Settlement
of Henry County, Illinois" (Ph.D. diss., University of Nebraska, 1970),
pp. 11–12; Jack E. Eblen, "An Analysis of Nineteenth-Century Frontier
Populations," *Demography,* no. 2 (1965): 404.

economic decline forced the breaking of ties with the old ways in order to survive in the new.[3] If self-sufficiency could be attained, isolation was a binding agent. But whatever the environmental interactions, the basic bond within was ethnicity, intensified by frontier conditions. Here, as rarely in the homeland, German Lutherans could cooperate with German Catholics and occasionally with German socialists. Such barriers, however, were seldom hurdled in strictly rural areas, but only in the looser ethnic communities that grew up in this country, associative communities of bank and marketplace, of immigrants falling together as similar particles form sandstone.

Ethnics could create subgroups within a larger community, breaking its homogeneity, fracturing its unity. They often chose to be exclusive, just as groups who had arrived earlier chose to exclude them. Merle Curti's scrutiny of a Wisconsin frontier county showed that Polish, Norwegian, and German groups were accepted in the early years of the settlement but that a decade or so later, in the 1870s, prejudice and separation clearly emerged. The Yankees always expected the minorities to conform to their ways. Jacksonville, Illinois, in 1849 still cherished its ideal of homogeneity, happily welcoming a colony of Portuguese because they were converts to Protestantism. Yet the Portuguese were diverted into a separate section of town, with their own church and their own economic contribution, chiefly domestic labor. Irish Catholics were similarly looked upon, and it was clear that the community did not want Negroes.[4] Seth Humphrey in the Dakotas seldom visited the nearby colony of Russian-Germans. When he did, his immigrant host usually cleaned his gun as they

[3] Compare the same process with individual foreigners: Ralph Mann, "The Decade After the Gold Rush," *Pacific Historical Review* 41 (November, 1972): 502; Luebke, "Ethnic Group Settlement," p. 425.

[4] Merle Curti, *The Making of an American Community*, pp. 98, 100; Don Doyle, *The Social Order of a Frontier Community*, pp. 128, 129, 137, 145, 148; John L. Shover, *First Majority—Last Minority*, p. 43.

talked, "as suspicious of me as I was of him."[5] In frontier Wheatland, Missouri, it was a group of Frenchmen, "the Ballou nation," that was the butt of the town's ridicule. Aliens were generally blamed for the decay of small-town life; the ethnics thought to bear "no historical connection with the place," which was "no longer a community as it once was."[6]

If we turn to the viewpoint of ethnics within their own colonies, and particularly those colonies migrating intact, the ethnics were far less willing to drop barriers and were far more intensely cooperative. Transplanting always threatened the survival of the group's traditional ways of doing and thinking. Addressing this central danger left little energy for utopianism, for visions of changing the host society. The ethnics might actively encourage fellow ethnics—fellow Jews, Irish, Swedes, or Welsh—but they did not imagine transforming American society. True, they could color an entire cultural landscape, like the Germans in parts of Wisconsin or the Swedes in Minnesota counties. Poles in the 1880s dreamed of a pure Polish county in central Nebraska. And a Negro colony leader once seriously proposed that Oklahoma be made an all-black state. But theirs was not a missionary purpose. It was, again, an awareness that only together could they preserve their ways. Alone, like a foreigner in a mining camp, a chilling phrase was like a chilling cultural nightmare: "Sickness thus overtook the stranger."[7] The group spelled survival.

[5] Seth K. Humphrey, *Following the Prairie Frontier*, p. 149. For similar segregation of Germans in Oklahoma see Allie B. Wallace, *Frontier Life in Oklahoma*, pp. 21–23. See also Hiram Drache, *Challenge of the Prairie*, pp. 234–36.

[6] Carl Withers, "Plainville, U.S.A.," in *Psychological Frontiers of Society*, ed. Abram Kardiner, pp. 58–59; Nathaniel Egleston, *Villages and Village Life*, p. 23.

[7] Meroe J. Owens, "John Barzynski, Land Agent," *Nebraska History* 36 (June, 1955): 91; Mozell Hill, "The All-Negro Communities of Okla-

But it might also spell genuine community, depending on
its willingness to recreate a new sense of place, its awareness of size as a factor in the quality of cooperative life,
and its devotion to overriding values.

"Oh, a Spring or Summer morning on the prairies!"
wrote a Swedish colonist. "How one then forgets all the
difficulties of pioneer life." A new sense of place was
dawning in a man whose adopted terrain was as different
from his native haunts as a moon plain. His family had
for generations been distinguished by a parish with its
church at the hub of life. A continental immigrant could
in the same way identify with a peasant village, "a fixed
point in which he knew his position in the world and his
relationship with all humanity." That village had been a
whole, one chorus, one valley, one sky, with everyone and
everything knitted together. Like the New England Puritan town, the peasant village was a natural model, an
assumed goal in the New World. The model was built
upon noncontiguous small landholdings, one man's lands
interspersed among others. There should also be land for
common pasturage and common woodcutting. Cooperative
work should be feasible and spontaneous, and common-
place. In the American West, however, land policy dictated individual holdings in large tracts, making difficult
the continuity of village forms. German Mennonites once
shrewdly commented to the railroad agents that ownership of land in common was a necessary condition of group
settlement.[8] A large, privately owned farm, of course,
proved highly attractive to Europeans. It was a compen-
sation that overcame mountains of anxiety, hardship, and

homa," *Journal of Negro History* 31 (July, 1946): 260; John Steele,
In Camp and Cabin, pp. 119–21.

[8] Olaf Olsson, quoted by Emory Lindquist, *Smokey Valley People*,
p. 63; Oscar Handlin, *The Uprooted*, p. 8; David Emmons, *Garden in
the Grasslands* (Lincoln, Nebr., 1971), p. 115.

pain. But at the same time it was a serious detriment to the continuation and growth of communal ties.

Mobility too cut like an acid into community life, speeding the assimilation or dispersal of ethnic colonies. The wider distribution of large immigrant groups like the Germans encouraged mobility, one reason that it was harder for them to maintain ethnic institutions than, say, for the Norwegians.[9] German religious colonies often proved an alternative to this rule.

Gypsies, however, were the grand exception to the catalytic quality of mobility. Although constantly moving, at least from spring to fall, they managed to preserve their ethnic community. As outcasts they were bound by the power of persecution and spoke a common language, a mother tongue, Romani. Organized into small bands and tribes, the families remained extremely vital. They held their own tribunals, and the breaking of a Gypsy law could bring excommunication from the community. Their economic system embraced work in common, and the income from their traditional trades, ranging from fortune-telling to coppersmithing, was largely shared. Their life-style gave them a common identity, from bright kerchiefs to a passion for God's highways. Indeed, their restlessness was appropriate in America. Their small bands of a dozen or so families, afoot or in wagons, straggled across the western roads between isolated farms. By the 1890s they were adding an occasional but characteristic dab of color to the frontier. To Allie Wallace in Oklahoma, Gypsy packs with silks, ivories, bracelets, and jewels were mental tapestries of adventure in foreign lands. Grace Snyder might label them "a seedy outfit" in public, but her description of the "bold, dark skinned people" would suggest that she too was intrigued by these nomadic ethnic communities.[10]

The Germans, the largest immigrant group on the Great

[9] Luebke, "Ethnic Group Settlements," p. 427.

Plains, usually migrated as families and were later drawn together as colonies or settlements. Thus Milwaukee after its beginnings in 1836 could be called an ethnic colony — echoing strains of "Die Lorelei" in the beer garden and "Ein feste Burge" in the church. There were turnvereins and coffee klatches. At the same time Germans shared a common interest in adapting to a new land, growing as part of a territory, state, and nation. All the while the community possessed the past, and there its people could return as for refreshment on a long journey, aided by the foreign-language newspapers, full of events of the homeland, often read word for word. But growth and heterogeneity came too. When possible, the one-third of the Catholic Germans separated from the Lutherans. Churches held together their own but did not bind the whole. The poor came to live in a vaguely drawn circle on the outskirts of town. Diversity made possible a welter of subgroups — music clubs, temperance societies, lodges like the Druids and the Sons of Herman, and non-German groups like the Harugari and the Wise Men. The *Gesellschaft* thrived while the *Gemeinschaft* weakened. Although heterogeneity had taken its toll of unity, it had created a broader society ready to respond to the pluralistic tenor of American life.[11]

Far more cohesive were those German colonies that migrated from Europe undivided. They were seldom new to the communal life. Some of them were Mennonites, children of harsh persecution after the Reformation, who in centuries of migrations to areas like Prussia and Russia had learned a cohesive fellowship that was "intimate and tight." In the 1870s they saw their sons being drafted into

[10] Wallace, *Frontier Life,* pp. 32–33; Grace Snyder, *No Time on My Hands,* pp. 154–55; Irving Brown, "The Gypsies in America," *Journal of the Gypsy Lore Society* 8 (1929): 145–76.

[11] Kathleen N. Conzen, *Immigrant Milwaukee, 1836–1860,* pp. 157, 163, 164, 135, 156, 64, 84, 154, 168, 160, 173.

the army, brutalizing their pacifist beliefs. The Mennonites moved again, many in little bands to the Great Plains, especially to Kansas, Nebraska, Iowa, and Missouri. They found that middle westerners tended to tolerate their differences more readily than did the people of the Dnieper or the Vistula. Still, these little islands of European culture lived apart, introducing to the West straw-burning ovens and Turkey Red wheat while holding firm to their German language and peculiar beliefs. To Gnadenau, in Kansas, "the meadow of grace," Jacob Wiebe had led thirty-four families of Mennonites in the spring of 1874. Within a decade visitors were noting how they had transformed the area with forests of Russian olive and mulberry and hedges that neatly defined their farmlands while suggesting the quiet and simple unity of the community.[12]

At the other end of the spectrum Jewish colonies seemed incapable of creating a new sense of place; at least they failed to adjust to agriculture on the Great Plains. In the 1880s and 1890s a dozen such colonies started in dugouts and soddies, eight in Kansas alone; but none lasted more than a few years. Many were the offspring of Om Olam, an organization supporting Russian and German Jewish groups in their move to the American West. At the same time men like Julius Goldman, of the Hebrew Emigrant Aid Society, searched modern Goshens to test Isaiah's plowshares and pruning hooks. At Bethlehem Yehudah in South Dakota thirty-two Jews farmed 165 acres and claimed that "all members constitute one family possessing equal rights and privileges." At Beersheba, near Dodge City, Kansas, sixty Jews built dugouts and a sod synagogue in the middle of a cattle trail. By 1883 they had eighteen houses and flowing wells, but little farming success. Some

---

[12] Edwin Gaustad, *Dissent in American Religion*, p. 132; John Hostetler, *Amish Society* (Baltimore, Md., 1963), pp. 27, 40–50; Kendall Bailes, "The Mennonites Come to Kansas," *American Heritage* 10 (August, 1959): 102–103.

tried the cattle business, but by 1884 the colonists had drifted away. They blamed poor soil and drought, though generally these were not bad years for farming. More likely they had simply not adapted to plains agriculture and its isolation.[13]

The size of the colony was always a factor in maintaining or undermining ethnicity. A larger mass encased cultural forms like a seedpod, whereas a small group invited infiltration. But, as we have so often seen, growth can be a danger to community, multiplying tensions and subgroups and undermining unity. The more polyglot the community, the faster was its decline into assimilation.[14]

The German Hutterites, one offshoot of the Reformation radicalism that had also bred the Mennonites, formed ethnic colonies of extraordinary unity. They proved unusually right for the West, at least when they claimed to need from the outside world only isolation and good water. Beyond these, "Each colony considers itself symbolic of Noah's ark, a God-given provision for living in a world that is otherwise hopelessly lost." The more isolated it was, the better, for the outside society lived by competition, a car-

---

[13] A Jewish colony at New Odessa, in Oregon, did little better. But Hebrew chicken farmers in Petaluma, California, prospered after 1903. By 1925 there were 100 families in that settlement, with an organized social life around a community center. One resident, Basha Singerman, said that "in the early days the whole Jewish community became like a family, like one big family." Zelda Bronstein and Kenneth Kann, "Basha Singerman, Comrade of Petaluma," *California Historical Quarterly* 56 (Spring, 1977): 25, 27; Leo Shpall, "Jewish Agricultural Colonies in the United States," *Agricultural History* 24 (July, 1950): 132–35; Elbert Sapinsley, "Jewish Agricultural Colonies in the West," *Western States Jewish Historical Quarterly* 3 (April, 1971): 159–60; A. James Rudin, "Beersheba, Kansas," *Kansas Historical Quarterly* 34 (Autumn, 1968): 286–96; Luebke, "Ethnic Group Settlements," p. 420; Robert S. Fogarty, "American Communes, 1865–1914," *Journal of American Studies* 9 (August, 1975): 158.

[14] Luebke, "Ethnic Group Settlements," pp. 428, 424.

nal sin. The Hutterites were a remnant of the Protestant Reformation that had colonized marginal areas of Russia for nearly a hundred years. In the 1870s, at the same time as the Mennonites did, they moved to America, setting up the Bon Homme colony in South Dakota in 1874. By then their beliefs were firmly directed against private property; they erected in its place "a communism of love" in both production and consumption, "the new *Gemeinschaft.*" Otherwise their culture remained German, and they contended that their faith was best expressed in the German language.

In 1878, when the first colony was crowded with fresh arrivals, a daughter colony, a *Neudorf,* was planned. The first branch was Tripp, thirty-six miles west. The process continued, and by the early twentieth century the Hutterites had nineteen colonies strung along the western border states and in Canada. They repeatedly demonstrated their sensitivity to size as a function of community. After an average of fourteen years, when a colony reached about 140 people, cell division began, new lands were purchased, and the split took place. Kinships were broken, but individual will had to be subordinated to the will of the community. The result was the perpetuation of "small, manageable, face-to-face domestic groups."[15]

Almost a generation earlier and five hundred miles south along the Iowa River, the Amana Society had worked out a similar destiny. Heirs of German pietism but followers of the particular vision of a self-lettered factory worker and servant girl, Barbara Heineman, they had moved as a colony to upstate New York. Yet they felt greater isolation essential to the preservation of their faith, and were soon seeking "a secluded, quiet place in the West." In summer, 1855, they found in central Iowa 26,000 acres of oak, hickory, and maple, meadows and fertile

[15] John A. Hostetler, *Hutterite Society,* pp. 1, 16–17, 126, 150, 185; Paul K. Conkin, *Two Paths to Utopia,* pp. 51–52.

fields to which they planted corn and grain. Eighteen hundred people eventually joined, but that number, too large in their minds for true community, was divided into seven separate villages, secluded German *dorfs* among the Iowa hills.

The Amana ideal was a community of loving, peaceful hospitality, simple as a Shaker room. Amana combined and preserved the German language and culture; in its separate villages it protected communality. Arriving members surrendered private property to the community, hoping to lose that air of accumulation characteristic of the outside world. The population remained remarkably stable, largely growing from within. As among the Hutterites and the Puritans, the divisiveness of democracy was avoided: the villages were run by a "great council" elected by the elders of the church. But cooperation was assumed. In periods of common need, such as sewing clothes, harvesting crops, or repairing machinery, everyone, no matter his trade, joined in. Responsibility was buttressed by the education of the young. Children were trained in those vocations needed by the community, and the communal schools were run "like a large household." Life held little frivolity, no cards or dancing, but visitors commented on the joy in work, unhurried, unpressured, careful, and varied. The eleven or twelve church meetings each week, however, served a social purpose. Houses were built with as little distinctiveness as possible, helping minimize individuality. Patents (important items for the future manufacturers of blankets and refrigerators) were issued in the name of the community, not an individual. "The 'me' spirit was subordinated to the 'we' spirit," they said. Amana lasted as a truly communal society until 1932 and then incorporated in such a way as to preserve as many as possible of the earlier traditions.[16]

[16] William R. Perkins and Barthinius L. Wick, *History of the Amana Society*, pp. 53, 70; Bertha M. H. Shambaugh, *Amana That Was and*

The value systems of ethnic colonies were usually heavy-laden with religion. Amana, resting in its Bible communism, felt faith to be "the only bond that can unite men in true fellowship." There were a few anticlerical Czech colonies, but they were balanced by other Czechs, especially Moravians, who were strongly religious.[17]

A striking example was the Irish colonization directed by the Roman Catholic church. After the success of the Mormons in Utah, the Irish began thinking of western colonization, but the movement was set afire in 1875 by recently ordained Bishop John Ireland in Saint Paul. Ireland was Irish-born, but his parents migrated, first to Vermont, then to Illinois, and finally to Minnesota. John became a firm-jawed, magnetic personality, capable of total absorption, like one "brooding over the enigma of life." One of his absorbing goals was Roman Catholic colonization in the West. By 1885, through various of his organizations, he had seen four thousand Catholic families emigrate to at least ten frontier settlements. To form a colony under the sponsorship of the Irish Immigration Society, the colonists had to be Roman Catholics with a priest in their ranks. Their hope was to create Catholic communities economically integrated into their surroundings, Catholic or not. These little villages, like De Graf, Clontarf, Currie, Graceville, predominantly Irish but with a few French, Germans, and Belgians, averaged about 650 people. Newcomers received five acres, and all members of the community under the supervision of the priest gathered to raise their new house. There were monthly fairs, races, suppers, community sings, and dances, but

Amana That Is, pp. 169, 94, 152, 115, 145–46, 86–87, 168, 148–49, 114, 160, 337–38; Frederick A. Bushee, "Communistic Societies," *Political Science Quarterly* 20 (December, 1905): 643.

[17] Perkins and Wick, *History of the Amana Society,* p. 65; Luebke, "Ethnic Group Settlements," pp. 418–19.

throughout, as on a Mexican rancho, life centered in the church—vespers, prayers for good harvests, triumphant "Te Dcums" when the crops were garnered, processions through the streets following the Blessed Sacrament. These villagers made "an extraordinary effort" to forge a community "in which their religious life could be fulfilled," in which religion was the base for social cohesion and like-mindedness.

The Roman Catholic colonization movement had withered by the 1890s from lack of general support. The communities it had nurtured remained. Those who had originally come for escape from the East or cities or poor farms tended to move on seeking something better. Those who had come with the positive expectation of religious community tended to remain. But in the effort to integrate economically with the rest of the society, heterogeneity inevitably followed. Roman Catholic colonies thereafter became little more than small towns on the middle border. Roman Catholicism in them remained strong, but a Hamlin Garland, perhaps with a slight brogue, might have emerged from any of them.[18]

Ethnic colonies held tightly to the family, endorsing all its traditional values. These immigrants seldom approached the West unless surrounded by spouses, children, and relatives. Even when Germans or Irish or Jews migrated as entire communities, the family formed the spine of communal life. Nowhere was this clearer than in colonies of Scandinavians.

In 1846 about twenty families of Swedish Nonconformist farmers, persecuted in Sweden for their religion, followed Eric Janson to ten thousand acres called Bishop Hill, Illinois. "I am come in Christ's place," Janson said,

---

[18] James Moynihan, *The Life of Archbishop John Ireland*, p. 383; James P. Shannon, *Catholic Colonization on the Western Frontier*, pp. 264, 265, 126, 53, 184, 175, 204–205, 244, 83.

Harvesting Grain, Bishop Hill, Illinois
Contemporary painting by Olof Krans, about 1848
Illinois Department of Conservation — Bishop Hill Historical Site

"to bring grace." He was an angular man, scar-faced with protruding teeth, but he was full of charm and eloquence. He led the colony through some wretched years, including a disastrous cholera epidemic, and by 1850 at least eight hundred people had followed him to Illinois. In that year they were rocked by the dissidence of John Root, whose wife preferred to stay in the colony rather than leave with him. Enraged, Root shot Janson. Although traumatic, the event was not lethal, and the colony prospered for a while. Family ties at Bishop Hill were never broken, though there was some problem over a doctrine of celibacy in the later years. Families lived separately, even with private accommodations in the ninety-five-room central building, the

"Big Brick." But they always ate in common and were clothed from a central store. By the late 1850s the railroads had destroyed their isolation, and the depression of 1857 hit their financial structure. Religious issues after Janson's death broke the unity of worship. By 1861 they were ready for the individualization of their property.[19]

Olaf Olsson, a minister of the Established Swedish church, in 1869 led another band of Swedes to thirteen thousand acres, called Lindsborg, near Salina, Kansas. A collection of families, thirty-five in all, offered "prayers of gratitude from the dugouts." Olsson held the group together with his kind, considerate personality. Although he was only twenty-eight years old, he had learned how a touch of mysticism could overcome stress. The family was even more helpful. Lindsborg never lost its sense of connection between family and church, conducting services in homes as well as in the *bolagshuset,* their central building. Each home was a self-contained unit, but it was also intimately tied to the whole, like the ship moored to the dock in Edward Shorter's metaphor of the extended family. The community provided the family with a midwife at time of birth. It gathered for a wedding. It offered festivities as on Midsummer's Eve or in work parties around cheese making. Through all these activities ran the love of music: a choir sang a Christmas concert within a year of settlement. These Swedes always thought that music enabled them to meet "the challenge of the incomplete but the possible." Their cultural equipment was serving them well.

Within a few years, however, other groups had moved into the area. Swedish Methodists arrived. Other outsiders opened a billiard parlor. The West was proving its threat. Doctrinal differences grew into ugly proportions. In the-

---

[19] Olov Isaksson, *Bishop Hill, Illinois,* pp. 36, 95; Michael A. Mikkelsen, *The Bishop Hill Colony,* pp. 45, 42, 60–63; Nelson, "Role of the Colonies," p. 136.

Swedish Ladies' Aid, Nebraska, about 1895
Nebraska State Historical Society

ology the groups disagreed over the meaning of Christ's
Atonement; in policy, over their connections with the
Augustana Synod. Neighbor was pitted against neighbor,
friend against friend. By 1877 the strength of the original
religious unity had evaporated, and heterogeneity had
taken its toll.[20]

Danish families were no different in their cohesiveness.

[20] Lindquist, *Smokey Valley People,* pp. 13, 51, 82, 14, 63. See also
Ruth Billdt, *Pioneer Swedish-American Culture in Central Kansas,*
pp. 24–32; J. I. Dowie, *Prairie Grass Dividing,* p. 27. Bethany College,
founded in 1881, was an effort to regain traditional forms.

Sod-house interior, Dannebrog, Nebraska, 1895
Nebraska State Historical Society

One of their main centers on the Great Plains was at
Dannebrog, Nebraska, settled in 1871 and named for the
Danish national flag, the white cross on red. Here young
Alfred Nielsen was raised, in the midst of families gathering for community events or converging on the folk school
for plays, lectures, and music. Family events were sub-
sumed in colony events, like Danish Constitution Day in
June, with parades and a great tug-of-war. When Alfred's
sister was married, two hundred people came. The community had taken a collection to furnish the house. The
wedding ceremony was followed by a midnight supper,
coffee and rum at 2:00 A.M., and dancing until dawn. It

192   COMMUNITY ON THE AMERICAN FRONTIER

was another occasion in which the family, church, and community merged. When the family suffered, so too did the community. The Sorensens abused their adopted six-year-old boy; he was taken from them and given to another family. The men of the colony visited the Sorensens and told them, "You are not wanted in this community." The Sorensens left.

These Danes had brought with them the cooperative movement then sweeping Denmark. In Dannebrog they organized a cooperative grain elevator, a lumberyard, a freighting association, a creamery, and a credit union. For many years these cooperatives were highly successful, reflecting a sense of standing or falling together. As Nielsen said, the Danes began as "economic collectivists," but as time went on and they grew more familiar with America, they changed to "economic individualists." "Little by little group solidarity became weaker." The cooperatives began to fail. The folk school closed. And Nielsen sadly reminisced, "Weeds grew where flowers had grown."[21]

If family attachments were particularly notable in ethnic colonies, class tensions, conversely, lay far in the background. European immigrants were hardly unaware that for generations their substance had been wasted on taxes and war chests for the pastimes of the gentry. America offered relief from that burden of supporting the aristocracy. On the other hand, not all colonists were peasants. There were occasions when the gentry itself colonized the West. Runnymede, for example, was a "jolly lot of men and women transported to the Kansas prairie." Most of them were second sons of titled Englishmen, sent for conversion into diligent farmers. Some donned cowboy outfits, playing a western role as Teddy Roosevelt was doing in Dakota about the same time. But with or without their spurs and chaps, the Englishmen brought along polo, tennis, and

[21] Alfred C. Nielsen, *Life in an American Denmark,* pp. 64–68, 62, 140.

Scotch whiskey. Unfortunately for the colony, an expected railroad never came, but the droughts of the 1880s hit hard. By 1892 the colony had largely dispersed. Their economic and cultural demands had proved too uncompromising for the frontier. In a very few years of western life, "We wore off the varnish, broke the bank, and turned out the lights."

Colonizing by English gentry had similar results elsewhere. At Victoria, Kansas, in the 1870s the colonists owned their land collectively but maintained hunt clubs (using coyotes for foxes) and sailed yachts on the river. The poor, when they came, were relegated to a separate section of town, making Victoria far more a combination of classes and cliques than a community. In the same area, perhaps because they were not wealthy, Welsh colonists adapted better to plains farming. At least three strictly Welsh colonies were established in Kansas alone. Their language and culture, especially their love of singing, certainly did not hamper, indeed must have enhanced, the cohesion of their work.[22]

Blacks used colonies in the West for different purposes. They emphasized less the past and more an adaptation to the larger American mode. With their eyes fixed on middle-class values — self-reliance, enterprise, high consumption — blacks exploited community forms as a means of achieving a bigger share of economic and social resources. Booker T. Washington interpreted one such colony in terms of land seekers, builders, bankers and merchants, and corporate action. During slavery a few black colonies for freed slaves

[22]Blanche Taylor, "The English Colonies in Kansas, 1870–1895," *Historical Magazine of the Protestant Episcopal Church* 41 (March, 1972): 31–34, 25, 30; Handlin, *The Uprooted*, p. 15; Carolyn B. Berneking, "The Welsh Settlers of Emporia," *Kansas Historical Quarterly* 37 (Autumn, 1971): 276–78; Phillips G. Davies, ed., "Welsh Settlements in Kansas," *Kansas Historical Quarterly* 43 (Winter, 1977): 448–68.

were formed in Canada and Ohio. Elgin, Wilberforce, and Carthegena, for example, were attempts to prepare blacks for participation in white society. Frances Wright, however, in forming her colony of freed slaves at Nashoba, Tennessee, in 1825 was not actually looking toward integration. Rather she saw the colony training its members for separate black community life.

After the Civil War and especially following Reconstruction, southern blacks used the Middle West as an escape from poverty and social oppression. During a few months in 1879, six thousand from Texas, Louisiana, and Mississippi migrated to Kansas alone. It was indeed an exodus out of bondage. Throughout Oklahoma, Kansas, and Nebraska, small black towns grew up, most of them ephemeral. Economic salvation was their first motive, and they needed outside help at first. Some, though, developed their own community institutions, churches, and schools and gradually grew strong.

A Joshua of the colony movement, Benjamin Singleton, was in his seventies at the time of the exodus, with whitening hair and goatee. A small bundle of lightning energy, he proclaimed, "I am the whole cause of Kansas immigration." Propelled by revelation and steeped in folk religion, along with a shrewd speculator's drive, he believed in segregated communities for the blacks.

Nicodemus, Kansas, which took its name from the plantation slave song that Singleton as a boy could have sung, was first settled in 1877, one of a dozen indirectly inspired by men like him. Its initial colonists with some resources survived the usual period of dugouts, tents, and tears, but they were faced shortly with a wave of poorer Negroes from farther south. By 1880 there were 484 people in the town. Rifts ran among them, especially between the old settlers and the newcomers, but a community in time emerged. A sense of distinction grew. In addition to patriotic holidays they celebrated dates of slave

The black subcommunity, Clermont, Iowa, about 1870
Iowa State Historical Society

emancipation.[23] They had their own lodges and death-benefit societies, baseball teams, band, and literary clubs.

Oklahoma had twenty-five such communities, partly explainable by the number of former slaves once owned by Indians in that territory. In 1890, Edward McCabe, once of Nicodemus and now leader of the black colony at Langston, even proposed Oklahoma as an all-Negro state. McCabe thought of his colony at Langston as a place "where the black man was to prosper and rule supreme in his own community." He was like another colonist who, thinking of his past role in society, said, "I don't always want to be led." Booker T. Washington saw these black colonies in terms of "dawning race consciousness," proof that Negroes could govern themselves. The move to colonies was thus a response to former conditions, like slavery, or a challenge thrown at the prevailing society. It was seldom a desire to work out forms of community as ends in themselves. Therefore, conditions in the outer society always had unusually severe impact. The colony at Langston, for example, was seriously drained by the Oklahoma land rushes of the 1890s and by a slow drift to cities for employment. These colonies were consequently like rafts in a surf of giant swells.[24]

[23] William H. Pease and Jane H. Pease, *Black Utopias*, pp. 2, 18; Nell I. Painter, *Exodusters*, pp. 184, 108; W. Sherman Savage, *Blacks in the West*, pp. 194, 199; Glen Schweedenmann, "Nicodemus: Negro Haven on the Soloman," *Kansas Historical Quarterly* 34 (Spring, 1968): 28; William L. Katz, *The Black West*, p. 313; Leonard Dinnerstein et al., *Natives and Strangers*, p. 212; Robert Athearn, *In Search of Canaan: Black Migration to Kansas, 1879–80*, pp. 167, 183–84. Norman Crockett, *Black Towns*, pp. 1–6, 174–75.

[24] Hill, "The All-Negro Communities," pp. 260, 265; Booker T. Washington, "Boley, a Negro Town in the West," *Outlook* 88 (January 4, 1908), reprinted in Katz, *The Black West*, pp. 315–16. In 1915, Deerfield, a black colony, was founded near Masters, Colorado; it lasted into the 1940s; Loveland *Reporters Herald*, April 22, 1946; *Rocky Mountain News*, February 2, 1973. The black colony Allensworth,

Ethnic awareness, said Michael Novak, the modern theologian, "is not self-enclosing; it is genuine community, honest and unpretending." The ethnic bond can initiate and ennoble community, as was exemplified on the Mexican rancho. In the American West that process worked in at least two ways. First, as we have seen, it has created subgroups within the larger community. Through lodges and associations ethnic culture provided a base for approaching the prevailing society. We have seen such groups undermining the *Gemeinschaft,* splitting the unity of the whole. In New Mexico in the 1890s, for example, the Alianza Hispano-Americana gave Mexicans all the benefits of a lodge plus cultural continuity. At the same time the Goras Blancas, a vigorously antiestablishment Mexican group, confronted rather than cooperated with the larger society. In either case their presence split the wider community while cementing the smaller.[25]

Second, ethnicity has infused and nurtured separate colonies. In the West, ethnics' "honest and unpretending communities" often succeeded in capturing community spirit remarkably well. The best of them exuded a sense of place, the traditional attachment to the soil now transplanted. They reverentially tended and loved the earth with more sensitivity than most American frontiersmen exhibited. Colonies that failed (like Jewish groups) were

---

near Bakersfield, California, in the 1920s, was an example of blacks reacting to city conditions and trying to organize their own colony. They proved unable to overcome problems like water supply, over which they had no control. Eleanor Ramsey, "Allensworth: A Study in Social Change" (Ph.D. diss., University of California, Berkeley, 1977).

[25] Michael Novak, *The Rise of the Unmeltable Ethnics,* p. xvi; Nancie L. Gonzalez, *Spanish-Americans of New Mexico,* pp. 88–90. Mexicans have not been discussed in this chapter because their numbers in the Southwest transcended colony status. Chinese have not been discussed because they were largely urban and hence less related to the frontier.

The Mexican subcommunity, Fourth of July, before 1900,
represented by the Alianza Hispano Americana, Tucson,
Arizona
Arizona Historical Society

often those with a lesser sense of place, developing less empathy with the peculiar qualities of the western terrain. The more successful brought the design of the peasant village, rich with close personal contact and laden with cooperative implications. Colonists who came without this peasant example, like the second sons of English gentry or former slaves, did less well. The village tradition rested on the family, which in turn insinuated itself into all of the community. Likewise, religion and community were often inseparable, and colonies like the Hutterites and Amana were communities simply because the colonists were children of God, though the name of their God was spelled in German.

In these colonies, except perhaps for those of the Hutterites, the frontier bolstered but little the forces working for community. True, it offered hardship and a reality for the metaphor of the wilderness. But it constantly tempered the ideal of stability. With its temptations to mobility, deeper attachments to place seldom lasted into another generation. The policy of establishing large, individualized farms in the West hindered the village ideal. The constant flow of new arrivals, both within and around the ethnic circle, injected heterogeneity and disunity. And the internal and external insistent pressures to assimilate into American society were drains, like slow hemorrhages, on traditional community values. Michael Novak's genuine community, "honest and unpretending," nourished by the juices of ethnicity, was frequent enough in the American West, but the frontier was not a congenial environment.

Chapter Nine

Cooperative Colonies:
"These Socialistic Paroxysms"

> Our Principles will, I trust, spread from Community to Community, from State to State, from Continent to Continent, until this system and these truths shall overshadow the whole earth, shedding fragrance and abundance, intelligence and happiness upon all the sons of men.
>
> Robert Owen, New Harmony, Indiana,
> July 4, 1826

GEORGE BERNARD SHAW, commenting on his play *Man and Superman,* chose John Humphrey Noyes as "one of those chance attempts at the Superman."[1] Indeed, Noyes, a tall, commanding figure from a prominent New England family, offered a Promethean vision, and he imagined a whole society following his lead. Noyes extolled the cooperative colonies of his day as "socialistic paroxysms." He intended to be positive. America, he felt, would be a different place because of these experiments. It was like a man who had experienced "a series of passional excitements and could never be the same being afterward." The models would be forever available. Having worked through "the ordeal of practical verification," they would stand as lessons in both their success and their failures.

Noyes was the founder in 1848 of the Oneida Community in upstate New York, perhaps the most encompass-

---

[1] George B. Shaw, *Man and Superman* (New York, 1903), p. 191.

ing social experiment in pre–Civil War America. During
the 1860s, late in Oneida's life, Noyes compiled a study
of American socialism, taking stock of where he and the
movement stood. He began with the manuscript of a
melancholy Robert Owen disciple who had visited American utopias, "wandering from grave to grave, patiently
deciphering the epitaphs of defunct 'phalanxes.'" America
was, he felt, "a laboratory in which socialisms of all kinds
have been experimenting." He found communitarianism,
as the modern historian Robert Fogerty finds it, far more
pervasive and strong than most Americans realize, far
more consistent and continuous, and far more relevant to
the social issues of their day.[2] Noyes was an idealistic
communist, at least in the sense that Shaw used the term,
one who proposes "to enrich the common fund rather
than to sponge upon it." Noyes, like all other utopian
socialists, hoped to abandon competitive values for those
of the group.

The models ranging along the socialist path varied from
those that cooperated on a very limited scale, like a colony
that might build together an irrigation system, to a com-
prehensive communism that abandoned all private holdings. In whatever manifestation the common life was
assumed superior. The model colony might be small, but
it was expandable, exportable, and repeatable. It might
advocate temperance or vegetarianism as a means of
reforming mankind. It seldom was revolutionary in the
Marxist sense. Instead, it leaned in the direction of per-
fectionism, the belief espoused by Noyes that man and
societies are malleable and, in the near future, perfectible.
As Victor Considerant proposed, ecstatic on the morning
of his Texas experimental colony, "one act of collective

[2] John H. Noyes, *History of American Socialisms,* pp. 24, 668, 2,
xix; Robert S. Fogarty, "American Communes, 1865–1914," *Journal
of American Studies* 9 (August, 1975): 146.

faith and this country is conquered."[3] Of course, religious colonies often doubted the possibility of a heaven on earth, but they all, religious or otherwise, sought a synthesis of actions and ideals. In this sense the frontier with its hardships and practical demands was a good ground for the utopian to engage in his battle to remodel the world.

Of the 100 pre–Civil War colonies studied by the historian Arthur Bestor, 73 or three-quarters, faced the frontier of their day. With more recent statistics Otohiko Okugawa listed 92 colonies between 1860 and 1919; of these, 62 were west of the Mississippi. The West, however, as Bestor pointed out, was not itself a prime mover toward utopianism; usually the impetus was a response to eastern industrial life. What the West gave was an expansive energy, a feeling of power: "No event was so insignificant that it might not affect the future character of an entire region." Western society was assumed to be plastic and flexible. Reform should come easier there than elsewhere, once the model was posed. The frontier offered freedom and a quiet environment. Unlike ethnic colonies that also profited from such conditions, the cooperative colonies postured optimistically, seeking only temporary seclusion, wishing ultimately to be noticed.[4]

The distance from their audience often raised questions, however. William Hinds, long a commune member, thought communitarianism was an alternative not to rural life but to "the specter of pauperism stalking" the cities. Robert Dale Owen worried that the message of his father's New Harmony would never be heard in England, where it was

---

[3] Laurence Veysey, *The Perfectionists* (New York, 1973), pp. 10–11; Victor Considerant, *The Great West*, p. 27.

[4] Arthur Bestor, "Patent-Office Models of the Good Society," in *Backwoods Utopias* (Philadelphia, 1970), pp. 239, 231–32, 233–34; Otohiko Okugawa, "Nineteenth-Century Communitarian Societies" (MS, Department of Sociology, University of Pittsburgh, 1974), pp. 48–49; the appendix contains a larger sample: of 124 colonies, 81 were western.

most needed. Noyes feared that communities lost too much meaning when divorced from urban conditions. Fixation on the land, he said, was a trap; cooperation could better be explored in a factory than on a farm.[5]

In 1825 it was the frontier, the banks of the Wabash in Indiana, to which Robert Owen brought his ideal society, to be called New Harmony. His vision had grown from the steamy industrialism of Scotland, where he had raised a model company town. Now he sought a place that was not a city but not quite a solitude. With fewer restrictions and more available land, America was a good place to initiate a classless society, the only springboard of permanent virtue. Private property should in time be abolished and with it marriage and the church.

Meanwhile the 26,000 acres Owen found in Indiana were both auspicious and ominous. The place was good because it was the former colony of the Rappites, followers of a German religious leader who had erected a communitarian village along the Wabash. George Rapp and Owen had corresponded, having common engagement in a great movement, a communitarian thrust that included Shakers, Mennonites, and socialists, all following similar paths to the new society. The place was ominous, however, because the Rappites had grown discontented here, disliking frontiersmen and wearying of mosquitoes and malaria. Yet it was good farmland encircled with hills, some already terraced with vineyards. One-quarter mile from the river was the settlement, with rows of young locust trees lining its streets. The Rappites planted a labyrinth, "an emblematic representation of the life these colonists had chosen," where one could wander for hours and fail to reach the little structure in the center. But after toil and confusion

[5] William Hinds, *American Communities*, p. 3; Noyes, *History of American Socialisms*, p. 19; Robert D. Owen, *Threading My Way*, p. 259.

came the cool repose of the grape arbor—peace and social harmony.

The first colonists arrived in early summer, 1825. When Owen joined them in January, 1826, there were already one thousand people, many more than the Rappites had accommodated. Serious problems arose, chiefly in housing and food supply. But still the colonists came, often in droves. Owen's son described them as "that heterogeneous collection of radicals, enthusiastic devotees to principle, honest latitudinarians, and lazy theorists, with a sprinkling of unprincipled sharpers thrown in." Random idealists of Europe and America were gathering on the Indiana frontier. One of them was Henry Pelham, a scholarly editor from Ohio, who had traveled in England and published books in Boston. Pelham was perhaps a typical colonist. He brought few if any practical frontier skills, yet he was buoyant with excitement. Three weeks after his arrival he had not yet seen the Wabash, one-quarter mile away; he was too much interested in the human beings around him and in the ideas of the colony.[6]

New Harmony built centralized structures that were intended eventually to be connected by enclosed passageways. Owen believed that workshops should be distant from living quarters. The structures reflected the philosophy that involved common property and social equality. To achieve these goals, no fewer than four constitutions, each the product of long debate, were adopted in New Harmony's short life.

"There is great charm in the good-fellowship," Robert Dale Owen found. New Harmonists called one another by given names, like brothers and sisters, often strolling

[6] Arthur L. Morton, *The Life and Ideas of Robert Owen*, p. 40; Charles Nordhoff, *Communistic Societies of the United States*, p. 89; Owen, *Threading My Way*, pp. 242–43, 286; William Pelham, *New Harmony as Seen by Participants and Travelers*, introduction by Caroline Pelham, pt. 1, and letter dated September 26, 1825.

together in the moonlight. But Robert Dale Owen, like so many others at New Harmony, was not adept at manual labor. After one day in the wheat fields his right arm was useless for forty-eight hours.[7] There was always time for debate, for interminable discussions of how the colonies should be run.

The land belonged to Robert Owen, but he had always said that in time he would turn it over to the community, maintaining that the colonists needed more education in cooperative life before assuming the responsibility. Owen's paternalism caused rancor, perhaps because it was not supported by a religious faith. The intellectuals grew dissatisfied with the inconveniences, and only a month after Owen arrived, the first dissidents left. Nearby they formed their own short-lived community. Another month, and another splinter group departed, this time an ethnic band of English farmers who had immigrated to Illinois in 1817 and then had joined Owen in a body. Now they set up their third colony, and it lasted far longer than New Harmony. Thus through quibbling debate the community dissolved in bits and pieces. Owen abandoned the place in June, 1827. He expected that seeds of his ideas would spring up anew. In that respect he was not completely wrong.[8]

New Harmony was a place of reason; Shalam, in New Mexico half a century later, shrouded its land with mystical meaning. Shalam lasted for nearly twenty years. According to legend, on an October morning in 1884, John Ballou Newbrough, a spiritualist, drove his buggy along the dusty roads out of Doña Ana, his eyes carefully blindfolded. Newbrough had heard angel voices since he was a boy among the oaks and log huts of Ohio in the 1820s. Although subsequently trained in medicine and dentistry, he became known for his *Oahspe,* a mystical tract com-

[7] Owen, *Threading My Way,* pp. 276, 281, 277.
[8] Bestor, *Backwoods Utopias,* pp. 48, 160, 176–77, 201.

posed from vibrations of lighted hands. It has held a small circle of devout readers since its publication in 1882. A few years later similar visions led him to New Mexico. Now on the desert east of the Río Grande, Newbrough's apparitions told him to stop the horses, and there he and twenty followers raised Shalam. It was conceived as "a place where the world would not live," and to it Newbrough brought "the babes the world would not have." Thus he designed for his people and these children "a land of peace and plenty." Newbrough combined a concern for the poor with his spiritualism. His sympathy resulted in the adoption of fifty orphans, abandoned children given to Shalam by the police of eastern cities. In Newbrough's thinking the world could be reformed through model colonization. A brotherhood of spiritualists could save the whole of mankind.[9] Among the mesas and mesquites of Shalam the colonists joined in a holy covenant to own nothing needed by others and to live an ascetic life rearing their orphans. They built impressive structures, like the Fraternum with its library, dining room, twenty bedrooms, ten bathrooms, and a playroom filled with toys and bird cages. A productive ranch and farm spread over the desert.

In 1891, Newbrough died of influenza. The colony continued for another decade, but problems multiplied. Members worked less, and outsiders had to be hired. The young people grew restive under the jibes of neighbors. In 1901, after returning many of the children to orphanages, Shalam ended its experiment of transforming a desert into a holy place.[10]

If place was a significant aspect of life at New Harmony

[9] Julia Keleher, "The Land of Shalam," *New Mexico Historical Review* 19 (April, 1944): 124–25, claims that Newbrough already had identified the rich Mesilla Valley lands and staged the blindfold act for the benefit of his followers. Stoes describes the incident in terms of a legend; K. D. Stoes, "The Land of Shalam," *New Mexico Historical Review* 33 (January, 1958): 16.

and Shalam, in other utopian ventures the number of people might be considered a more crucial question. About the time Robert Owen was leaving Indiana, Charles Fourier was formulating a similar philosophy in Paris. Like Owen, Fourier felt deeply the evils of industrialism and was equally firm in his belief that all classes would unite when they witnessed the cooperative way. A lonely bachelor, he envisioned communities called phalanxes, whose best size would be 1,600. In contrast, Robert Owen had believed the optimum to be between 800 and 1,200, interestingly close to New Harmony's population.[11] In his numbers Fourier sought a balance between kinds of production, as well as among varieties of temperament, for which he devised his subgroupings, called series. The series were combined into an association that lived together in a phalanstery where all activities of spirit, mind, body, work, and play were harmonized. Private property and the family were maintained within the association. These customary attitudes made possible a sizable following, including twenty-seven colonies in America. One was as far west as Iowa, and at least a dozen were in the Old Northwest.

The Wisconsin Phalanx, which called itself Ceresco, for the goddess of grain, never approached Fourier's desired size, but it did enlarge from 20 members in 1844 to 180 before it liquidated six years later. Born in a lyceum meeting in the frontier town of Southport (now Kenosha), the experiment was kindled by readings and discussions of Fourier. Among the students was Warren Chase, who became a trusted leader. Only thirty years old, he had already moved from New Hampshire to Michigan to Wis-

[10] Stoes, "Land of Shalam," pp. 1–23; Jim Dennon, *The Oahspe Story*, pp. 17–23; Fogarty, "American Communes, 1865–1914," p. 155. The Newbrough philosophy was revived in the 1950s at the Essenes of the Kosmon colony; Laurence Veysey, *The Communal Experience*, p. 43.

[11] Bestor, *Backwoods Utopias*, p. 74.

consin, and after the colony he would add Missouri and California to the places he called home. Now he led these converted Fourierists to the Wisconsin prairie, to a fertile region of oak groves and clear streams.

As good Fourierists they raised a central phalanstery with apartments and a dining hall, the latter the gathering place too for musicals, weekly cotillions, and no fewer than three weddings in one subsequent summer. Their lyceum meetings continued every Tuesday night. They tried to divide their work into series, but no Fourierist colony was ever large enough to practice that theory adequately. They worked hard, nonetheless, trying also to eliminate intoxication, quarreling, and "profane swearing." The moralism inspired Noyes's observation that they were a nearly perfect society.[12] He was also impressed by their financial integrity: at their dissolution they claimed a profit on their original investment of 108 percent.

Yet these students of the French master were disturbed in their isolation by the rise nearby of a town, Ripon. The colony's "good principles," said Chase, were in "bad company." Land values mushroomed, and speculative fever rose. By the end of the 1840s the California-gold mania had lured away its toll of members. Chase became a spiritualist and was replaced as president. In the circumstances the temptations to capitalize on their land were too great to prevent them from selling. One annual report concluded sadly, "This generation is not yet ready." Chase echoed, "It was prematurely born, and tried to live before its proper time and, of course, must die and be born again." Noyes called it "deliberate suicide," unable to fathom why so prosperous an experiment should so weakly resist the temptations of frontier speculation.[13]

[12]Noyes, *History of American Socialisms*, p. 418.

[13]Warren Chase, *The Life-Line of the Lone One*, pp. 120–27, 129; Warren Chase, quoted in S. M. Pedrick, "The Wisconsin Phalanx at Ceresco," *Proceedings of the State Historical Society of Wisconsin* 50 (1902): 224, 210, 221; Noyes, *History of American Socialisms*, p. 448;

At the other end of the Great Plains, European Fourierists were trying their hand at utopia. Victor Considerant had become, in his early twenties, a disciple of Charles Fourier and had resigned from the French army to follow his teacher. Forced to leave Europe because of his radical demonstrations, he used the frontier to test the principles of association. With the help of American Fourierists, he found an initial twelve thousand acres in Texas across the Trinity River from what would become Dallas. In April 1855, with hopes as fresh as the spring grass, the first colonists arrived from France, Belgium, Switzerland, and Germany. "We should associate with heart and hands in a work which our collective mind acknowledges as the grandest enterprise conceivable by Man," wrote Considerant. "The Promised Land is reality."

They called their colony Reunion, the assembly of mankind in one big family. Group after group continued to arrive until they reached some four hundred, far too many for the facilities. Still they were lighthearted enough to laugh at the grasshoppers and the drought of the first summer. But soft grass dried upon the barren hills of winter. During the grim storms and in the crowded houses, it grew harder to laugh. Unlike the Wisconsin Phalanx and more like New Harmony, this colony was filled with scientists, musicians, and tradesmen, but included only two farmers. Practically speaking, there was little chance for these Fourierists facing the frontier. By 1858 they had begun to scatter. In their minds, however, they failed because "they could not withstand the feeling of individualism which thrived so strongly and so universally in this country."[14] Two important antidotes to that indivi-

---

Montgomery E. McIntosh, "Co-operative Communities in Wisconsin," 1903, pp. 101, 102, 105–106.

[14] Considerant, *The Great West*, pp. 26, 27; Ermance Rejebian, "La Reunion," *Southwestern Historical Quarterly* 43 (April, 1940): 477; John W. Reps, *Cities of the American West*, p. 149.

dualism, religious faith and long personal acquaintance (once advocated by Noyes as essentials to community), were lacking at Reunion. They had not brought values strong enough to counterbalance their serious deficiencies in frontier agriculture.

Noyes spoke from the heart and from experience when he identified religion as an essential of the cooperative life. "Earnest religion may be relied upon to carry association through to the attainment of all its hopes." It was the "soul's environment" that the socialist was trying to redesign. Such a religious intent certainly infused Noyes's leadership at Oneida, and he was aware that the anti-religious stance of Robert Owen had not helped New Harmony overcome its frontier problems. Indeed, Owen had been joyful about the West precisely because he expected there "less hypocrisy concerning religion." The Fourierist tradition stood somewhere between Noyes and Owen. At the Wisconsin Phalanx, for example, denominations took turns worshiping in the dining hall, but there was no intrinsic connection between its religion and its cooperative life.[15]

Quite different was an experiment in religious communism mounted by the Mormons in a hot southern valley of Utah. The Mormons produced an astonishing number of people willing to sacrifice for the whole. That was why Richard Ely, the Wisconsin economist, considered them so nearly "a perfect piece of social mechanism." The machinery was geared to unity. "If ye are not one, ye are not mine," said Joseph Smith in his revelation on stewardship. In this same vision he saw the saints surrendering all surplus to the community. The wealth would then be redistributed according to wants and needs. During the early persecutions of the church the full implementation

[15] Noyes, *History of American Socialisms*, pp. 656, 26, 412; Karl Bernhard, New Harmony as Seen . . ., pt. 2 [from Karl Bernhard, *Travels Through North America* (1828), 2:105–24].

of stewardship had to be postponed. But through all the trials and migrations these latter-day Puritans repeatedly covenanted together, pledging themselves to the common good. At Nauvoo, for example, on the eve of their exodus to Utah, they joined in yet another such holy agreement: ". . . to stand by and assist each other, to the utmost of our abilities."[16]

Their migration west did not lack those who ate too much and gave too little, but still it was an archetype of self-sacrifice and cooperative organization. Moreover, these wagon-train communities did not disperse at the end of the trail. Mormon settlement in the Great Basin was saturated with the peasant village ideal. As with the Puritans, families received town lots as well as farmland on the outskirts. Thus a traditional setting facilitated their cooperative doctrine and helped support life in an arid environment. Irrigated agriculture, as Richard Ely said, depended upon "a compact society, well-knit together." The Mormons supplied water cooperatively, dug irrigation ditches and wells, fenced jointly, raised houses, and bridged the streams together. They worked to provide food for their own poor. Polygamy, a particularly active practice after the 1860s, functioned like the *compadre* system, constantly confirming bonds between the family and the community. In some areas the doctrine of stewardship was kept alive with families giving all their property to the church.[17] In others, like Brigham City, cooperatives reinforced agricultural and factory production. Mormon

[16] Richard Ely, "Economic Aspects of Mormonism," *Harper's* 106 (April, 1903): 668; Leonard Arrington, *Great Basin Kingdom* (Cambridge, Mass., 1958), pp. 5–6; Leonard Arrington, Feramorz Fox, and Dean May, *Building the City of God*, pp. 360, 41.

[17] John W. Reps, *Town Planning in Frontier America*, pp. 410–21; Ely, "Economic Aspects of Mormonism," p. 669; Arrington, Fox, and May, *Building the City of God*, pp. 63–78.

settlement was a patchwork of cohesive communities.

In the 1870s the Mormons began building intentional colonies. At that time the United Order of Enoch, a part of Joseph Smith's earlier revelation on stewardship, was revived by Brigham Young himself. Towns like Richfield and Saint George were converted into models with hundreds of Mormons surrendering most of their private property, thereby combating "the feeling of 'Mine'" while avoiding the evils of "grasping individualism." Yet Brigham Young's hope that all Mormon cooperation would be perfected in small, integrated villages was seldom realized. Saint George and Richfield kept to their communal faiths for no more than five years. Kanab wrenched and split into competing versions of cooperation that embittered almost a whole generation.

In contrast, the little village of Orderville in arid southern Utah achieved Mormonism's highest goals. In the early spring of 1875, ninety-four Mormons and their children entered a solemn covenant that they were all equals as children of God; the earth bore sufficient resources if God's people acted as stewards of his gifts. They were to love one another as one family and hold their possessions in common. As a group they had already known hardships, having pioneered for the church a rugged area along the Muddy River. That had been a miserable experience in which they had learned much about survival.

At Orderville they decided to house each family separately but without private kitchens. They ate in a central hall, where their worship and social gatherings also took place. The kitchen served three meals a day to an average of eighty families for five years. Bugles and bells called the colony to meals, to prayers, to work, and to play.

Orderville shaped a very nearly self-sufficient economy, producing its own food, clothing, soap, brooms, wooden buckets, silk, leather products, woolens, and furniture. It grew a surplus of cotton, whose export provided capital.

A midwife corps and an herb doctor offered medical care. The absolute equality of all labor was replaced in a few years by a work-credit system, but women's labor always counted less than men's. The common storehouse distributed all items according to want and need, as approved by a committee of three women.

The accomplishments notwithstanding, and although all new members were carefully screened, some colonists were less interested than others in working. The community did little to penalize them, and jealousy arose. When some families withdrew, the colony returned property far beyond what was their due. One man, found guilty of "loitering and trifling his time away," left the colony, but he received his full share for the sake of his children.

About 1880 the region around Orderville felt a surge of mining prosperity. Young colonists began comparing their homespun ways with the affluence abroad, forgetting that their envy was directed at the richest outsiders, not the poor. Nevertheless, discontent arose. In 1880 common dining was not restored after a flood destroyed the ovens. In the following years families grew more self-centered. A wage system was adopted. "Limited stewardship" took the place of common ownership. New plans and proposals multiplied almost as rapidly as constitutions at New Harmony. Still, Orderville prospered and would have continued as a highly cooperative colony had not the federal government moved strenuously to enforce the antipolygamy laws. After 1885, Orderville leaders, many of whom held plural wives, were prosecuted and imprisoned. The church suggested that the colony disband and the members reluctantly voted "to discontinue their operations in utopia," auctioning off their property and distributing the proceeds.

Orderville's decade left an afterglow. Reminiscences were uniformly positive, and most recalled "the closest approximation to a well-ordered supremely happy, Chris-

Union Colony Building, Greeley, Colorado, 1870
Colorado Historical Society

tian life that it was possible to achieve in human society."[18] Looking backward, these people agreed that they never felt better or lived more happily than when they were devoting themselves to the common good. After the death of Brigham Young, the admission of Utah as a state, and the end of outside pressures on Mormonism, the impetus for cooperative colonization waned. The church, perhaps realizing, as Christopher Lasch said, how demanding was "the conception of a secular community organized in accordance with religious principles," turned to less practical theology and, above all, economic individualism as its interpretation of the good life.[19]

Not all the values of cooperative colonies were religious, especially when focused on one barrier to social change like drunkenness, unhealthful dress or diet, or inhibition of sexual expression. Temperance, for example, could lead to stronger families and fairer government; vegetarianism could reduce aggressiveness and so promote cooperation. These reformist approaches, though sounding priggish or unsympathetic with human foibles, often posed serious assaults on major social problems—the irresponsibility of large-scale food processing, the anomie of industrialism, or unjust inequalities for women.

Colorado in the 1870s and 1880s, with its rapid economic development following mining booms, was a par-

[18] Arrington, Fox, and May, *Building the City of God,* pp. 201, 140, 220; they tithed as a group, not individually, and donated special help to the building of the Saint George Temple. Total assets increased from $21,000 in 1875 to $79,000 in 1883; ibid., pp. 276, 282, 292, 293; Reps, *Cities of the American West,* p. 336.

[19] Orderville was the model for a chain of Mormon settlements extending southward to Mexico. The more remote the area, the more perfect for cooperative experimentation, Brigham Young believed. Most were in Arizona, but one was in Mexico, where from 1893 to 1895 former Orderville colonists helped establish a cooperative community at Cave Valley. Christopher Lasch, *World of Nations,* p. 68.

Greeley Fire Department competing in Longmont, Colorado, about 1890
Western History Department, Denver Public Library

ticularly interesting region for reformist settlements. There were colonies for urban poor, for labor unions, for women, for temperance, and for diet.[20] The most famous of these, the Union Colony that established Greeley, included the

[20] Olive Wright, "Colony for Women. San Luis Valley, Colorado," *Denver Tribune Republican*, October 25, 1885, p. 14; "Amity Colony, (Salvation Army)," *Denver Times*, March 12, 1899; *Harper's Weekly*, September 7, 1901.

Early buildings, Greeley, Colorado, 1870
Western History Department, Denver Public Library

temperance cause as part of its initial purpose. Its founder, Nathan Meeker, worked with Horace Greeley, the onetime Fourierist, on the *New York Tribune*. Bitten with the cooperative idea, he sought abstainers to found a colony in Colorado. The members arrived on their twelve thousand acres early in 1870. Each family was allotted land in the mile-square townsite and a farm in the surrounding countryside. They planned a cooperative irrigation system and a common fence around all the farmland. By May four hundred people had come. They labored hard on the water ditch and the fence, but they also had a concert band and a vocal society, a newspaper and a hotel. They collected a library and organized a dramatic society that produced a smashing run of *Ten Nights in a Bar Room.*

The colonists thought of themselves as an example, "free from the baneful liquor traffic and its attendant vices and immorality." They claimed neither to smoke tobacco nor to chew it, and the bachelors in their common housing conversed without oaths and vulgarities.

Within a year cracks appeared. An outsider tried to erect a saloon, and the colony had to raise two hundred dollars to buy him out. Inequalities sharpened as wealthier members acquired larger and larger parcels of land. Speculators bought into the colony, and their activities made the original members angry enough to gather around the hotel and use "inflammatory language." The old-timers were labeled "old fogeys" and "growlers." Subgroups, like the Oddfellows Lodge, arose. The unity was gone. Greeley ceased to be a colony and incorporated itself as a "normal" frontier town the following year.[21]

Likewise, women's rights or diet reform could offer values that motivated single-issue colonies. The removal of impositions by men upon women, for example, might unfetter society, and a colony based on such principles might lead the way. Communalism was not a major thrust for the women's movement, but in the West there was at least one colony in Belton, Texas. In 1884 the Sanctified

[21] As quoted in James F. Willard, ed., *Union Colony at Greeley,* p. 336; Willard, *Union Colony,* pp. 297, 351; *Colorado Miner* (Georgetown, Colo.), March 31, 1870, and April 21, 1870; for a temperance colony in the Texas Panhandle, the Clarendon Colony, see Mari Sandoz, *Cattlemen from the Río Grande,* p. 184. The Union Colony had a rival "dry" colony called the St. Louis–Western; James F. Willard and Colin Goodykoontz, eds., *Experiments in Colorado Colonization,* p. xxx.

Sisters there vowed celibacy, separated from their husbands, and lived together in the Women's Commonwealth. They ran their colony, including an economically successful hotel, for fifteen years.[22] In a similar way diet was occasionally raised to a primary issue. Henry Clubb in 1855 led a vegetarian colony that raised its "white banner of 'peace and goodwill'" along the Neosho River in Kansas. In 1884, Isaac Rumford organized a similar colony called Joyful near Bakersfield, California. They ate an Edenic diet of grated apple, mashed almonds, pounded raisins, and a mix of oats and wheat called grainia. In both colonies diet was seen as the catalyst for a society ruled by Christianity and love. Neither Belton nor the diet colonies were important in themselves, yet in the aggregate of all reform colonies they represented an impressive use of the frontier for communal purposes.[23]

The family was abandoned in very few cooperative colonies. Most felt like Charles Nordhoff that a commune's chief asset was its reproduction of the values of family life. Noyes saw the common idea of socialism and religion to be unitary families in unitary homes, "where daily meetings and continuous criticism are possible."[24] Of course, Noyes, Owen, and most socialists hoped to improve upon the possessiveness and insularity of the nuclear family.

The Mormons were trying to do the same, though they

[22] Fogarty, "American Communes, 1865–1914," p. 152; Otohiko Okugawa, "Nineteenth-Century Communitarian Societies," (MS), appendix, unpaged.

[23] Veysey, *The Communal Experience*, p. 60; Maren Lockwood, "The Experimental Utopia in America," *Daedalus* 2 (Spring, 1965): 407–408; Joseph G. Gambone, ed., "Kansas—A Vegetarian Utopia," *Kansas Historical Quarterly* 38 (Spring, 1972): 65–87; Robert Hine, *California's Utopian Colonies* (New Haven, Conn., 1966), p. 140.

[24] Noyes, *History of American Socialisms*, p. 27.

built on a hierarchy within the family that was seen by outsiders as possessive. For them the family had to be integrated into the community, bound to the goals of the society. At Orderville a woman colonist once washed clothes for nearby miners, and instead of surrendering the money to the common treasury, she spent it on her children. The colony called her to task, forgave because of her past faithfulness, and enjoined her to go and sin no more.[25] The Mormon community might be a family writ large, but the family must be subservient to the community's needs and will.

The cooperative colony was also an arena of class conflict, though the utopian socialist earnestly expected otherwise. Even minimally cooperative colonies were in effect deriding the capitalist values of the middle classes. Nathan Meeker at Greeley praised all colonies because they circumvented and counteracted land speculation. Furthermore, a whole arm of the cooperative-colony movement stemmed from workingmen's clubs and labor unions. While it was difficult for individual laborers to move west, it was possible for workingmen to combine their resources to buy frontier land.[26]

The Colorado Cooperative Colony (later called Nucla) was designed by labor unionists and socialists in 1894 near Pinon. Its socialists were alienated, however, when the majority voted in favor of private ownership of land. But the collective continued to own all buildings, and the produce was the property of the group, which in turn sold

[25] Arrington, Fox, and May, *Building the City of God*, p. 278.
[26] Willard, *Union Colony at Greeley*, p. 4. Good examples would be the Chicago Colony of Longmont, Colorado, and the German cooperative colony of Wet Mountain, Colorado, both in the 1870s. Ibid., pp. xvii, xxiv. *Denver Daily Tribune*, March 6, 1871; *Harper's Weekly*, March 26, 1870.

Early Main Street looking south, Nucla, Colorado
Colorado Historical Society

it back to the members at cost. Their supreme communal
effort centered on an irrigation system. Surprisingly aware
of western ecology, they parceled the land according to
the water supply. Each holding was small until the water
could be increased. This environmental approach, they

felt, was made possible by their abandonment of capitalism's greediness. They did dream of affluence, however, even planning an opera house for which they debated the color of the plush seats. Some members eagerly sought to abandon the collective once their water arrived. The committed socialists were once again disgusted by the quick reversion to thoughts of personal property. As Nucla's historian wrote, "Private enterprise had seemingly put a curse upon those who were seriously contemplating utopia." By 1909 only the ditch remained cooperative.[27]

In the Middle West socialist colonization was often associated with ethnicity. With French roots like those of Fourierism, followers of Etienne Cabet in 1860 brought to Iowa a thriving Gallic experiment called Icaria.[28] Elsewhere European immigrants bore radical ideas that had motivated the revolutions of 1848 and 1871. Danish socialists, for example, formed a colony in Kansas in 1877. Its leader, Louis Pio, inspired by the Paris Commune of 1871, had organized the first Danish section of the Socialist International. Fomenting strikes and demonstrations, he had been sentenced to four years at hard labor. A few years after his release he was bribed by the police to leave. He collected a group of socialists, including some Germans, and emigrated to Kansas. In jail he had read of the Mormon trek to Utah and wondered if socialists too might benefit from a little isolation. Once on the colony land, the members debated interminably, reflecting that bubbling time in socialist theory, not yet a decade after *Das Kapital.* The theoretical differences stirred up traditional national feuds, and eventually the Germans decided that they could no longer live with the Danes. The colony split apart. As usual, there were other problems. One of them was the general unpreparedness for the frontier. As urbanites they were terrified of Kansas creatures. Pio even tied his trouser legs to keep the snakes from crawling

[27] Ellen Peterson, "Origins of the Town of Nucla," *Colorado Magazine* 26 (October, 1949): 252–58; Duane D. Mercer, "The Colorado Co-operative Company, 1894–1904," *Colorado Magazine* 44 (Fall, 1967): 293–306.

[28] Albert Shaw, *Icaria;* Hine, *California's Utopian Colonies,* pp. 59–64.

up. Yet intellectual disputes remained the critical venom in their community life.[29]

These labor and socialist enterprises, "by poor men for poor men," were widespread in the Far West between the 1870s and World War I. Setbacks to labor's cause would often initiate thoughts of retreat and model colonization. Thus in 1883 the Knights of Labor in Minneapolis founded a cooperative land association. The resulting colony, the Pioneer Land Company, began in 1886 on 253 acres by a lake in Crow Wing County, in western Minnesota. Like the Colorado Cooperative Colony it was environmentally oriented, prohibiting "manufactories," carefully preserving the natural resources, keeping at least one-fourth of the land in timber, and protecting native groves of oak, maple, and hickory. In the process the slow decline of membership was a measure of success, like the death of one way of life providing nourishment for another.[30]

About the same time in San Francisco the International Workingmen's Association under a socialist leader, Burnette G. Haskell, considered escape from the city's frustrations. It took up land in the tranquil Sierra Nevada foothills for the Kaweah Cooperative Commonwealth. Kaweah lasted from 1885 to 1890, its history punctured with land-title problems, intensifying the colonists' bitterness with the capitalist system. They were convinced, though with little proof, that their colony was persecuted by big timber and railroad interests, another reflection of the conflict between the upper class and the workingman. In 1890 the federal government appropriated their land to become part of Sequoia National Park. "The capitalist press,"

[29] Kenneth E. Miller, "Danish Socialism and the Kansas Prairie," *Kansas Historical Quarterly* 38 (Summer, 1972): 156–68; Julius Braunthal, *The History of the International*, 1:227–28.

[30] Albert Shaw, *History of Cooperation in the United States* (Baltimore, Md., 1888), pp. 243–54.

they wrote, "used their banal reporter's English to stab us to death; the lumber monopoly of the San Joaquin went to Congress behind our back. . . . We were poor. We were ignorant. We were jeered at. But no man dare say but we were honest."[31]

A few years later, in 1896, a national radical party, the Brotherhood of the Cooperative Commonwealth, laid plans for socializing the state of Washington and thereafter, like shock troops, to take state by state until the nation was won. It would all begin with a small colony, an encampment that could easily demonstrate the strength of its cause to a frontier whose capitalist institutions were not firmly entrenched. In 1897 socialists gathered on 280 acres along Puget Sound to form Equality, named for the recently published novel of Edward Bellamy. "We are the advanced guard of a mighty host," proclaimed one of its leaders. At its height there were 300 socialists in the colony. They ate three meals a day together, sang together, listened to lectures and debates at lyceums, and even offered prayer meetings twice a week for the devout. But their economic management did not match their spirit, and their production was low. It was hard to predict the workforce, whose numbers varied in one of the best years from 115 to 300. According to one observer, 15 percent of the members remained "conscious individualists," and at least half of those who came had no philosophy at all. Basic individualism was masquerading as socialism. In 1903 they dropped to thirty-eight. By then the various armies of revolution had abandoned model building for more class-conscious unity in the industrial centers of the world.[32]

Another Washington colony was an experiment in anarchism called Home. In 1896, having already tried to live together according to the ideas of Edward Bellamy, these

[31] Burnette G. Haskell, "Kaweah," *Out West* 17 (September, 1902): pp. 316–17.

nonconformists moved on to cooperative anarchism. On small holdings of two acres each, members lived as they pleased. Laws, they assumed, were deterrents to the best in human behavior. A gathering of true individualists would produce the moral society. As a community they were "individuals united by their very differences."

At one time nearly five hundred people lived at Home. Neither traditional family structures nor merely "mutual living arrangements" caused comment. Vegetarians supped with omnivores; religionists sat down with atheists. Almost all of them grew vegetable gardens, and many raised chickens. One woman lived in a wigwam; two men, in the stump of a hollow tree. There was a transvestite, and some colonists swam nude in Puget Sound. Small groups studied Yoga and physical culture. Violence was shunned, and self-reliance extolled; still, most of the community turned out to build houses for newcomers.

Emma Goldman paid Home a long visit in 1898. The mother figure of American radicalism with "a heart that embraced the world," concluded that the colony was a dead end. It had withdrawn from the turmoil of revolution, more interested in "vegetables and chickens than in propaganda."

By 1908 the individualistic homogeneity, if such it can be called, was splintering. New groups of members entered, one of which was called "the prudes." They objected to the nudity, though they were accused of watching the swimmers through field glasses. External hostility had been increasing, especially after President William McKinley's assassination by an anarchist in 1901. Patriotic organizations targeted Home as a hotbed of radicalism. Federal officials arrested three members for publishing in the

[32] Charles P. LeWarne, *Utopias on Puget Sound, 1885–1915*, pp. 55, 63, 74; Frederick A. Bushee, "Communistic Societies in the United States," *Political Science Quarterly* 20 (December, 1905): 635–36, claims the membership higher and the acreage lower.

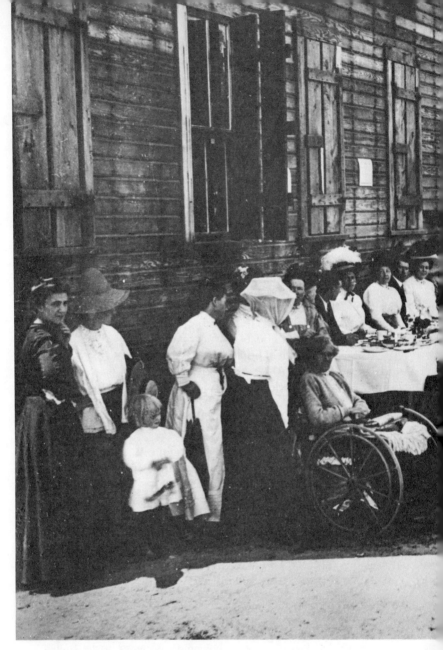

Picnic at Home Colony, Puget Sound, about 1898
Washington State Historical Society

colony paper an article on free love. In spite of bickering and hostility, however, Home continued as a colony until 1921.[33]

The Promethean vision of John Humphrey Noyes—a whole society following the beacon of a small cooperative community—was no more achieved in the West than elsewhere. Noyes may have been right that the frontier's infatuation with agricultural land hampered the dream rather than unloosing it. Nevertheless, the frontier was available, unformed, presumably still flexible in attitude, and plastic in its institutions. It invited a welter of cooperative experiments, from the devoutness of Orderville to the composite morality of Home, from the intellectualism of New Harmony to the mysticism of Shalam, from the business acumen of the Wisconsin Phalanx to the radicalism of Equality, from the short-lived vegetarianism of Joyful to the unified temperance at Greeley. They were incarnations of the emerging pluralism of nineteenth-century American life, in which the frontier was a principal participant.

Considering their disparities and frustrations, it is not surprising that one historian of such colonies called them "foolish monuments to the community idea."[34] The long view of history may well retain the noun "monument" but reject the adjective. It certainly was not foolish to imagine the frontier as an opportunity to change society for the better. It was not foolish to idealize small groups of families working and playing closely together. It was not foolish to affirm traditional values, which is what they generally did, in the face of a rapidly changing society. In their desire to withdraw from that world of flux and competition, someday to return with the answers, they did not realize that the competitive industrialism

[33] LeWarne, *Utopias on Puget Sound*, pp. 174, 176, 168, 171–76, 186, 190, 200.

[34] Walter Burr, *Small Towns*, p. 54.

they were fleeing had preceded them on the frontier. They had in fact escaped but little. Speculators, railroads, laissez-faire economics were already rampant. Mobility colored hopes of stability. Few colonists could resist the temptations of quick wealth, better land, and the presumed joys of untrammeled freedom.

Daniel Boorstin could have used these cooperative colonies as reflections of the penchant for community building in the West. Like torches bringing light to the wilderness, these clusters of believers demonstrated the American genius at self-government. But, as with small towns, wagon trains, mining camps, or ranches, the politics of cooperative colonization were subjected to severe strains on the frontier. Internal tensions became lethal under continuing assaults on stability and homogeneity. These colonists were foolish only because they expected the frontier to free them from their pasts. It was a setting for disillusion rather than light.

Epilogue

After the Frontier

With the passing away of the days when there were
unlimited opportunities for individual activity there is
coming to America an increase of the social sense, an
increased feeling of social responsibility.

F. J. Turner, "High School and City" (1895)

IN 1940 THE UNBUTTONED CITIZENS of Wheatland, Missouri,
their days patterned with neighborly visits, borrowing
plows and wheelbarrows, sharing garden vegetables or
wild honey, still perceived the pioneer past to be better
than the present. Frontiersmen, they felt, knew how to
work together, understood the true meaning of cooperation, and lived in a close-knit community of a kind un-
obtainable in the twentieth century.[1] Clearly Wheatlanders
yearned for unity, some communal Eden. Yet as modern
men and women they surely enjoyed the tangy fruit of
pluralism while tasting new varieties of community. Perhaps their thoughts on the present were causing their sense
of reality to shift, like pioneers whose receding memories
were of nearly forgotten amenities. Succumbing to the
weakness of longing, they were downgrading the values of
the present.

The modern commune movement acts on a similar desire for unity. By the early 1970s young people were

---

[1] Carl Withers (pseud. James West), "Plainville, U.S.A.," in *Psychological Frontiers of Society*, ed. Abram Kardiner, pp. 74–75.

gathering in as many as ten thousand communes, hiving off like Puritans into modern versions of the cooperative village.[2] At the same time they frequently resorted to the rhetoric of the frontier, assailing the future with their eyes on the past. And their efforts were not insignificant, to judge from the writings of Paul Goodman, Charles Reich, Theodore Roszak, Jean François Revel, Buckminster Fuller, and Philip Slater.

David Ruth, who left Harvard in 1972 to join Twin Oaks, a prominent Virginia experiment, later wrote that a major thrust among communes "recalls the early pioneer spirit," especially in its sense of interdependence with one another and with the land. The pioneer way could restore deeper experiences of friendship and rootedness that have become little more than encumbrances to a mobile society. Self-descriptions by communes come to sound like replays of western history: "They chose the cheapest, most remote land they could find and began building their homes and their culture." The new frontiersmen read advice their ancestors would have found in trail guides or almanacs: Take care lest your burning pile alkalize the water supply; use kerosene to remove ticks intact; look for trust to grow between those who survive together the hard winter.[3]

In the *Ultimate Frontier,* Richard Keininger, leader of an Illinois commune, described frontiersmen as braving all hardships "for the satisfaction of having conquered

[2] Statistics on communes vary widely depending on definition. The *New York Times,* December 17, 1970, estimated 2,000 communes in America, using a narrow definition. Judson Jerome, *Families of Eden* (New York, 1974), p. 17, lists well over 30,000.

[3] David Ruth, "Commune Movement in the Middle 1970s," *Communities,* no. 23 (November-December, 1976), p. 22; Anonymous, "United US Stand," *Communities,* no. 11 (December, 1974), p. 3; Owen Lindsay, "Pioneer Health," *Communities,* no. 2 (February, 1973), pp. 39–41; Anon., "Deep Valley Farm," *Communities,* no. 4 (July, 1973), p. 42. See also *Morning Star Scrapbook,* p. 56.

nature." Sounding like the citizens of Wheatland, he pointed to the time when "men of various backgrounds subordinated their differences and pulled together." Keininger, like most other communards, would see the frontier community as encouraging motivation for the common good because of its smallness and self-sufficiency, hence providing a balance point between the individual and the state.[4]

In 1967, Lou Gottlieb, a folk musician, "tall, frizzlybearded, with a nose like a Babylonian patriarch," planned a commune with a friend, Ramon Sender Morningstar. They would use the thirty acres Gottlieb owned in northern California. The land would be open to "the naked, homeless, and harmless." No one would be turned away who came in good faith and loved the land. In this spirit Gottlieb determined to deed his property to God. The ranch was named Morning Star from the final sentence of Thoreau's *Walden*. Within the first year nearly a hundred representatives of the counterculture came to this "free sanctuary." "Huts, shacks, lean-to's, and tents sprouted like mushrooms. Om's and chants floated across the starlit meadows."

One of their neighbors, eight miles away, was a young blond, bearded architect from Yale, Bill Wheeler. With inherited money he had bought 320 acres as a site for his studio and home. In the summer of 1968, as the result of a neighborly visit, he was converted to the ideals of Morning Star. "I wondered whether in the American land-rights system there could be a radical experiment in which a substantial number of people lived together on a piece of land and did not destroy it." He followed Morning Star's lead, "and the land called, opening itself."

Wheeler loved his land. "The Ridge held magic for me,

<hr/>

[4]Richard Keininger, *Ultimate Frontier*, pp. 210, 213; E. F. Schumacher, *Small Is Beautiful* (New York, 1973), p. 72, cautions against assuming consequences in human behavior from community size.

it was where I wanted to spend the rest of my life." Within a short time its "spacious and lyrical" acres sheltered some two hundred people. Each newcomer chose his own piece of land and built what he wanted. One of them, a man named Larry, a "noisy frontiersman" Wheeler called him, acted as "a midwife" to the opening of the Ridge. They named the place Ahimsa (meaning "harmlessness"), and it slowly formed "a tribe, a village, a community in a truly organic way,"[5] based on Morning Star's "voluntary primitivism." Neighborhoods assumed different characteristics —the Front Gate, the Knoll, the Yacht Club, the East Canyon, the Back of the Land. Their "biodegradable architecture" ranged from tight cabins to hollow tree stumps. Life was spontaneous and eclectic. The wooden cross raised for an Easter sunrise later became a Maypole. Sunday was often a festive occasion, something of a ritual with cleansing, dressing, and communal eating. Drugs were used as a means of introspection, and Timothy Leary's visit to Morning Star was a memorable moment.

They hoped "to reach backward for roots, simplicity, and the tribal experience."[6] That reach was often directed at the American Indian analogue. A carved wooden sign of Native American design greeted one at the gate to Morning Star. Gottlieb felt that they had registered their dissatisfaction with the prevailing culture in the same way that the Plains Indians had voted against a leader by leaving camp. Likewise, deeding the land to God would bring them closer to Indian beliefs. Sender read Indian prophecies at the morning gatherings, and he instituted the "Sun

[5] Ramon Sender Morningstar, "Home Free" (MS, 1978, Special Collections, University of California Library, Riverside), pp. 6, 42, 107, 111, 148; Ron E. Roberts, *New Communes*, p. 52.

[6] Sara Davidson, "Open Land," *Harper's* 240 (June, 1970): 94; Robin Richman, "Happy Hippie Hunting Ground," *Life* 63 (December, 1967): 66.

Yoga," based on an American Indian dance and including a ritual of gazing into the sun.

As communities Morning Star and Wheeler's Ranch faced the hurdle of the constant drifting in and out. But there were other problems. Hepatitis occasionally assumed serious proportions. The frontier remedies for it, radishes, ginseng, and special herb teas were prescribed. In the fall of 1968 racial tensions surfaced around the black members. There were drug excesses, as when punch was overdosed with LSD on the near-tragic so-called Black Sunday. But most difficult for community was the absence of unity among the various paths to self-awareness, between the competing teachings of Jesus or Buddha, Gurdjieff or Ramakrishna, Adelle Davis or Rudolph Steiner. Only the land, the place, held them together. The only common value was that "the Earth is Mother, and must be treated as such."

Instability waxed in the lack of an authority or political structure. With the exception of a few rules against cars, detergents, and open burning, regulations were avoided. The residents were heirs to an anarchic communal tradition that stretched back to Josiah Warren and included the colony of Home on Puget Sound. At Wheeler's, "The felt need for anarchy," said the *Modern Utopian*, "is more real than the need for community."[7]

External antipathies mounted quickly, from deflating tires of parked cars to charges in the courts. Beginning in 1968 raids and arrests were directed at drug violations and irregularities in building codes. In 1971, for example, thirty colonists were arrested in one raid alone. Gottlieb's deed to God was thrown out of court. Harassment stimulated deeper feelings of kinship with exploited frontiersmen and despised Indians. Members felt that outsiders

---

[7] Sender Morningstar, "Home Free," pp. 136, 63, 199; Stanley Krippner and Don Fersh, "The Mystical Experience and the Mystical Commune," *Modern Utopian* 4 (Spring, 1970): 7.

looked on them as "smelly savages"; they faced like a native tribe the prospect of extinction. America, Wheeler said, "won't let us be Indians again."

Late in 1968, Morning Star East was set up among the piñon plateaus near Taos, New Mexico. A sporadic exodus followed from the original site and from Wheeler's Ranch. But confrontations with the authorities did not lessen. In October, 1969, sheriff's bulldozers moved on the original Morning Star, and in two days most of the houses were in splinters. One naked member followed the machines reading from the Old Testament, while others played sadly on flutes and guitars. Over three years later, in May, 1973, Wheeler's place received similar treatment. "Bull-dozer tracks scar the ground for years. It hurts Mother." After the first day of destruction the residents ritually burned their own places throughout the foggy night. It was like the Divets' firing of the tragic homesteaders' cabin on the Great Plains.[8] At Wheeler's, heartbreak was deep among those modern pantheists, those romanticizers of the primitive, those idealists hoping to lead America out of the cities, those experimenters with a community based on a mythic and tribal sense of place.

Influencing Wheeler's Ranch were the books and ideas of Stephen Gaskin, a tall, gaunt San Francisco teacher with wire-rimmed spectacles. Gaskin preached personal fulfillment and decried the power of the modern state, but he looked forward to the organization of his own followers into "a sleazy, poor, multi-million dollar corporation." Gaskin had experienced the modern state in the form of the United States Marines, which he had joined at the age of seventeen. Leaving the corps after the Korean War, he earned bachelor's and master's degrees in English at San Francisco State College. He increasingly associated with the counterculture in the Bay area, and by 1968 was known as the popular teacher of a Monday night experi-

[8] Sender Morningstar, "Home Free," pp. 263, 339, 341, 343.

mental course. The class ranged freely over the spiritual reawakening in Zen and Yoga, mystical Christianity and LSD. "When Stephen talks," one of his disciples said, "a white light flows in the room."[9]

Partly to spread his message and partly to get out of the city, Gaskin led some two hundred of his followers on a caravan trek across the continent. On Columbus Day, 1970, over twenty of their converted school buses and vans wound out of San Francisco. Lecturing, singing, and camping together for four months, they returned in January, their numbers larger and their unity stronger. They now wished to convert their nomadic company into a community of place, and in good frontier sequence their overland trail preceded the taking up of land.[10]

On their caravan they had been attracted to fertile, inexpensive farming country in Tennessee. Eventually the group settled on over seventeen hundred acres sixty miles southwest of Nashville. By 1977, seven hundred adults and three hundred children were living on this land, and ten satellite colonies had already hived off to other places. At The Farm in Tennessee they began with a desire to escape the city but with little agricultural skill. Unlike the colonists at Wheeler's Ranch, however, they were willing to organize and work hard to dispel the image of city drifters. It was not easy, for some of their Tennessee hillfolk neighbors eyed them curiously as "technicolor Amish," weird as a Martian landing party.[11]

[9] Ibid., p. 271; *New York Times,* February 17, 1973, April 5, 1971; *San Francisco Chronicle,* November 6, 1977.

[10] Other nomadic communes include the Hog Farm, Hugh Romney, *Hog Farm and Friends* (New York, 1974). See also Project America, Richard Goering, "Project America," *Communities,* no. 23 (November–December, 1976), pp. 44–47.

[11] Anonymous, "Stephen Gaskin and The Farm," *Mother Earth News,* no. 45 (May–June, 1977), p. 10; Peter Jenkins, "Walk Across America," *National Geographic* 151 (April, 1977): 492. See also Peter Jenkins, *A Walk Across America,* pp. 181–210.

Construction of geodesic dome, The Farm, near Summertown, Tennessee, 1978
Stephen Gaskin and The Farm

In 1975 about 45 percent of The Farm's colonists were married, but by then most of the earlier group marriages had reverted to monogamy. The large proportion of children was central to their ideals of changing the future. Material possessions were shared, and a simple life affirmed. Home-grown vegetables and grains, especially soybeans, formed their vegetarian diet. The commune tried to meet weekly for food and fellowship.[12]

[12] John Rothchild and Susan Wolf, *Children of the Counter-Culture* (New York, 1976), p. 180. Laurence Veysey, *Communal Experience*, p. 312, describes a commune where meals are characterized by energy gained in common and then "consumed" in silence.

Digging sweet potatoes, The Farm, near Summertown,
Tennessee, 1979
Stephen Gaskin and The Farm

Work was a form of meditation, a Yoga. It's just "you
and the dirt and God," said Gaskin. The fourteen adult
crews plus children's brigades produced food for themselves and enough sorghum and soybeans for sale. Construction gangs took jobs outside and earned up to a thousand dollars a week. The colonists built a dozen communal
structures, including a schoolhouse, a laundry, a printshop,

a flour mill, a canning facility, and a meeting hall. They provided their own musicians, teachers, and midwives.[13]

The Farm was officially incorporated as a church, but its values were eclectic—a Fourieristic mix of Emersonian Oversoul and Newbrough spiritualism blended with telepathy and auras and combining Zen, Yoga, Islam, and Christianity. Christ has already returned, now in the hearts of thousands of people. Beyond telepathy or any other messages communion is the recognition of human oneness. Human relationships are clarified in the religious experience, which enables one to see "the natural wiring diagram of the way human energy is moved to relate with the universe." The diagram proves that all men, brothers in one family, can live together in harmony. In the rituals of this religion marijuana became a sacrament, which has plunged them into trouble with the law. But marijuana clearly led beyond mere pleasure. One visitor, after a long stay at The Farm, reported to the *National Geographic,* "In all the time I was there, I saw and felt a lot of simple goodness, far more real and lasting than any smoke cloud."

With seven years of pioneering over, The Farm remains alive and prosperous. There has grown a stable core population, including three-fifths of the original 270 settlers. Values seem firmly set in the context of pioneering—simplicity, work, hardship, and natural childbirth. Gaskin refers to his frontier Oklahoma ancestors, proud of that tradition, except that now he cheers for the Indians. Whatever its future, it is not an exaggeration to say that The Farm glories in its frontier rhetoric and life-style.[14]

Even more than at Gaskin's Farm or at Wheeler's Ranch, the image of the small pioneer farm imbues life at Camp Joy, a commune near Santa Cruz, California. Jim Nelson

[13] Anonymous, "Gaskin," *Mother Earth News,* p. 10.

[14] Stephen Gaskin, *Caravan,* pp. 7, 10, 225, 239; Jenkins, "Walk Across America," p. 492; *Phoenix* (San Francisco State University), February 25, 1976.

Sunday-morning wedding service, The Farm, near
Summertown, Tennessee, January, 1976
Paul Kagan

and Beth Benjamin met in the late 1960s at Joan Baez
concerts and antiwar demonstrations. At the University
of California, Santa Cruz, they worked together in The
Garden, seedbed of the ideas of Theodore Reich and Alan
Chadwick. Like Lou Gottlieb, Reich and Chadwick
preached a love and reverence for the earth, but Chadwick and his students went on to explore horticultural
methods and practical techniques. In 1971 Jim and Beth,
now married, were offered the use of nearly four acres of
land called Camp Joy in nearby Boulder Creek. In the

early spring the Nelsons and four others moved into an old barn. There in a drafty loft Beth gave birth to her first child. The barn served as living quarters for years while priorities went to planting, harvesting, and building a new barn for the animals. No chemicals or power-driven machines were used. Large numbers of crops, rigorously rotated, were interspersed for pest control in heavily composted raised beds. Onions, tomatoes, squash, corn, and beans mingled with flowers and herbs. Fruit trees lined the berry patches, and all were fertilized from the goats and chickens. With some justification one of the members said they had created a Garden of Eden.

Housing was perfected more slowly. The old barn was renovated in time for the winter of 1972. A small kitchen was sufficient to preserve in large glass jars on open shelves much of the first harvest. Drying onions and herbs hung from the rafters, their smells combining with the aroma of the wood stove on winter evenings. A tipi and a geodesic dome rose. In the second year the community grew to twelve people, including three children. In 1973, after a series of confrontations with the county over building-code irregularities, planning and construction of a large communal dwelling began. For the next five years the house consumed the community's spare energy. Built of salvaged lumber and hand-split shingles, it included common rooms and a kitchen, upstairs sleeping quarters, showers, and a laundry.

The land was the heart of the community. The earth was not only cherished, though; it was intensely cultivated, following Chadwick's principles, and thereby the colony would demonstrate the feasibility of small farming in an urban environment. This goal ultimately held the group together through the years, especially in 1974, when a faction grew restive and proposed moving into a completely rural surrounding. Most felt that the experiment in self-sufficiency and local marketing was too significant to abandon. By then the commune was providing the major part of its own food and selling to nearby stores and restaurants.

Construction of communal building, Camp Joy, Boulder Creek,
California, 1974
Beth Nelson

Camp Joy was working on the narrow cash base of a pioneer farm. Like E. F. Schumacher, whose *Small Is Beautiful* appeared about that time, Camp Joy was seeking new economics of smallness. At the same time there was always another dimension, an animistic reverence for the spirit of the soil and the color and life it enveloped. Plants were seeded and set out according to the phases of the moon. Short and extralong germinating seeds, for example, were planted only a few days before or after the new moon, "taking advantage of the full sum of the forces of nature, including gravity, light, and magnetism." The harvest at Camp Joy provided the year's high ritual. It was celebrated on the first full moon after the first fall frost, when the tomatoes and squashes ceased to bear. Nature, not a political figure, determined the date of the feast. In attending to the rhythms of soil and season, the individual grew more sensitive to "the aching sweetness of the fava bean blossoms with the light of afternoon slanting through the green." As another member said, "Our bond is a love of gardening and a love of growing things."[15]

The drought of 1976–77 dealt a blow because the farm relied on natural water supplies. As the water from their spring diminished, the members were forced to plant less, which in turn provoked "an identity crisis." As the income slipped, outside work held the nucleus together, and gardening receded as the focus of their lives. It was a difficult period, remotely analogous to times when the pioneer farmers faced the hardships of the plains. Yet they persevered, and even through the difficulties, as an original member, Michael Stusser, put it, the camp "evolved into a close family."[16] Through cooperation and sharing in the work and the harvest, a community was forming.

Ironically, not long after he wrote, Stusser left Camp

[15] John Jeavons, *How to Grow More Vegetables* (Palo Alto, Calif., 1974), p. 36; Beth Nelson to author, April 5, 1975; Boulder Creek (Calif.) *Log,* June 9, 1978.

Joy for a Buddhist retreat. His departure was not untypical. Except for four or five at the center, comings and goings have been frequent. People went away because of desires for greater privacy or more organization, but most often simply for personal reasons, sometimes no more than a restless search for change. The conflicts were probably normal tensions, but mobility may remain a serious barrier to full community at Camp Joy.

Substantial numbers of modern communes, such as spiritual or issue-oriented collectives, take little or no thought of the frontier model. But Wheeler's Ranch, Gaskin's Farm, and Camp Joy represent those that do. They are the ones most concerned with a sense of place, with devotion to the land and nature, and with personal fulfillment through small, integrated arrangements. Furthermore, the values their members hold in common are not as commanding as the traditional religious exaltation of the group over the individual, and in this sense these particular communards may be even more like frontiersmen than they think.

Whenever community thrived on the frontier, it was framed by a sense of place. The scooped shape of a mountain, the peculiar sound of a night wind, a familiar horizon cradling the dead and the unborn—these were means by which the self was joined to the environment. The phenomenon, already a tradition in the American South, is expressed in emotions like those of the farmer who considered his land "as much me as my own arms and legs." But the presumption went deeper. As an old Kentuckian once said, "People could have no devotion to each other that they did not give at the same time to the place they had in common."[17] As an extension of self, this localism

[16] Michael Stusser, "Making Idle Land Produce," *Organic Gardening and Farming* 20 (April, 1973): 58. Stusser, although he left Camp Joy, subsequently settled in a similar garden project in northern California.

[17] I-Fu Tuan, *Topophilia*, p. 97; Wendell Berry, *The Memory of Old Jack*, p. 185. See also Wendell Berry, *Unsettling of America*, pp. 4, 123.

was also the source of the regional history that is so important to new countries and frontiers. Identification with that history reinforced identification with the environment and with its people. In this manner the building stones of community were initially gathered.

In the Puritan town the total environment—the plan of the village common and its radiating farmlands, its central chapel and meeting house—surrounded the individual and insinuated a respect for order. Farther west similar effects were created in the small towns, at least the covenanted ones, with their churches, main streets, and town squares. The experience was well known to ethnic colonists like the Hutterites and the Amanans as they dug their tools and lives into a new soil. Shalam's reverence for its desert sands was a more mystical expression of the same feeling. Everywhere the Far West seemed to specialize in arousing the emotions of place—wilderness for the trapper, open range for the rancher, "That's my mountain!" for Agnes Cleaveland. Yet if these responses were the masonry of community, no social structure was inherent in them. They were stones thrown in the river to make a ford, and the act implied no plans for a bridge. Indeed, in the Far West not only was structure lacking in the interaction between place and community, but the setting itself often became an obstacle. The West embraced little of the enclosed, protective space of the Puritan town; it was a grand, windy, usually unpeopled vista that frequently cast a blue haze of distance over social intent.

Those who would not capture a sense of place were likely to have trouble with stable community. For Jewish colonists, as an example, the Great Plains region with its alien demands and its festering loneliness remained distasteful. For others, interference with attachment could come from intellectual distraction. So it was with Danish socialists and French Fourierists. At New Harmony the theoretical debates caused one man to go three weeks without even noticing the river. Likewise, speculative fever could distort pride of place into boosterism, usually a superficial mockery of the deeper emotion, because the land was seen in terms of transfer and profit, not as an extension of self through time.

Understandably, de Tocqueville saw the westerner as incessantly speculating and moving on, like Seth Humphrey's family, always settling, never settled. Even as late as the 1940s and 1950s the majority of those changing residence sounded much like pioneers—rural, nonfarming young men. In this "ceaseless stir and transformation" each frontiersman remained a stranger to the fate of the rest.[18] His deliberate choice of mobility, monotonously interrupting the psychological adjustment to new environments, repeatedly grew into a context for others who cherished a sense of place. If stability was the rooted plant, restlessness imbued place with all the fragility of uprooted life.

Puritans moving from their village out to farmlands set a pattern in which identity was dashed by transiency. Reproductions of that movement followed like variations on a theme—miners bivouacking until their women and the corporations came, farmhands and cowboys wandering and drifting, ethnics seeking assimilation. All the while increasing division of labor and growing attachment to professions were undercutting place, and agglomeration into larger economic units weakened the uniqueness of localities. For instance, time zones were imposed on the town zenith; the demands of mobility skewed the position of the sun for the benefit of the railroads. As Don Doyle said of Jacksonville, Illinois, the chief hope for community lay in the cultivation of institutions serving mutual strangers.

The changes that chipped away at a sense of place were generally associated with growth, a problem because the loss of smallness drastically influenced the quality of life.

[18] Alexis de Toqueville, *Democracy in America,* 2:166, 311; Donald Bogue et al., *Subregional Migration in the United States,* 1:17–21.

Maximizing size ultimately dictated lower levels of co-operation, participation, and face-to-face contacts. Sometimes larger numbers were an advantage. The smaller scale always bred dangers; those integrated close contacts, for example, could magnify jealousy, wretchedness, and dullness. But whatever its drawbacks, the small group, the timeless, critical clue to human personalities, remained the only context in which certain values like sharing could be fully realized.[19] Because the frontier contained small settlements and their concordant values, it was logical to expect a revitalization of community.

Where communities seemed the most vigorous—the Puritan town, the Hutterites, Amana, Orderville, the Mexican rancho, the Wisconsin Phalanx—numbers ranged around two hundred. But, since others that were less successful—wagon trains, midwestern farm neighborhoods, mining camps—were roughly commensurate, the effects of size on quality appear uncertain. In the latter cases size was determined by the pressures of survival or economic need, and in such situations factionalism seemed unusually high. Collective memory had a hard time developing where growth was courted. Neighborliness then bound neighbors and restrictive associations, but not the total community. Because in the stresses of frontier development few communities could protect themselves from growth and its companion heterogeneity, the strengths which time draws out of smallness seldom matured.

Still, as long as group values held firm, neither mobility nor growth was sufficient to break a community. The outward proof of communal beliefs lay in the willingness to share. Sharing ornamented the calluses of work and worry. Labor and anxiety were the common lot, uniting farmers

---

[19] Robert Nisbet, *Social Bond,* pp. 89–90. For the import of the frontier on mobility see Gordon W. Kirk, Jr., *Promise of American Life.* The John Baskin quote that follows is from *New Burlington: The Life and Death of an American Village,* p. 12.

as they did ranchers. And they were woven together by common things, as in John Baskin's words, "themselves in the presence of each other, work, dislike, judgment, death," all the ambiguities and contradictions of living. Mutual hardship inspired a sense of local uniqueness, and, as in overlanders, it aroused in them a feeling of participation in a historic movement. Collective anguish strengthened the common culture of ethnic colonies. The natural setting for group values growing out of hardships was the self-sufficient, integrated village.

When functioning in communities, values such as sharing and cooperation, like islands in a stream, were surrounded and influenced by prevailing economic theories. The frontier was a competitive milieu, and competition was seldom congenial to the concept of community. Before competitive ideals could predominate among the Puritans, their tribal orientation had to be minimized. And seldom did the thrust return to the tribal. Although the old behavior never died, community tended to become collected individuals, cooperating chiefly for economic purposes, with subdivisions splintering and realigning periodically. The process enthroned imperious individualists like cattlemen, who disdained the public good and derided collective action. The result was harmonious with the Jeffersonian concept of the independent yeoman farmer, so antithetical to the village ideal. When the cooperative colony and the modern commune called for popular ownership and joint production, they challenged important frontier values.

There were always unwitting allies of that challenge, within and without the community circle. Religion, for one, had never ceased proposing the brotherhood of man. And sharing was as much a religious value as it was an economic or social one. Indeed, the fellowship of a mutual faith remained the most effective embodiment of group ideals. John Winthrop's community was a homogeneous worshiping congregation. From the hierarchical Mexican rancho celebrating holy days to the more democratic Protestant small town seeking leadership in the cause of order, the church filled the center. And almost all the immigrant communities would agree with Amana that "faith was the only bond that could unite people." Single issues might be elevated to cosmic proportions, but they never generated the selfless transcendence of an Orderville so joyful in working for the common good.

For community, however, no one should contend that religion was a universal blessing. In the most religiously committed colonies like Lindsborg or Bishop Hill, it was tendentious theological dispute that broke the harmony. In small towns lines between Protestants and Catholics were cracks in the unity. Nevertheless, no other force so consistently asserted the beneficial reality of brotherhood, of mutual awareness, of the incorporation of individuals and events into a larger whole.

Perhaps the secret of communities like Orderville lay in their discerning the point where the self was diminished but not demeaned, where the individual and the society respected the needs of one another. From the group's standpoint the individual will had to be checked for the good of the whole, as when Amana filed its patents only in the name of the community. But on the frontier such demands were risky. As Orderville, the Wisconsin Phalanx, many a ranch and mining camp, and countless small towns all learned to their sorrow, frontier temptations could easily draw off membership. Adherents of the ideas of Ralph Waldo Emerson took less well to restrictions than the sons of philosophers like Brigham Young. The surrender of individuality to the community, the "act of internal secession," as Veysey called it, was rare. Possibly that was why the small town found itself engaged in superficial gossip as its individuals resisted more active commitment and responsibility.

The frontier's more fundamental temptation may have been toward philosophical anarchy. Like tree trunks falling into a swollen stream, trappers, ranchers, miners, immigrants, and colonists from New Harmony to Home succumbed to this ethic. The modern commune often slips into the same waters, measuring its progress primarily in self-awareness and personal fulfillment.[20] Whenever anarchy and community confront one another, time acts as a crucial element, time for the changes in motivation so that sharing may become synonymous with self-realization. The frontier seldom if ever provided a sufficient period for that evolution.

If the individual stood above the community, there was a constant inclination for the family also to draw apart. True, towns like Dedham in the seventeenth century, Dannebrog, or the Mexican rancho were strong enough to reach into and control household life. And the big happy family was the ultimate metaphor for the ideal frontier community. In spite of that platitude, however, the frontier family, in this sense nuclear, was not likely to merge with the community. For most miners, ranchers, or settlers, kinship events—baptisms, weddings, funerals, and Thanksgiving—had ceased to be community occasions. The family and the community tended to walk separate, though not distant, paths.

When closest to Old World conditions—Mexican ranchos or ethnic transplanting—community was built upon hierarchy and class. A natural division of obligations followed. Class had less meaning, however, in most early-frontier situations where wealth and power were more evenly distributed. As time went on, faith in economic and social mobility attenuated class differences and left the illusion of harmony. But that dilution of class consciousness was usually short-lived. In most communities land speculation quickly made some wealthier than others. Economic subcultures with self-conscious life-styles drained identity from the larger community. Wider markets serving farm and town stretched class horizons, a change that Max

[20] Veysey, *Communal Experience,* p. 7; Daniel Boorstin, *Decline of Radicalism,* pp. xiii–xvi; Veysey, "Communal Sex and Communal Survival," *Psychology Today* 8 (December, 1974): 73–78.

Weber, Thorstein Veblen, and Frederick Jackson Turner all found destructive of frontier community. "What is the meaning of this city?" asked T. S. Eliot. "Do you huddle close together because you love each other? What will you answer? 'We all dwell together to make money from each other'? or 'This is a community'?"[21]

Against the shifting nature of American community march the little band of cooperative colonies, sometimes in mild protest, as in Dannebrog's cooperatives, sometimes with shrill voices, as at Equality or Kaweah, sometimes in response to new freedom, as in Negro colonies. Their expectations fresh as a winter star, they proposed to overcome unhappy conditions and statuses. They saw the prevailing society less and less capable of resolving internal tensions, while the politics of vigilantes and boosters exacerbated rather than healed the conflicts. From the colonists' viewpoint the absence of group values left wagon trains bickering and mining camps drowning in litigiousness. Without question the cooperative champions were the product of eastern urban life, yet their uses of and presence on the frontier distorted their protest almost as quickly as the same environment warped other efforts at community.

So it was that the frontier wrestled with what Martin Buber called "the primary aspiration of history," a genuine community. Buber could have identified the American West, as he did his own Israeli desert, as a collective environment, congenial to community, because his prerequisites of heartache and hardship were there aplenty. Certainly in the frontier's early primitive phases sharing and mutual trust surmounted the barriers of restlessness and privatization. By "persuading settlers to seek their own kind," as Howard Lamar once said, the West magnified public values.[22] Yet paradoxically, in the call of every

---

[21] T. S. Eliot, "Choruses from 'The Rock,'" *Complete Poems and Plays, 1909–1950* (New York, 1952), p. 103.

meadowlark at sunset, the frontier seemed to inject a sigh and a longing and so encourage the same people to disperse.

When New Englanders first moved from town to farmland, those who transgressed against the sedentary ancestral ways tended to value independence and property over participation in village life.[23] The frontier must always have sifted, tirelessly screening, to lure the lovers of separation. Consequently much of the population would have been unsympathetic to the frequent close contacts of classic community. Even the stoutest ethnic colonies, as Alfred Nielsen said, felt the frontier environment slowly deteriorate their collective instincts.

Occasionally early frontier conditions weakened economic laissez faire, but more often the debilitation was a mere softening of the harsh effects of that competition. While expectations were aglow with expansion and prosperity and as long as the competitive society appeared so little troubled, cooperation seemed far less compelling. Then, too, the West held a peculiar affinity for the central government; from thence came its cheap land, its protection from Indians, the engineering of its roads and communications. This attachment was a covert rejoinder to localism, an undermining of the values Royce tied to provincialism. "The woof of time is every instant broken and the generations effaced," as de Tocqueville said, and frighteningly so on the frontier.[24] The rapidity of the economic development left little time for new guidelines to crystallize.

In a fragmented society where loneliness vies with frustration, the search for wholeness has special meaning.[25]

[22] Howard R. Lamar, "Public Values and Private Dreams," *South Dakota History* 8 (Spring, 1978): 128.

[23] Richard Bushman, *From Puritan to Yankee* (Cambridge, Mass., 1967), p. 33.

[24] De Tocqueville, *Democracy in America*, 2:105.

[25] Michael Fellman, *The Unbounded Frame*, p. xv.

Today at Wheeler's Ranch, at Camp Joy, at The Farm, and in hundreds of other colonies, people try to carve community out of atomization, to reintroduce *Gemeinschaft* into the *Gesellschaft*. They deal, as we have, with a prescriptive community based on a sense of place, upon integrated lives bound together by values that reach beyond self-interest. If the ongoing search involves these same elements, then it is proper to maintain that definition in looking back on our frontier. Otherwise we may be in danger of losing the model, of settling for a series of associations, and of not understanding the nature of the nineteenth-century efforts and experiments. If the modern world in its size and complexity will realistically permit only the disengaged and associative, we should still keep clearly in mind the alternative. Neither summer haze nor years of air pollution must cause us to forget or redefine a blue sky with white clouds.

Those who prefer pluralism and association to a close-knit community can advance a convincing case. They seek a less restrictive life rich in movement and variety. They point out that historically the village has not been a complete joy; else how explain the desire of millions to escape its narrow confines? The collective, wherever it has existed, can tyrannize and inflict injury as readily as can the individual. Communality may be good for the primitive and poor, but it becomes increasingly irrelevant as society grows economically complex and socially sophisticated—that is, when society leaves its simplest pioneer beginnings. The real distortion, they would say, lies in overlooking the great amount of community spirit surrounding modern urban conditions.[26]

What these sociological commentators are describing is, once again, association, not integrated community. Their model is one of limited involvement and consequently en-

---

[26] Morris Janowitz, *The Community Press in an Urban Setting*, pp. 210–11.

tails easy withdrawal, reduced commitment, and minimal effectiveness. Not everyone in a traditional community has wanted to leave or to see the cooperation individualized. For the men and women of Dannebrog and Orderville, in spite of apparent failure, the community example remained clear and attractive. They and their intellectual offspring would agree with D. H. Lawrence: "Men are free when they belong to a living, organic, believing community, active in fulfilling unfulfilled, perhaps unrealized purposes, not when they are escaping to some Wild West."[27]

It might seem ironic, then, that commune people now praise the model of the pioneer community when the frontier so debilitated collectivism. Indeed, other Americans have "a queasy feeling," as Jackson Putnam recently observed, that frontiersmen made many wrong choices.[28] Perhaps the modern commune might even concur, but it would add that the pioneer did not go far enough toward the collective or that his wrong choices were actually a lack of persistence. B. F. Skinner has wondered whether a cooperative community might not succeed our long courtship with liberalism and personal dignity. If the frontier was our period of supreme individualism, then in this proposition genuine community could emerge from it. Such a transition is a frequent expectation of the commune movement, and the question what follows liberalism could be rephrased to ask what follows our historic love affair with the frontier. Ferdinand Toennies was persuaded that industrialism might spiral upward into some higher version of the lost *Gemeinschaft*. We could eventually achieve a variant of frontier society, one of mutual respect and in-

[27] D. H. Lawrence, *Studies in Classic American Literature* (Garden City, N.Y., 1951), p. 17.
[28] Jackson Putnam, "Turner Thesis and the Westward Movement," *Western Historical Quarterly* 7 (October, 1976): 404; Werner J. Cahnman, "Toennies in America," *History and Theory* 16 (1977): 150.

tuitive communality, such as that which made Max Weber
so merry when visiting early Oklahoma.

Toennies notwithstanding, the experience of the pioneer
community cannot seriously instruct the industrial society.
Gulfs separate them, except that the modern world desperately requires cooperation and seeks more effective
channels for decentralization. History is never a one-way
trend, but the new must always encase parts of the old.
At the levels of cooperation and decentralization the great
historic cycles may yet turn. If we apply Toennies to America, the fruition of the cooperative community, like the
slow blossoming of the maguey, may have to wait until
the full effect of the westward movement is spent. Meanwhile, those who cherish the common good and persevere
in the cultivation of an integrated society should be thought-
fully aware of the so loosely tied, so quickly unbound communities on the American frontier.

BIBLIOGRAPHY

Adams, Andy. *Log of a Cowboy*. Boston, 1931; reprint ed., Lincoln, Nebr., 1964.

Adams, Herbert. "Common Fields in Salem." See Sims, Newell L. *Rural Community*.

———. *Germanic Origins of New England Towns*. Baltimore, Md., 1882.

Alderson, Nannie. See Smith, Helena H. *Bride*.

Allen, James B. *Company Town in the American West*. Norman, Okla., 1966.

Allen, Ruth. *Chapters in the History of Organized Labor in Texas*. Austin, Texas, 1941.

Anderson, Sherwood. *Home Town*. New York, 1940.

———. *Poor White*. New York, 1925.

———. *Winesburg, Ohio*. New York, 1919; reprint ed., Garden City, N.Y., 1960.

Anderson, Wilbert L. *Country Town: A Study of Rural Evolution*. 1906; reprint ed., New York, 1974.

Angell, Robert C. *Free Society in Moral Crisis*. Ann Arbor, Mich., 1958.

Arensberg, Conrad M. *Culture and Community*. New York, 1965.

Arrington, Leonard, et al. *Building the City of God: Community and Cooperation Among the Mormons*. Salt Lake City, Utah, 1976.

Athearn, Robert G. *In Search of Canaan: Black Migration to Kansas, 1879–80*. Lawrence, Kans., 1978.

Atherton, Lewis. *Cattle Kings*. Bloomington, Ind., 1961.

———. *Main Street on the Middle Border*. Bloomington, Ind., 1954.

Bach, Robert L., and Smith, Joel. "Community Satisfaction, Expectations of Moving, and Migration." *Demography* 14 (May, 1977):147–67.

Bailes, Kendall. "The Mennonites Come to Kansas." *American Heritage* 10 (August, 1959):30.

Baltzell, Edward D. *Search for Community in Modern America.* New York, 1968.

Bancroft, Hubert Howe. *History of California.* 7 vols. San Francisco, 1884–90.

Barker, Eugene C. *Life of Stephen F. Austin.* Austin, Texas, 1925.

Barnes, Cass G. *Sod House.* Lincoln, Nebr., 1970.

Barth, Gunther. *Instant Cities: Urbanization and the Rise of San Francisco and Denver.* New York, 1975.

Baskin, John. *New Burlington: The Life and Death of an American Village.* New York, 1976.

Bassett, T. D. Seymour. "The Quakers and Communitarianism." *Bulletin of Friends Historical Association* 43 (Autumn, 1954): 84–100.

Becker, Carl. "Kansas." In *Everyman His Own Historian.* New York, 1935.

Beijbom, Ulf. "The Printed Word in a Nineteenth-Century Immigrant Colony: The Role of the Ethnic Press in Chicago's Swede Town." *Swedish Pioneer Historical Quarterly* 28 (April, 1977):82–96.

Bemis, Edward W., et al. *History of Cooperation in the United States.* Baltimore, Md., 1888.

Bender, Thomas. *Community and Social Change in America.* New Brunswick, N.J., 1978.

Bendix, Reinhard. *Max Weber: An Intellectual Portrait.* Garden City, N.Y., 1960.

———, and Lipset, S. Martin, eds. *Class, Status and Power.* New York, 1966.

Benne, Kenneth D. *Group Dynamics and Social Action.* New York, 1950.

Bercovici, Konrad. *Story of the Gypsies.* New York, 1928.

Bernard, Jessie S. *Sociology of Community.* Glenview, Ill., 1973.

Berneking, Carolyn B. "Welsh Settlers of Emporia: A Cultural History." *Kansas Historical Quarterly* 37 (Autumn, 1971): 269–80.

Berry, Don. *Majority of Scoundrels: An Informal History of the Rocky Mountain Fur Co.* New York, 1961.

Berry, Wendell. *Memory of Old Jack.* New York, 1974.

———. *Unsettling of America.* San Francisco, 1977.

Berthoff, Rowland. *British Immigrants in Industrial America, 1790–1950.* Cambridge, Mass., 1953.

———. *An Unsettled People.* New York, 1971.

Bestor, Arthur. *Backwoods Utopias.* Philadelphia, 1970.

Bidwell, Percy W. "Agricultural Revolution in New England." *American Historical Review* 26 (July, 1921):683–702.

Billdt, Ruth. *Pioneer Swedish-American Culture in Central Kansas.* Lindsborg, Kans., 1965.

Billington, Ray A. *America's Frontier Heritage.* New York, 1966.

———. *Frederick Jackson Turner: Historian, Scholar, Teacher.* New York, 1973.

Bishop, Claire H. *All Things Common.* New York, 1950.

Bloomberg, Susan, et al. "A Census Probe into Nineteenth Century Family History: Southern Michigan, 1850–1880." *Journal of Social History* 5 (Fall, 1971):26–45.

Blouet, Brian, and Lawson, Merlin, eds. *Images of the Plains: The Role of Human Nature in Settlement.* Lincoln, Nebr., 1975.

Blumenthal, Albert. *Small-Town Stuff.* Chicago, 1932.

———. *Sociological Study of a Small Town.* Chicago, 1932.

Blumin, Stuart. *Urban Threshold: Growth and Change in a 19th Century American Community.* Chicago, 1976.

Boatright, Mody. "Myth of Frontier Individualism." See Hofstadter, Richard, and Lipset, S. Martin. *Turner.*

Bodenhamer, David J. "Law and Disorder on the Early Frontier: Marion County, Indiana, 1823–1859." *Western Historical Quarterly* 10 (July, 1979):323–36.

Bogue, Allan G. *From Prairie to Corn Belt.* Chicago, 1963.

———. "Social Theory and the Pioneer." See Hofstadter, Richard, and Lipset, S. Martin. *Turner.*

———, et al, eds. *West of the American People.* Itasca, Ill., 1970.

Bogue, Donald, ed. *Applications of Demography.* Oxford, Ohio, 1957.

———, et al. *Subregional Migration in the United States, 1935–1940.* 2 vols. Oxford, Ohio, 1953–57.

Boorstin, Daniel. *The Americans.* 3 vols. New York, 1958–73.

———.*Decline of Radicalism.* New York, 1969.

———. *Republic of Technology.* New York, 1978.

Borthwick, John D. *Three Years in California.* Oakland, Calif., 1948.

Bowden, Martyn. "Desert Wheat Belt, Plains Corn Belt." See Blouet, Brian, and Lawson, Merlin, eds. *Images.*

Bradfield, Richard M. *Natural History of Associations.* London, 1973.

Bradbury, John. "Travels in the Interior." See Thwaites, Reuben, G. *Travels.*

Bradford, William. *Of Plymouth Plantation, 1620–1647.* Edited by Samuel E. Morison. New York, 1952.

Branch, E. Douglas. *Westward.* New York, 1930.

Braunthal, Julius. *History of the International.* 2 vols. New York, 1967.

Bridenbaugh, Carl. *Cities in the Wilderness.* New York, 1938.

Briggs, John E. "Grasshopper Plagues in Iowa." *Iowa Journal of History and Politics* 13 (July, 1915):349–91.

Bright, John, ed. *Kansas.* New York, 1956.

Bronson, Kenneth C. "Local Press and the Changing Community." *Kansas Historical Quarterly* 42 (Spring, 1976):48–54.

Bronstein, Zelda, and Kann, Kenneth. "Basha Singerman, Comrade of Petaluma." *California Historical Quarterly* 56 (Spring, 1977):20–33.

Brown, Dee. *Gentle Tamers.* Lincoln, Nebr., 1958.

Brown, Irving. *Gypsy Fires in America.* New York, 1924.

———. "Gypsies in America." *Journal of the Gypsy Lore Society* 8 (1929): 145–76.

Brown, Richard M. *Strain of Violence.* New York, 1975.

BIBLIOGRAPHY   263

Brown, Robert E. *Middle-Class Democracy and the Revolution in Massachusetts.* Ithaca, N.Y., 1955.

Brownell, Baker. *Human Community.* New York, 1950.

Brunner, Edmund. *Village Communities.* New York, 1927.

Buber, Martin. *Paths in Utopia.* Boston, 1949.

Buell, Jennie. *One Woman's Work for Farm Women.* Boston, 1908.

Buffum, Edward G. *Six Months in the Gold Mines.* Los Angeles, 1959.

Burr, Walter. *Small Towns.* New York, 1929.

Bushee, Frederick A. "Communistic Societies in the United States." *Political Science Quarterly* 20 (December, 1905): 625–64.

Cabeza de Baca, Fabiola. *We Fed Them Cactus.* Albuquerque, N.Mex., 1954.

Cahnman, Werner J. "Toennies in America." *History and Theory* 16 (May, 1977):147–67.

Calhoun, Arthur. *Social History of the American Family.* 3 vols. Cleveland, Ohio, 1917–19.

Cather, Willa. *My Antonia.* Boston, 1946.

Caughey, John W. *Gold Is the Cornerstone.* Berkeley, Calif., 1948.

———. *Their Majesties the Mob.* Chicago, 1960.

Chase, Warren. *The Life-Line of the Lone One.* Boston, 1857.

Chittenden, Hiram M. *History of the American Fur Trade of the Far West.* 2 vols. Stanford, Calif., 1954.

Clappe, Louise Amelia K. (Dame Shirley). *Shirley Letters.* New York, 1949.

Clark, Dan. *Middle West in American History.* New York, 1937.

Clarke, Ada B. "Pothook Pioneer: A Remembrance." *Nebraska History* 39 (March, 1958):41–56.

Clay, John. *My Life on the Range.* Norman, Okla., 1962.

Cleaveland, Agnes. *No Life for a Lady.* Boston, 1941.

Cleland, Robert G. *Cattle on a Thousand Hills.* San Marino, Calif., 1951.

———. *This Reckless Breed of Men.* New York, 1950.

Clifton, James. *Prairie People.* Lawrence, Kans., 1977.

Clyman, James. *James Clyman, Frontiersman.* Edited by Charles Camp. Portland, Oreg., 1960.

Colman, Peter. "Restless Grant County." In *Old Northwest.* Edited by Harry Scheiber. Lincoln, Nebr., 1969.

Colton, Walter. *Three Years in California.* Stanford, Calif., 1949.

Cone, Carl B. "Iowa Firemen's Association." *Iowa Journal of History and Politics* 42 (July, 1944):227–65.

Conkin, Paul K. *Two Paths to Utopia.* Lincoln, Nebr., 1964.

Connor, Seymour, and Skaggs, Jimmy. *Broadcloth and Britches: The Santa Fe Trade.* College Station, Texas, 1977.

Considerant, Victor. *Great West.* New York, 1854.

Conzen, Kathleen N. *Immigrant Milwaukee, 1836–1860.* Cambridge, Mass., 1976.

Cook, Edward M., Jr. *Fathers of the Towns.* Baltimore, Md., 1976.

Cook, Harold J. *Tales of the 04 Ranch.* Lincoln, Nebr., 1968.

Corning, Howard M. *Willamette Landings.* Portland, Oreg., 1973.

Coser, Lewis A. *Functions of Social Conflict.* Glencoe, Ill., 1956.

Cotton, James H. *Royce on the Human Self.* Cambridge, Mass., 1954.

Coy, Owen C. *The Great Trek.* Los Angeles, 1931.

Crews, Harry. *Childhood: The Biography of a Place.* New York, 1978.

Crockett, Norman L. *Black Towns.* Lawrence, Kans., 1979.

Curti, Merle. *Making of an American Community.* Stanford, Calif., 1959.

Dale, Edward E. *Cow Country.* Norman, Okla., 1965.

———. *Frontier Ways.* Austin, Texas, 1959.

Dane, G. Ezra. *Ghost Town.* New York, 1941.

Davidson, Sara. "Open Land: Getting Back to the Communal Garden." *Harper's* 240 (June, 1970):91–102.

Davies, Phillips G., ed. "Welsh Settlements in Kansas." *Kansas Historical Quarterly* 43 (Winter, 1977):448–69.

Davis, James E. *Frontier America, 1800–1840: A Comparative Demographic Analysis of the Settlement Process.* Glendale, Calif., 1977.

Davis, Ronald L. "Community and Conflict in Pioneer St. Louis, Missouri." *Western Historical Quarterly* 10 (July, 1979): 337–55.

Dawley, Alan. *Class and Community: The Industrial Revolution in Lynn.* Cambridge, Mass., 1976.

Debo, Angie. *Prairie City.* New York, 1944.

Decker, Peter. *Fortunes and Failures: White Collar Mobility in 19th-Century San Francisco.* Cambridge, Mass., 1978.

De Groot, Henry. *Recollections of California Mining Life.* San Francisco, 1884.

Delano, Alonzo. *Life on the Plains and Among the Diggings.* Auburn, N.Y., 1854; reprint ed., New York, 1973.

Demos, John. "Families in Colonial Bristol, R.I." *William and Mary Quarterly* 25 (January, 1968):40–67.

———. *Little Commonwealth: Family Life in Plymouth Colony.* New York, 1970.

Dennon, Jim. *Oahspe Story.* Seaside, Oreg., 1965.

De Quille, Dan. *Big Bonanza.* New York, 1947.

De Voto, Bernard. *Across the Wide Missouri.* Boston, 1947.

Dick, Everett. *Sod-house Frontier.* Lincoln, Nebr., 1954.

———. *Vanguards of the Frontier.* New York, 1941.

Diggins, John P. "Consciousness and Ideology in American History: The Burden of Daniel J. Boorstin." *American Historical Review* 76 (February, 1971):99–118.

Dinnerstein, Leonard., et al. *Natives and Strangers: Ethnic Groups in the Building of America.* New York, 1979.

Dorfman, Joseph. *Thorstein Veblen and His America.* New York, 1934.

Douglass, Harlan. *Little Town.* New York, 1919.

Dowie, J. I. *Prairie Grass Dividing.* Rock Island, Ill., 1959.

Doyle, Don H. *Social Order of a Frontier Community: Jacksonville, Illinois, 1825–1870.* Urbana, Ill., 1978.

———. "Social Theory and New Communities in Nineteenth Century America." *Western Historical Quarterly* 8 (April, 1977):151–65.

Drache, Hiram. *Challenge of the Prairie.* Fargo, N.Dak., 1970.

Drukman, Mason. *Community and Purpose in America.* New York, 1971.

Dykstra, Robert R. *Cattle Towns.* New York, 1968.

Ebbutt, Percy G. *Emigrant Life in Kansas.* London, 1886; reprint ed., New York, 1975.

Eblen, Jack E. "An Analysis of Nineteenth-Century Frontier Populations." *Demography,* no. 2 (1965):399–413.

Egleston, Nathaniel. *Villages and Village Life with Hints for Their Improvement.* New York, 1878.

Ellis, Anne. *Life of an Ordinary Woman.* Boston, 1929.

———. *Plain Anne Ellis: More About the Life of an Ordinary Woman.* Boston, 1931.

Ely, Richard. "Economic Aspects of Mormonism." *Harper's* 106 (April, 1903):667–78.

Fairchild, Grace. *Frontier Woman.* Edited by Walker Wyman. River Falls, Wis., 1972.

Faragher, John M. *Women and Men on the Overland Trail.* New Haven, Conn., 1979.

"The Farm: Excerpts from the January 1975 Farm Report." *Communities* 13 (March–April, 1975):18–19.

Fatout, Paul. *Meadow Lake: Gold Town.* Bloomington, Ind., 1969.

Faulk, Odie. *Dodge City.* New York, 1977.

Fehrenbach, T. R. *Lone Star.* New York, 1968.

Fellman, Michael. *The Unbounded Frame: Freedom and Community in Nineteenth Century Utopianism.* Westport, Conn., 1973.

Ferguson, Charles W. *Fifty Million Brothers: A Panorama of American Lodges and Clubs.* New York, 1937.

Filley, Horace C. *Cooperation in Agriculture.* New York, 1929.

Fischer, Christiane, ed. *Let Them Speak for Themselves: Women in the American West, 1849–1900.* Hamden, Conn., 1977.

Fite, Gilbert. *Farmer's Frontier.* New York, 1966.

Fogarty, Robert S. "American Communes, 1865–1914." *Journal of American Studies* 9 (August, 1975):145–62.

———. *American Utopianism.* Itasca, Ill. 1972.

Fox, Dixon R. *Sources of Culture in the Middle West.* New York, 1934.

Frantz, Joe B., and Choate, Julian E., Jr. *American Cowboy:*

The Myth and the Reality. Norman, Okla., 1955.

Freeman, Susan. *Neighbors.* Chicago, 1970.

French, Robert M. *Community: A Comparative Perspective.* Itasca, Ill., 1969.

Fried, Albert, ed. *Socialism in America.* Garden City, N.Y., 1970.

Friedrich, Carl, ed. *Community (Nomos: II).* New York, 1959.

Frink, Maurice; Jackson, W. T.; and Spring, Agnes. *When Grass Was King.* Boulder, Colo., 1956.

Frisch, Michael H. *Town into City: Springfield, Massachusetts, and the Meaning of Community, 1840–1880.* Cambridge, Mass., 1972.

Fuss, Peter. *Moral Philosophy of Josiah Royce.* Cambridge, Mass., 1965.

Gaines, Marlene. "The Early Sacramento Jewish Community." *Western States Jewish Historical Quarterly* 3 (January, 1971): 65–85.

Galeski, Boguslaw. "Models of Collective Farming." In *Cooperative and Commune: Group Farming in the Economic Development of Agriculture.* Edited by Peter Dorner. Madison, Wis., 1977.

Galpin, Charles J. *The Social Anatomy of an Agricultural Community.* Madison, Wis., 1915.

Gambone, Joseph G., ed. "Kansas—A Vegetarian Utopia: The Letters of John Milton Hadley, 1855–1856." *Kansas Historical Quarterly* 38 (Spring, 1972):65–87.

Garland, Hamlin. *Son of the Middle Border.* 1914, reprint ed., New York, 1952.

Garrard, Lewis H. *Wah-to-yah and the Taos Trail.* Norman, Okla., 1955.

Gaskin, Stephen. *Caravan.* New York, 1972.

———. *Monday Night Class.* San Francisco, n.d.

Gates, Paul W. *Farmer's Age.* New York, 1960.

———. "Frontier Estate Builders and Farm Laborers." See Hofstader, Richard and Lipset, S. Martin. *Turner.*

Gaustad, Edwin S. *Dissent in American Religion.* Chicago, 1973.

———. *Historical Atlas of Religion in America.* 1962; rev. ed.,

New York, 1976.

Gide, Charles. *Communist and Co-operative Colonies.* New York, 1930.

Gillespie, Charles B. "A Miner's Sunday in Coloma." *Century* 42 (June, 1891):259–69.

Goist, Park. *From Main Street to State Street: Town, City, and Community in America.* Point Washington, N.Y., 1977.

Goldschmidt, Walter. *As You Sow.* Montclair, N.J., 1947.

Gonzalez, Nancie L. *Spanish-Americans of New Mexico.* Albuquerque, N.Mex., 1969.

Gowans, Fred R. *Rocky Mountain Rendezvous: A History of the Fur Trade Rendezvous, 1825–1840.* Provo, Utah, 1976.

Grant, Charles S. *Democracy in the Connecticut Frontier Town of Kent.* New York, 1961.

Grant, Roger H. "Portrait of a Workers' Utopia: The Labor Exchange and the Freedom, Kan., Colony." *Kansas Historical Quarterly* 43 (Spring, 1977):56–66.

Greever, William S. *The Bonanza West.* Norman, Okla., 1963.

Gregg, Josiah. *Commerce of the Prairies.* Norman, Okla., 1954.

Gressley, Gene M. *Bankers and Cattlemen.* New York, 1966.

Greven, Philip Jr. *Four Generations: Population, Land, and Family in Colonial Andover, Mass.* Ithaca, N.Y., 1970.

Griswold, Don L. and Jean H. *The Carbonate Camp Called Leadville.* Denver, Colo., 1951.

Gross, Paul S. *Hutterite Way.* Saskatoon, Canada, 1965.

Gudde, Edwin. *California Gold Camps.* Berkeley, Calif., 1975.

Guenther, Richard L. "A History of the Welsh Community of Carroll, Nebraska." *Nebraska History* 46 (September, 1965): 209–24.

Gutman, Herbert. *Work, Culture, and Society in Industrializing America.* New York, 1976.

Hafen, LeRoy R. *Mountain Men and the Fur Trade of the Far West.* 10 vols. Glendale, Calif., 1965–.

Hagen, Norris C. *Three North Dakota Settlers Reminisce.* New York, 1958.

Hale, Will. *Twenty-four Years a Cowboy and Ranchman in Southern Texas and Old Mexico.* Norman, Okla., 1976.

Haley, J. Evetts. *XIT Ranch of Texas and the Early Days of the Llano Estacado.* Norman, Okla., 1953.

Haller, William. *Puritan Frontier.* New York, 1951.

Hamburg, James F. "Paper Towns in South Dakota." *Journal of the West* 16 (January, 1977):40–42.

Handlin, Oscar. *The Uprooted.* New York, 1951.

Hannon, Jessie G. *Boston-Newton Company Venture: From Massachusetts to California in 1849.* Lincoln, Nebr., 1969.

Hargreaves, Mary W. "Homesteading and Homemaking on the Plains." *Agricultural History* 47 (April, 1973):156–63.

Harris, Charles W., and Rainey, Buck, eds. *The Cowboy: Six-shooters, Songs, and Sex.* Norman, Okla., 1976.

Haskell, Burnette G. "Kaweah." *Out West* 17 (September, 1902):300–22.

Hastings, Lansford W. *Emigrants' Guide to Oregon and California.* Princeton, N.J., 1932.

Hayden, Dolores. *Seven American Utopias: The Architecture of Communitarian Socialism, 1790–1975.* Cambridge, Mass., 1976.

Hicks, Granville. *Small Town.* New York, 1946.

Hill, Mozell. "The All-Negro Communities of Oklahoma." *Journal of Negro History* 31 (July, 1946):254–68.

Hillery, George A., Jr. *Communal Organizations: A Study of Local Societies.* Chicago, 1968.

———. "Definitions of Community: Areas of Agreement." *Rural Sociology* 20 (June, 1955):111–23.

Hinds, William. *American Communities.* 1878; reprint ed., Gloucester, Mass., 1971.

Hofstadter, Richard, and Lipset, S. Martin. *Turner and the Sociology of the Frontier.* New York, 1968.

Holloway, Mark. *Heavens on Earth: Utopian Communities in America, 1680–1880.* New York, 1966.

Hostetler, John A. *Hutterite Society.* Baltimore, Md., 1974.

———, and Huntington, Gertrude E. *Hutterites in North America.* New York, 1967.

Howe, Edgar W. *The Anthology of Another Town.* New York, 1920.

———. *Plain People*. New York, 1929.

———. *Story of a Country Town*. Boston, 1927.

Humphrey, Seth K. *Following the Prairie Frontier*. Minneapolis, Minn., 1931.

International Congress of Arts and Science, Universal Exposition, Saint Louis, 1904. *Congress of Arts and Science*. Edited by Howard Rogers. 8 vols. Boston, 1905–1907.

Isaksson, Olov. *Bishop Hill, Illinois: A Utopia on the Prairie*. Stockholm, Sweden, 1969.

Jackson, W. Turrentine. *Treasure Hill: Portrait of a Silver Mining Camp*. Tucson, Ariz., 1963.

Janowitz, Morris. *The Community Press in an Urban Setting: The Social Elements of Urbanism*. Chicago, 1967.

Jaramillo, Cleofas. "Shadows of the Past." In *The New Mexico Hispano*. New York, 1974.

Jarchow, Merrill E. *The Earth Brought Forth: A History of Minnesota Agriculture to 1885*. Saint Paul, Minn., 1949.

Jenkins, Jeff. *The Northern Tier, or Life Among the Homesteaders*. Topeka, Kans., 1880.

Jenkins, Peter. "Walk Across America." *National Geographic* 151 (April, 1977):466–99.

———. *Walk Across America*. New York, 1979.

Jones, Oakah L., Jr. *Los Paisanos*. Norman, Okla., 1979.

Jordan, Terry G. "The Origin and Distribution of Open-Range Cattle Ranching." *Social Science Quarterly* 53 (June, 1972): 105–21.

Kagan, Paul. *New World Utopias*. New York, 1975.

Kanter, Rosabeth M. *Commitment and Community: Communes and Utopias in Sociological Perspective*. Cambridge, Mass., 1972.

Katz, William L. *The Black West*. Garden City, N.Y., 1973.

Keleher, Julia. "The Land of Shalam: Utopia in New Mexico." *New Mexico Historical Review* 19 (April, 1944):123–34.

Kelson, Benjamin. "Jews of Montana." *Western States Jewish Historical Quarterly* 3 (January–July, 1971):113.

Kerr, William G. *Scottish Capital on the American Credit Frontier*. Austin, Texas, 1976.

Kieninger, Richard. *Ultimate Frontier*. Chicago, 1963.

Kinneman, John. *Community in American Society.* New York, 1947.

Kirk, Gordon W. Jr. *Promise of American Life: Social Mobility in a Nineteenth Century Immigrant Community, Holland, Michigan, 1847–1894.* Philadelphia, 1978.

Kirk, Russel. *The Roots of American Order.* LaSalle, Ill., 1974.

Knight, Oliver. "Toward an Understanding of the Western Town." *Western Historical Quarterly* 4 (January, 1973): 27–42.

Koerselman, Gary H. "Quest for Community in Rural Iowa: Neighborhood Life in Early Middleburg History." *Annals of Iowa* 41 (Summer, 1972):1006–20.

———. "Church and Community Life in Early Middleburg History." *Annals of Iowa* 40 (Spring, 1971):631–40.

König, René. *Community.* New York, 1968.

Kuklick, Bruce. *Josiah Royce: An Intellectual Biography.* Indianapolis, Ind., 1972.

Kutak, Robert I. *The Story of a Bohemian-American Village.* Louisville, Ky., 1933.

Lamar, Howard R. "Public Values and Private Dreams: South Dakota's Search for Identity, 1850–1900." *South Dakota History* 8 (Spring, 1978):117–42.

———. *Trader on the American Frontier: Myth's Victim.* College Station, Texas, 1977.

Langum, David J. "Pioneer Justice on the Overland Trails." *Western Historical Quarterly* 5 (October, 1974):421–39.

Lapp, Rudolph M. *Blacks in Gold Rush California.* New Haven, Conn., 1977.

Larsen, Lawrence H. *Urban West at the End of the Frontier.* Lawrence, Kans., 1978.

Lasch, Christopher. *World of Nations.* 1962; reprint ed., New York, 1973.

Lasky, Melvin J. *Utopia and Revolution.* Chicago, 1976.

Lavender, David. *Westward Vision.* New York, 1963.

Lea, Tom. *King Ranch.* 2 vols. Boston, 1957.

Lee, Katie. *Ten Thousand Goddam Cattle.* Flagstaff, Ariz., 1976.

Levy, Daniel. "Letters About the Jews of California: 1855–58."

Western States Jewish Historical Quarterly 3 (January, 1971): 86–112.

LeWarne, Charles P. *Utopias on Puget Sound, 1885–1915.* Seattle, Wash., 1975.

Lewis, Faye C. *Nothing to Make a Shadow.* Ames, Iowa, 1971.

Lindquist, Emory. *Smokey Valley People.* Lindsborg, Kans., 1953.

———. *Vision for a Valley.* Rock Island, Ill., 1970.

Lingenfelter, Richard E. *Hardrock Miners.* Berkeley, Calif., 1974.

Lockridge, Kenneth A. *A New England Town: The First Hundred Years.* New York, 1970.

Lockwood, George B. *New Harmony Communities.* New York, 1971.

Lockwood, Maren. "Experimental Utopia in America." *Daedalus* 2 (Spring, 1965):401–18.

Lubbig, John C. *Journal of a Fur-Trading Expedition on the Upper Missouri.* New York, 1964.

Luebke, Frederick C. "Ethnic Group Settlement on the Great Plains." *Western Historical Quarterly* 8 (October, 1977): 405–30.

———. *Immigrants and Politics: The Germans of Nebraska 1880–1900.* Lincoln, Nebr., 1969.

Lyman, George D. *Saga of the Comstock Lode.* New York, 1934.

Lynd, Robert and Helen. *Middletown.* New York, 1929.

McConnel, John L. *Western Characters.* New York, 1853; reprint ed., New York, 1975.

McCoy, Joseph G. *Cattle Trade of the West and Southwest.* Kansas City, Mo., 1874; reprint ed., Ann Arbor, 1966.

McIntosh, Montgomery E. "Co-operative Communities in Wisconsin." *Proceedings of the State Historical Society of Wisconsin,* 1903, pp. 99–117.

MacIver, Robert M. *On Community, Society, and Power.* Chicago, 1970.

McLeod, Martin. "Diary." Edited by Grace Nute. *Minnesota History* 4 (November, 1922):350–439.

McWilliams, Wilson C. *Idea of Fraternity in America.* Berkeley, Calif., 1973.

Magoffin, Susan S. *Down the Santa Fé Trail and into Mexico.* New Haven, Conn., 1926.

Malin, James C. *Grassland of North America.* Lawrence, Kans., 1947.

――――. "The Turnover of Farm Population in Kansas." *Kansas Historical Quarterly* 4 (November, 1935):339–72.

Mann, Ralph. "Decade After the Gold Rush: Social Structure in Grass Valley and Nevada City, Calif., 1850–1860." *Pacific Historical Review* 41 (November, 1972):484–504.

Marcy, Randolph B. *Prairie Traveler.* New York, 1859.

Mayhew, Ann. "A Reappraisal of the Causes of Farm Protest in the U.S. 1870–1900." *Journal of Economic History* 32 (June, 1972):464–75.

Meltzer, George. "Social Life and Entertainment on Kansas Frontier, 1854–1890." Master's thesis, University of Wichita, Kans., 1941.

Mercer, Duane D. "Colorado Co-operative Company, 1894–1904." *Colorado Magazine* 44 (Fall, 1967):293–306.

Mikkelsen, Michael A. *Bishop Hill Colony.* Baltimore, Md., 1892.

Miller, James M. *Genesis of Western Culture.* Columbus, Ohio, 1938.

Miller, Kenneth E. "Danish Socialism and the Kansas Prairie." *Kansas Historical Quarterly* 38 (Summer, 1972):156–68.

Miller, Nyle H., ed. "An English Runnymede in Kansas." *Kansas Historical Quarterly* 41 (Spring–Summer, 1975):22.

Miller, Perry, and Johnson, Thomas H. *Puritans.* New York, 1938.

Minar, David W. *Concept of Community.* Chicago, 1969.

Mintz, Sidney, and Wolf, Eric. "Analysis of Ritual Co-parenthood." *Southwestern Journal of Anthropology* 6 (Winter, 1950):341–68.

Mitzman, Arthur. *Sociology and Estrangement: Three Sociologists of Imperial Germany.* New York, 1973.

Miyakawa, T. Scott. *Protestants and Pioneers.* Chicago, 1964.

Modell, John. "Family and Fertility on the Indiana Frontier, 1820." *American Quarterly* 23 (December, 1971):615–34.

Morgan, Dale L. *Jedediah Smith: And the Opening of the West.*

Lincoln, Nebr., 1953.

Morgan, Edmund S. *American Slavery, American Freedom: The Ordeal of Colonial Virginia.* New York, 1975.

———. *Puritan Family.* Boston, 1956.

Morning Star Scrapbook. By Unohoo et al. Occidental, Calif., 1973.

Mortensen, Daniel R. "Process of Community Development in a Frontier Town: Sonora, California, 1848–1860." Ph.D. dissertation, University of Southern California, 1977.

Morton, Arthur L. *Life and Ideas of Robert Owen.* New York, 1962.

Moynihan, James. *Life of Archbishop John Ireland.* New York, 1953.

Moynihan, Ruth B. "Children and Young People on the Overland Trail." *Western Historical Quarterly* 6 (July, 1975): 279–94.

Muir, John. *Story of My Boyhood and Youth.* Madison, Wis., 1965.

Mulford, Prentice. *Prentice Mulford's Story.* Oakland, Calif., 1953.

Muller, Dorothea R. "Church Building and Community Making on the Frontier, a Case Study: Josiah Strong, Home Missionary in Cheyenne, 1871–1873." *Western Historical Quarterly* 10 (April, 1979):191–216.

Myers, Sandra. *Ranch in Spanish Texas, 1691–1900.* El Paso, Texas, 1969.

Nelson, Lowry. *American Farm Life.* Cambridge, Mass., 1954.

———. *Rural Sociology.* Minneapolis, Minn., 1969.

Nelson, Ronald E. "The Role of Colonies in the Pioneer Settlement of Henry County, Illinois." Ph.D. dissertation, University of Nebraska, 1970.

New Harmony as Seen by Participants and Travelers. Philadelphia, 1975.

Nielsen, Alfred C. *Life in an American Denmark.* Des Moines, Iowa, 1962.

Nisbet, Robert A. *Quest For Community or Community and Power.* New York, 1953.

———. *Social Bond.* New York, 1970.

———. *Sociological Tradition.* New York, 1966.

———. *Twilight of Authority.* New York, 1975.

Nordhoff, Charles. *Communistic Societies of the United States.* New York, 1875.

Nordyke, Lewis. *Great Roundup: The Story of Texas and Southwestern Cowmen.* New York, 1955.

Novak, Michael. *Rise of the Unmeltable Ethnics.* New York, 1972.

Noyes, John H. *History of American Socialisms.* 1870; reprint ed., New York, 1966.

O'Kieffe, Charley. *Western Story: Recollections.* Lincoln, Nebr., 1960.

Owen, Robert D. *Threading My Way: An Autobiography.* 1874; reprint ed., New York, 1967.

Owens, Meroe J. "John Barzynski, Land Agent." *Nebraska History* 36 (June, 1955):81–91.

Painter, Nell I. *Exodusters: Black Migration to Kansas After Reconstruction.* New York, 1976.

Parkman, Francis. *Oregon Trail.* Edited by E. N. Feltskog. Madison, Wis., 1969.

Pattie, James O. *Personal Narrative.* 1962; reprint ed., New York, 1966.

Paul, Rodman. *Mining Frontiers of the Far West 1848–1880.* New York, 1963.

———. *California Gold.* Cambridge, Mass., 1947; reprint ed., Lincoln, Nebr., 1965.

Pearson, Norman H. "The American Writer and the Feeling for Community." *English Studies* 43 (October, 1962):403–12.

Pease, William H. and Pease, Jane H. *Black Utopias.* Madison, Wis., 1963.

Pedrick, S. M. "Wisconsin Phalanx at Ceresco." *Proceedings of the State Historical Society of Wisconsin* 50 (1902):190–226.

Pelham, William. See *New Harmony as Seen by Participants and Travelers.*

Perkins, William R., and Wick, Barthinius L. *History of the Amana Society.* Iowa City, 1891; reprint ed., Westport, Conn.,

1976.

Perrigo, Lynn I. "Law and Order in Early Colorado Mining Camps." *Mississippi Valley Historical Review* 28 (June, 1941–42):41–62.

Peterson, Ellen. "Origins of the Town of Nucla." *Colorado Magazine* 26 (October, 1949):252–58.

Peterson, Richard H. *Bonanza Kings.* Lincoln, Nebr., 1977.

———. "The Frontier Thesis and Social Mobility in the Mining Frontier." *Pacific Historical Review* 44 (February, 1975): 52–67.

Pickett, Calder M. *Ed Howe: Country Town Philosopher.* Lawrence, Kans., 1968.

Pierson, George W. *The Moving American.* New York, 1973.

Plant, Raymond. *Community and Ideology.* London, 1974.

"Plowboy Papers: Stephen Gaskin and The Farm." *Mother Earth News* 45 (May–June, 1977):8–20.

Pomeroy, Earl. "Josiah Royce, Historian in Quest of Community." *Pacific Historical Review* 40 (February, 1971):1–20.

Pole, Jack R. "Daniel Boorstin." *Pastmasters.* Edited by Marcus Cunliffe and Robin Winks. New York, 1969.

———. *Pursuit of Equality in American History.* Berkeley, Calif., 1978.

Poplin, Dennis. *Communities.* New York, 1972.

Porter, Kenneth W. *John Jacob Astor, Businessman.* 2 vols. Cambridge, Mass., 1931.

———. *Negro on the American Frontier.* New York, 1971.

Powell, Sumner C. *Puritan Village.* Middletown, Conn., 1963.

Putnam, Jackson. "Turner Thesis and the Westward Movement: A Reappraisal." *Western Historical Quarterly* 7 (October, 1976):377–404.

Raaen, Aagot. *Grass of the Earth: Immigrant Life in the Dakota Country.* Northfield, Minn., 1950.

Ramsey, Eleanor. "Allensworth: A Study in Social Change." Ph.D. dissertation, University of California, Berkeley, 1977.

Redfield, Robert. *Little Community.* Chicago, 1955.

Reed, Charles S. "Life in a Nebraska Soddy." *Nebraska History* 39 (March, 1958):57–73.

Rejebian, Ermance. "La Reunion: The French Colony in Dallas County." *Southwestern Historical Quarterly* 43 (April, 1940): 472–78.

Reps, John W. *Cities of the American West.* Princeton, N.J., 1979.

————. *Town Planning in Frontier America.* Princeton, N.J., 1965.

Robbins, William. "Community Conflict in Roseburg, Oregon, 1870–1885." *Journal of the West* 12 (October, 1973):618–32.

Roberts, Ron E. *New Communes.* Englewood Cliffs, N.J., 1971.

Rohrbough, Malcolm J. *The Trans-Appalachian Frontier: People, Societies, and Institutions 1775–1850.* New York, 1978.

Rojas, Arnold. *California Vaquero.* Fresno, Calif., 1953.

————. *Last of the Vaqueros.* Fresno, Calif., 1960.

————. *Vaquero.* Charlotte, N.C., 1964.

Rölvaag, Ole E. *Giants in the Earth.* New York, 1927; reprint ed., New York, 1964.

Rose, Harold. "The All-Negro Town." *Geographical Review* 55 (July, 1965):362–81.

Ross, Jack C. *Assembly of Good Fellows: Voluntary Associations in History.* Westport, Conn., 1976.

Rothman, David. *Discovery of the Asylum.* Boston, 1971.

Royce, Josiah, *California.* New York, 1948; reprint ed., Santa Barbara, 1970.

————. *Hope of the Great Community.* New York, 1916.

————. *Philosophy of Loyalty.* New York, 1908.

————. *Problem of Christianity.* Chicago, 1968.

————. *Race Questions, Provincialism, and other American Problems.* New York, 1908.

Royce, Sarah E. *A Frontier Lady.* New Haven, Conn., 1932.

Rudin, A. James. "Beersheba, Kansas." *Kansas Historical Quarterly* 34 (Autumn, 1968):282–98.

Ruede, Howard. *Sod House Days: Letters from a Kansas Homesteader, 1877–1878.* Edited by John Ise. New York, 1937.

Russell, Osborne. *Journal of a Trapper.* Edited by Aubrey L. Haines. Portland, Oreg., 1955.

Sanders, Irwin. *Community.* New York, 1966.

Sanford, Mollie. *Mollie.* Lincoln, Nebr., 1959.

Sandoz, Mari. *Cattlemen from the Río Grande Across the Far Marias.* New York, 1958.

———. *Old Jules.* Boston, 1935; reprint ed., Lincoln, Nebr., 1962.

Sapinsley, Elbert. "Jewish Agricultural Colonies in the West: The Kansas Example." *Western States Jewish Historical Quarterly* 3 (April, 1971):157–69.

Savage, W. Sherman. *Blacks in the West.* Westport, Conn., 1976.

Schaar, John. *Loyalty in America.* Berkeley, Calif., 1957.

Schafer, Joseph. *Social History of American Agriculture.* New York, 1936.

Schwendemann, Glen. "Nicodemus: Negro Haven on the Solomon." *Kansas Historical Quarterly* 34 (Spring, 1968):10–31.

Sender, Ramon, and Wheeler, Bill, eds. "Home Free: A History of Morning Star Ranch and Wheeler's Ahimsa." Copy of typescript, 1978. Special Collections Library, University of California, Riverside.

Shambaugh, Bertha M. H. *Amana That Was and Amana That Is.* Iowa City, Iowa, 1932.

Shannon, Fred A. *Farmer's Last Frontier.* New York, 1945.

———. *American Farmer's Movements.* Princeton, N.J., 1957.

———. "Culture and Agriculture." *Mississippi Valley Historical Review* 41 (June, 1954):3–20.

Shannon, James P. *Catholic Colonization on the Western Frontier.* New Haven, 1957; reprint ed., New York, 1976.

Shaw, Albert. *History of Cooperation in the United States.* Baltimore, Md., 1888.

———. *Icaria.* New York, 1884.

Sherif, Muzafer, and Sherif, Caroline. *Groups in Harmony.* New York, 1953.

Shinn, Charles H. *Mining Camps.* 1965; reprint ed., New York, 1970.

Shorter, Edward. *Making of the Modern Family.* New York, 1975.

Shover, John L. *First Majority—Last Minority: The Transformation of Rural America.* De Kalb, Ill., 1976.

Shpall, Leo. "Jewish Agricultural Colonies in the United States." *Agricultural History* 24 (July, 1950):120–24.

Siberts, Bruce. *See* Wyman, Walker D.

Sims, Newell L. *A Hoosier Village.* New York, 1912.

———. *The Rural Community: Ancient and Modern.* New York, 1920.

Siringo, Charles A. *Lone Star Cowboy.* Santa Fe, N.Mex., 1919.

———. *Texas Cowboy.* Lincoln, Nebr., 1950.

Smalley, Eugene V. "The Isolation of Life on Prairie Farms." *Atlantic* 72 (September, 1893):378–82.

Smith, C. Henry. *Mennonites of America.* Goshen, Ind., 1909.

———. *Story of the Mennonites.* Newton, Kans., 1957.

Smith, Duane A. *Rocky Mountain Mining Camps: The Urban Frontier.* Bloomington, Ind., 1967.

Smith, Helena H., ed. *A Bride Goes West.* New York, 1942.

———. "Pioneers in Petticoats." *American Heritage* 10 (February, 1959):36.

———. *War on Powder River.* New York, 1966.

Smith, Henry N. *Virgin Land: The American West as Symbol and Myth.* Cambridge, Mass., 1950.

Smith, Jedediah. *Southwest Expedition of Jedediah Smith, 1826–27.* Edited by George R. Brooks. Glendale, Calif., 1977.

Smith, Page. *As a City upon a Hill: The Town in American History.* New York, 1966.

Snyder, Albert B., and Yost, Nellie. *Pinnacle Jake.* Caldwell, Idaho, 1951.

Snyder, Grace. *No Time on My Hands.* Caldwell, Idaho, 1963.

Sonnichsen, Charles L. *Cowboys and Cattle Kings.* Norman, Okla., 1950.

Steele, John. *In Camp and Cabin.* New York, 1962.

Stein, Maurice R. *The Eclipse of Community.* Princeton, N.J., 1960.

Steiner, Michael C. "The Significance of Turner's Sectional Thesis." *Western Historical Quarterly* 10 (October, 1979): 437–66.

Stewart, Elinore P. *Letters of a Woman Homesteader.* Lincoln, Nebr., 1961.

Stoes, K. D. "The Land of Shalam." *New Mexico Historical Review* 33 (January–April, 1958):1.

Stone, Lawrence. *The Family, Sex and Marriage in England, 1500–1800.* New York, 1977.

Stork, Byron C. *Pioneer Days in Montana.* New York, 1952.

Suttles, Gerald D. *Social Construction of Communities.* Chicago, 1972.

Taber, Clarence W. *Breaking Sod on the Prairies.* Yonkers-on-Hudson, N.Y., 1924.

Taylor, Blanche. "English Colonies in Kansas 1870–1895." *Historical Magazine of the Protestant Episcopal Church* 41 (March, 1972):17–36.

Taylor, Carl C. *Farmers' Movement.* New York, 1953.

———, et al. *Rural Life in the United States.* New York, 1949.

Thernstrom, Stephen. *Other Bostonians.* Cambridge, Mass., 1973.

———, and Knights, Peter. "Men in Motion." *Journal of Interdisciplinary History* 1 (Autumn, 1970):7–35.

Thomas, Robert D. *The Man Who Would Be Perfect: John Humphrey Noyes and the Utopian Impulse.* Philadelphia, 1977.

Throne, Mildred. "Population Study of an Iowa County in 1850." *Iowa Journal of History* 57 (October, 1959):305–30.

Thwaites, Reuben G., ed. *Early Western Travels, 1748–1946.* 23 vols. Cleveland, Ohio, 1966.

Tobey, Ronald. "How Urbane Is the Urbanite?" *Historical Methods Newsletter* 7 (September, 1974):259–75.

Tocqueville, Alexis de. *Democracy in America.* 2 vols. New York, 1945.

Toennies, Ferdinand. *Community and Society.* Edited by Charles P. Loomis. East Lansing, Mich., 1957.

———. "Present Problem of Social Structure." See International Congress of Arts and Science.

———. *On Sociology.* Edited by Werner J. Cahnman and Rudolf Heberle. Chicago, 1971.

Trotzig, E. G. "Early Swedish Settlements in the Dakota Territory." *Swedish Pioneer Historical Quarterly* 28 (April, 1977): 106–17.

Tuan, I-Fu. *Topophilia: A Study of Environmental Perception, Attitudes, and Values.* Englewood Cliffs, N.J., 1974.

Turner, Frederick, J. *The Frontier in American History.* 1920; reprint ed., New York, 1953.

———. "Problems in American History." See International Congress of Arts and Science.

Unruh, John D., Jr. *Plains Across.* Urbana, Ill., 1979.

U.S., Congress, Senate. *Report of the Country Life Commission.* 60th Cong., 2d sess., Sen. Doc. 21. Washington, D.C., 1909.

Veblen, Thorstein. *Absentee Ownership and Business Enterprise in Recent Times.* 1923; reprint ed., New York, 1938.

Veysey, Laurence. *Communal Experience.* New York, 1973.

———. "Communal Sex and Communal Survival." *Psychology Today* 8 (December, 1974):73–78.

Victor, Frances F. *River of the West.* Hartford, Conn., 1870; reprint ed., Danville, Calif., 1974.

Vidich, Arthur, and Bensman, Joseph. *Small Town in Mass Society: Class, Power and Religion in a Rural Community.* Princeton, N.J., 1958.

Vogt, Evon, and O'Dea, Thomas. "Comparative Study of the Role of Values in Social Action in Two Southwestern Communities." *American Sociological Review* 18 (December, 1953): 645.

Wade, Richard C. *Urban Frontier.* Cambridge, Mass., 1959.

Walker, Williston. *Creeds and Platforms of Congregationalism.* Boston, 1969.

Wallace, Allie B. *Frontier Life in Oklahoma.* Washington, D.C., 1964.

Warner, Sam Bass. *Urban Wilderness.* New York, 1972.

Warren, Roland L. *Community and America.* Chicago, 1963.

———. *Perspectives on the American Community.* Chicago, 1966.

Washington, Booker T. "Boley, a Negro Town in the West." *Outlook* 88 (January 4, 1908):28–31.

Weaver, David B. "Early Days in Emigrant Gulch." *Contributions to the Historical Society of Montana* 7 (1910):73–96.

Webb, Walter P. *Great Plains.* Boston, 1931.

Weber, Marianne. *Max Weber.* New York, 1975.

Weber, Max. *From Max Weber: Essays in Sociology.* New York, 1946.

———. "The Relations of the Rural Community to Other Branches of Social Science." See International Congress of Arts and Science.

Wenger, John C. *Mennonite Church in America.* Scottdale, Pa., 1966.

West, James. See Withers, Carl.

Weston, Richard. *A Visit to the United States and Canada in 1833.* Edinburgh, Scotland, 1836.

"Wheat Fields of the Columbia." *Harper's Monthly* 69 (September, 1884):500–15.

White, William Allen. *Autobiography.* New York, 1946.

Wiebe, Robert. *The Search For Order.* New York, 1967.

———. *Segmented Society.* New York, 1975.

Willard, James F., ed. *Union Colony at Greeley.* Boulder, Colo., 1918.

———, and Goodykoontz, Colin, eds. *Experiments in Colorado Colonization: 1869–1872.* Boulder, Colo., 1926.

Williams, Blaine T. "Frontier Family: Demographic Fact and Historical Myth." In *Essays on the American West.* Edited by Harold M. Hollingsworth. Austin, Texas, 1969.

Williams, George H. *Wilderness and Paradise in Christian Thought.* New York, 1962.

Wilson, R. Jackson. *In Quest of Community.* New York, 1968.

Wiltsee, Ernest A. *Pioneer Miner and the Pack Mule Express.* San Francisco, 1931.

Winner, Dorothy. "Rationing During the Montana Gold Rush." *Pacific Northwest Quarterly* 36 (April, 1945):115–20.

Winslow, Ola E. *Meetinghouse Hill: 1630–1783.* New York, 1952.

Winters, Donald L. *Farmers Without Farms: Agricultural Tenancy in Nineteenth-Century Iowa.* Westport, Conn., 1978.

Withers, Carl (pseud. James West). "Plainville, U.S.A." In *Psychological Frontiers of Society.* Edited by Abram Kardiner. New York, 1945.

Woods, Daniel B. *Sixteen Months at the Gold Diggings.* New York, 1851.

Wooster, Clarence M. "Meadow Lake City and a Winter at Cisco in the Sixties." *California Historical Society Quarterly* 18 (June, 1939):149–56.

Wyman, Walker D., and Siberts, Bruce. *Nothing but Prairie and Sky.* Norman, Okla., 1954.

Yambura, Barbara S., and Bodine, Eunice W. *A Change and a Parting: My Story of Amana.* Ames, Iowa, 1960.

Zabel, Orville H. "Community Development: Another Look at the Elkhorn Valley." *Nebraska History* 54 (Fall, 1973):383–98.

Zimmerman, Carle. *The Changing Community.* New York, 1938.

Zuckerman, Michael. *Peaceable Kingdoms: New England Towns in the Eighteenth Century.* New York, 1970.

Index